WHATEVER HAPPENED TO...?

ACKNOWLEDGEMENTS
The authors would like to thank the following for their help in the making of this book.
Bob & Tricia, Mick Bovee, Mal Cook, Anne Holmes, Sue Johnson, Val (who did the typing), . . . and Erica. Special thanks to Gene Pitney.

PHOTO CREDITS
Andre Csillag, Nigel Dickson, EMI, Epoque Ltd., Fantasy Records, Dezo Hoffman Ltd., Infinity Records, Island Records, Alan Johnson, London Features International, Jan Persson, Barry Plummer, Record Mirror, Pye Records, David Redfern Ltd., Rex Features, SKR Photos International, Brian Sommerville Ltd., Sounds, South London Photo Agency, Syndication International, Universal Pictorial Press, Virgin Records, Chris Walter Photography, Brian Worth,

ALBUM CREDITS
Bizarre, Bronze Records, Capitol Records, Columbia, Elektra, EMI, Epic, Island, London, MGM, Mountain Records, Phillips, Phonogram, Chess, Polydor, Straight Records.

Titles in the
PROTEUS ROCKS
series:

This edition published 1982 by Book Club Associates,
by arrangement with Proteus Books

United States
PROTEUS PUBLISHING CO., INC.
733 Third Avenue
New York, N.Y. 10017
distributed by:
THE SCRIBNER BOOK COMPANIES, INC.
597 Fifth Avenue
New York, N.Y. 10017

United Kingdom
PROTEUS (PUBLISHING) LIMITED
Bremar House,
Sale Place,
London, W2 1PT.

ISBN 0 906071 40 2 (p.b)
     0 906071 46 1 (h.b)

First published in US 1981
First published in UK 1981
© 1981 Howard Elson and John Brunton.
All rights reserved.

DL.B.28486 – 1982
Printed by Printer Industria Grafica sa
Barcelona, Spain

WHATEVER HAPPENED TO...?

The Great Rock and Pop Nostalgia Book

HOWARD ELSON
AND
JOHN BRUNTON

BOOK CLUB ASSOCIATES
LONDON

FOREWORD

Whatever happened to . . . **MARVIN RAINWATER** or **KAY STARR?**

Do you remember . . . **THE SEARCHERS** or **RICK NELSON?**

What about . . . **THUNDERCLAP NEWMAN, LOBO,** or **CREEDENCE CLEARWATER REVIVAL?** Great names from the '50s and '60s and '70s, who for a while were top of everyone's pops and then seemed to fade from the public's view almost as fast as they became big stars.

Showbusiness is littered with many hundreds of people who have tasted outstanding success and reigned supreme in the international Hit Parades. They came, they saw, they certainly conquered . . . and then they were gone. But where exactly *did* they go? Just because they were no longer in the all-seeing eye of the world's media, didn't necessarily mean they had gone into retirement. Far from!

In actual fact, many of the so called 'fading' (as the media would have us believe) stars went on to bigger and better things, or their careers changed direction dramatically to encompass and explore other showbusiness avenues in record production, songwriting, acting, television, sessions . . . the list is endless.

Like the delightful **Lesley Gore,** who enjoyed massive '60s hits with songs like 'It's My Party', 'Judy's Turn To Cry' and 'Sunshine, Lollipops and Rainbows'. Just recently, she's had a great success as a songwriter, penning the lyrics for the brilliant movie 'Fame'. Like **Wink Martindale,** whose great world-wide hit 'Deck of Cards' sold millions of copies and inspired many people. He turned his talents to the demanding world of television and today hosts one of America's top TV Quiz shows. And like **Peter Asher,** one half of Peter And Gordon whose hits included 'World Without Love', 'True Love Ways' and 'Nobody I Know'. Today, he is a highly-acclaimed record-producer, the mastermind and mentor behind Linda Ronstadt.

There are others, too, who left the business altogether to pursue new things and carve highly successful careers for themselves *away* from the hurly-burly of showbusiness.

Joey Dee – remember 'Peppermint Twist'? – is now an antique coin dealer in Florida. **Brian Poole,** who had many hits with The Tremeloes in the early 1960s, is a master butcher, running his own business just outside London. And gravel-voiced singer **Hurricane Smith,** the former record engineer who worked on many Beatles' tracks, breeds racehorses!

Some, however, have found lucrative livings for themselves in the plushest international nightclubs and cabarets, or by touring the world in rock 'n' roll revival shows. As big a star today, as they always were . . . and a handful more have gone off on their own in search of other dreams and ideals, like singer-songwriter **Cat Stevens,** now a converted and devout Muslim.

We all love nostalgia – and showbusiness nostalgia will never die, it's so very much a vital part of the business. Turn on any radio anywhere in the world, and the revived 45 shows are proving to be some of the most popular on air, while, 'Where Are They Now?' programs are top-raters on television. The reason is simple. People, of all ages, and all nationalities, indulge themselves in their own particular favorite songs, and singers, that bring the memories flooding back to them in abundance. They're playing our song . . . remember when?

This book recaptures some of those moments. Some of those times, and some of the people who made them all possible, and made them so special to all of us. It is *not* a hitch-hikers guide to the fallen idols of the industry, or a fanfare to the one-hit wonders now down on their luck.

But a salute to over 200 people who, during the last forty years, have made millions more happy; who have given hours of pleasure; who have written their own pages in the history of popular music. And they must always be remembered for doing just that . . .

For as long as there is popular music, people will always remember – and when a certain record is played that sets their minds wandering back to another time, another place, another . . . – they will always wonder Whatever Happened To . . . . . ?

Gene Pitney

CONTENTS

AMERICA
American. Male.
Vocal/Instrumental group.
*Original line-up: Gerry Beckley
(guitar/vocals); Dewey Bunnell
(guitar/vocals); Dan Peek
(guitar/vocals).*

It's often strange how a band or artist who goes down well in America fails to establish themselves in Britain, and vice versa.

One such group in particular, with an oddly ironic name, is America.

British record buyers flooded shops with demands for copies of 'A Horse With No Name', boosting it to Number 3 in the charts early in 1972. But afterwards, they lost interest in the three-man band. Yet in America they are established as one of the country's most successful chart bands.

The three-man band – all sons of American servicemen based abroad – met, ironically again, at school in London, England. There, Gerry Beckley, Dewey Bunnell and Dan Peek, started composing songs.

They finally formed America in 1969, with 'A Horse With No Name' galloping into the charts three years later.

Unfavorable comparisons were made with Crosby, Stills, Nash and Young, and the trio were accused of imitation. But back in the States, their bland, acoustic style has since guaranteed a number of platinum and gold discs for album releases.

THE ANIMALS
British. Male. Vocal/Instrumental Group.
Original line-up: Eric Burdon (vocals); Alan Price (keyboards/vocals); Hilton Valentine (guitar); Chas Chandler (bass); John Steel (drums).

The Animals were formed in Newcastle-upon-Tyne, England, at the turn of the 1960s – but started life as The Alan Price Combo. In 1962, the four-piece outfit was joined by a young art student, Eric Burdon, whose raucous, blues-cum-soul orientated voice blended brilliantly with the big blues instrumental sound created by

AMERICA — (l-r): Dewey Bunnell, Gary Beckley, Dan Peek

the other members. The sound the group created – and the feeling they put across on stage – added to their gutsy act, drove their audiences to nickname them Animals. The name stuck.

The band established a huge following in the North East of England, and their reputation soon spread to London where producer Mickie Most signed them to a recording contract. Their first single – 'Baby Let Me Take You Home' – was a minor hit, early in 1964, but it was just the lull before a devastating storm which reached fever pitch in the summer of '64 when they released 'The House Of The Rising Sun'. Burdon's wailing, crying voice poured out the sad story of a poor boy's plight in New Orleans – and the record topped hit parades all over the world, including those of Britain and America. Eric Burdon became the image of The Animals:

face contorted as he sung, his compact body, bent and tense with effort, entirely oblivious of the world beyond his music.

In their years at the top The Animals gained respect as one of the world's foremost (white) rhythm and blues groups. They had nine massive hit singles, including 'I'm Crying' (1964), 'Don't Let Me Be Misunderstood' (1964), 'We've Gotta Get Out Of This Place' (1965), and 'Bring It On Home To Me' (1965), and several hugely successful albums.

The group disbanded in 1966, though Alan Price left a year earlier to concentrate on his own solo career and has enjoyed great success in his own right ever since, clocking up many hit singles: 'I Put A Spell On You' (1966), 'Hi Lilli, Hi Lo' (1966), 'Simon Smith And His Amazing Dancing Bear' (1967), 'The House That Jack Built' (1967), 'Don't Stop The Carnival' (1968) and 'Jarrow Song' (1974). In 1971, he teamed up with Georgie Fame (see **Georgie Fame**) and together they toured extensively and appeared on their own BBC Television series 'Fame And Price'. They had one hit as a duo in 1971 – 'Rosetta' – before going their own separate ways, which for Alan later meant writing the score for the movie 'Oh Lucky Man' *and* turning his hand at acting, to star in the title role of the film 'Alfie Darling'.

Chas Chandler, with John Steel as his assistant, went into management and later discovered Jimi Hendrix, playing in the Cafe Wha in New York's Greenwich Village. He brought Hendrix to Britain in 1966, became his manager – until his tragic death in 1970 – and helped make him a superstar. Chas later worked his own kind of management magic on another of his discoveries, Slade. Today, he heads his own record company Cheapskate Records in London, England.

Hilton Valentine, like Price, set out on his own solo career, making an album – 'All In Your Head' in 1969 – but his success was short-lived.

Eric Burdon, on the other hand, formed his own group – Eric Burdon And The (New) Animals, featuring Barry Jenkins (drums), Danny McCulloch (guitar), Vic Briggs (keyboards) and John Weider (bass/violin) – and for two years enjoyed success with a string of international hits: 'Help Me

THE ANIMALS — (top); — LP 'Animal Tracks', (bottom, l-r): John Steel, Chas Chandler, Eric Burdon, Hilton Valentine, Alan Price

Girl' (1966), 'Good Times' (1967) and 'San Franciscan Nights' (1967). In 1968, he disappeared from the music scene, only to resurface two years later in America, fronting the group War, with whom he recorded two albums. In 1971, he made an LP with one of his great blues' idols, Jimmy Witherspoon, and in 1973 and 1976, he toured Britain, before slipping back into semi-retirement in France, and later on the West Coast of America, where he occasionally resurfaces for gigs.

In 1976, the original Animals – Burdon, Price, Valentine, Steel and Chandler – re-formed briefly to record a brand new album, which through a series of disputes and contractual difficulties was never released.

APHRODITE'S CHILD
Greek. Male. Vocal/Instrumental Group.
Original line-up: Vangelis Papathanassiou (organ); Demis Roussos (bass); Lucas Sideras (drums).

Formed in Athens, Greece, by

APHRODITE'S CHILD — (l-r): Lucas Sideras, Vangelis, Demis Roussos

singer Demis Roussos in the mid-1960s Aphrodite's Child clocked up several hit records in their homeland and elsewhere on the Continent. Their biggest success came in 1968 with the monster-selling 'Rain And Tears' – though it was their only British hit record.

The group's music was deeply rooted in Greek traditionalism and they even adapted national folk songs to contemporary treatment.

The group split up in 1971, with Roussos setting out on his own singing career, which culminated in British hit singles – 'Happy To Be On An Island In The Sun' in 1975, followed a year later by his chart-topping EP 'The Roussos Phenomenon'. Vangelis Papathanassiou also went solo and made several solo albums. Then in 1979, he and Jon Anderson recorded the hit album 'Jon And Vangelis', from which their chart single 'I Hear You Now' was taken. In 1981, Vangelis composed the music for the score of the movie 'Chariots Of Fire' which was chosen for the year's British Royal Film premiere.

PETER ASHER
British. Male. Singer/Producer.

Peter Asher, brother of English actress Jane Asher, rose to fame, and subsequent fortune, in 1964 as one half of the successful singing duo Peter and Gordon.

With partner Gordon Waller – they met when they were pupils at London's famous Westminster School – Peter topped the British hit parade with the Paul McCartney song 'World Without Love'. It was rapidly followed by a series of best-selling singles – 'Nobody I Know', 'True Love Ways', 'To Know You Is To Love You', 'Woman', 'Baby I'm Yours' and 'Knight In Rusty Armour' (a massive hit in America, which failed to register in Britain).

When the duo split in 1967, with Gordon Waller following his own solo singing career, Peter (born London, June 22, 1944) became head of A and R for the Beatles' ill-fated Apple record company. He made several signings for the label, including James Taylor whom he produced and managed.

Asher later moved to America's West Coast, and formed his own management company in Los Angeles. In 1974, he started what has continued to be an outstanding association with singer Linda Ronstadt and produced the album that finally established her among the elite of world stars – 'Heart Like A Wheel'.

THE ASSOCIATION
American. Male. Vocal/Instrumental Group.

Original line-up: Gary Alexander (guitar); Ted Bluechel (drums); Russ Giguere (guitar); Terry Kirkman (vocals); Jim Yester (guitar); Brian Cole (bass).

Formed in California in February 1965, The Association enjoyed a brief reign in the international music charts during the mid-'60s. They were clean-cut and had immense style – and their music, which relied on intricate six-part vocal harmony, became known as 'the new American' sound.

During 1966 the group chalked up two massive American Top Ten hits with 'Along Comes Mary' and 'Cherish' (their first American Number 1) and both songs sold over a million copies. They were followed by the obscure 'Pandora's Golden Heebie Jeebies', the wistful 'Windy' which topped the U.S. charts in 1967, and 'Never My Love' which reached the Number 2 slot. Their albums 'And then

THE ASSOCIATION — pictured in London in 1967

. . . Along Comes The Association' and 'Insight Out' both sold over a million.

In 1968, they enjoyed their only British success with 'A Time For Living'. Four years later, they left Warner Brothers Records and switched to Columbia, but recording success eluded them.

However, the group, which during its early stages had played gigs in Los Angeles clubs and colleges *and* even had a residency at Disneyland, turned to the U.S. cabaret circuit and supper clubs, where they have carved a new and exciting career.

CHET ATKINS
American. Male. Instrumentalist.

One of the 'all time greats' of the guitar, and one of the most respected musicians around, Chet Atkins was born Chester Burton Atkins in Luttrell, Tennessee, on June 20, 1924. His father was a music teacher who specialized in piano.

Legend has it that young Chet was fascinated by country music – Jimmie Rodgers was his idol – and before long, he had swapped an old antique pistol for an old guitar in order to

make his own kind of music.

What is certain, however, is that Chet taught himself to play the instrument during his school days and by the time he had graduated from High School, he was broadcasting with Bill Carlisle And The Dixieland Swingers on Radio WNOX in Knoxville, Tennessee. Besides being featured on guitar for those early broadcasts, Chet was often heard playing country fiddle – another of the instruments he had mastered. Next followed a stint working in Nashville for the celebrated Carter Family.

In 1946, he was signed to a recording contract by RCA executive Steve Sholes and he was used as a studio guitarist for RCA-Nashville sessions. Within ten years, Chet had become Head of RCA-Nashville operations and he was working and recording with such artistes as Jim Reeves, Elvis Presley and The Everly Brothers (see **The Everly Brothers**).

During this time, he also discovered Roy Orbison (see **Roy Orbison**), Don Gibson, Connie Smith, Dottie West, Charley Pride, Roger Miller and Boots Randolph . . . and set them all on the road to stardom.

Atkins combined his studio activities by performing in Nashville's famous Carousel Club during the early '60s with a group of musicians who were later to be hailed as the 'fathers' of the Nashville Sound, including Floyd Cramer (see **Floyd**

CHET ATKINS — the legendary guitar master

Cramer) on piano, whom Chet had discovered in 1955; Bob Moore on bass, Grady Martin on guitar; Buddy Harman on drums; and Hank Garland on guitar. He also found the time to record his own singles and albums. To date he has had over 100 albums released worldwide.

In 1968 he was appointed as RCA Records' Division Vice President in charge of Popular Artists and Repertoire, and has since then combined two careers of heading the RCA-Nashville office *and* performing in his own right. In 1973, he was elected to the distinguished Country Music Hall of Fame.

Now known simply as 'Mr. Nashville', Chet Atkins is a well-established millionaire – though legend has it that his wife Leonna still cuts his hair!

He still combines his two careers as executive-cum-performer, and regularly tours the world, playing his very own, very distinctive kind of music. Indeed, in 1980 he undertook a lengthy European tour.

A musician of exceptional ability, having played guitar with the Atlanta Symphony Orchestra, Chet Atkins is quite simply one of the best-known guitarists in the world. A point illustrated by American writer Melvin Shestack.

Chet and songwriter John D. Loudermilk (see **John D. Loudermilk**) had taken their wives on a Caribbean cruise vacation when one night they got together for an impromptu jam session on board ship.

"The next day," Chet told the writer, "one of the people who'd been sitting around listening, came up to me and said: 'Say, you sure can play that guitar.' I thanked him – and then the man added, 'I'll tell you one thing, though, you ain't no Chet Atkins!' "

FRANKIE AVALON
American. Male. Singer.

Frankie Avalon was a child prodigy – and won his first talent show at the age of six, singing 'Give Me Five Minutes More'. Besides singing, he learnt to play piano – and by the age of 12, was playing local dance hall engagements with a band called Rocco And The Saints – which featured Bobby Rydell on drums. The group later played a summer residency at the Steele Pier in Atlantic City. At about the same time, he was a regular television performer, appearing on the 'Jackie Gleeson Show', 'The Paul Whiteman Show' and Ray Anthony's program.

His father later bought a local night club where young Frankie became a popular performer. In 1956, however, the venue burned down and Frankie's father spent several months in hospital, which meant that both he and his sister had to work after school to pay the medical bills.

Frankie earned *his* money singing, and was discovered by Chancellor Records' Bob Marcucci and Peter de Angelis and signed to their label. His first releases 'Teacher's Pet' and 'Cupid' were minor hits in 1957, and coincided with his movie debut in 'Disc Jockey Jamboree'. However, it was his appearances on the top TV show 'American Bandstand' that really lit the blue touch paper to his career and like his friend Fabian (see **Fabian**) who followed an identical path to success, Frankie Avalon became a teen-idol.

In 1958, he clocked up his first million-seller with 'Dede Dinah', rapidly followed by three more multi-selling singles in 1959 – 'Venus', which was Number 1 in America for

FRANKIE AVALON — '60s hearthrob

five weeks, 'Just Ask Your Heart' and 'Why'. Both 'Venus' and 'Why' made the British charts in the same year. And between 1958 and 1962, he enjoyed twenty-four major American chart singles.

During the 1960s, however, his career veered sharply towards films, and he starred in many. 'The Alamo', 'Guns of Timberland', 'The Carpetbaggers', 'Panic In The Year Zero', 'Castalian', 'I'll Take Sweden', 'Voyage To The Bottom Of The Sea', 'Skidoo', 'The Million Eyes Of Samuru' and numerous 'beach' and 'bikini' movies. He combined his acting commitments with major nightclub appearances throughout America including the famous Copacabana in New York.

Nicknamed "The Young Sinatra" and "Golden Boy" in his singing hey day, Frankie Avalon was born Frank Avallone of Italian stock, in Philadelphia, on September 18, 1940. He has continued to develop his career in motion pictures – he starred in 'Grease' in 1978 – and made numerous appearances on television in America running the gamut of the entertainment world from drama series, comedy and singing spectaculars.

The father of eight children, Frankie Avalon's teen-idol days may be long gone, but he has emerged as a much more mature, and talented artiste in recent years.

B

BADFINGER
British. Male. Vocal/Instrumental Group.
Original line-up: Peter Ham (Guitar); Ron Griffith (guitar); Tom Evans (bass); Mike Gibbons (drums).

Despite having tremendous potential, three million-selling international Top Ten hits *and* an American chart-topping single during the early 1970s, Badfinger *never* really established themselves as a force-to-be-reckoned-with in international pop music. They had plenty of opportunity *and* the backing and resources of The Beatles through Apple, but somehow they never quite made it to the top.

The group was formed in the mid-1960s in Swansea, and as The Iveys were soon established playing one-nighters in the South Wales youth clubs and dance halls – and indeed, they created quite an impression. So much so, that singer David Garrick signed them as his backing group. Next stop was London and an appearance at the famous Flamingo Club where they were spotted by Beatles' road-manager Mal Evans who in turn recommended them to Apple. However, they weren't signed to the label until 1968 when Paul McCartney personally took an interest in the group, after hearing a demo-tape.

A year later, they changed their name to Badfinger on McCartney's suggestion and were featured on the soundtrack of the Peter Sellers/Ringo Starr (see **Ringo Starr**) movie 'The Magic Christian', from which they scored their first Top Ten hit with 'Come And Get It'. They had to wait a whole year for their next chart success, 'No Matter What'.

In 1971, Badfinger were featured on George Harrison's massive bill at the Bangladesh concert in Madison Square Garden and twelve months later enjoyed their third major chart single with 'Day After Day' which reached number one in America. However, earlier that year, Harry Nilsson recorded the Tom Evans/Peter Ham composition – 'Without You' – and took it to the very top of the

BADFINGER — (l-r): Ron Griffith, Peter Ham, Tom Evans, Mike Gibbons

British and American charts.

The group continued to perform together for a further three years, without consolidating their early promise. Then, on April 24, 1975 – following a fit of depression that some say was brought on by the group's lack of consistent success – Peter Ham, Badfinger's musical inspiration, was found hanged in his home in Surrey. A verdict of suicide was later recorded by the coroner. The rest of the group decided to call it a day shortly afterwards, and went their own separate ways.

GINGER BAKER
British. Male. Instrumentalist.

Peter Baker was born in Lewisham, London on August 19, 1939 – and took his name 'Ginger', not unnaturally, from the color of his hair.

At school he became a champion racing cyclist, and also played trumpet, but later switched to drums ... And indeed, he started his musical career playing drums in several traditional jazz bands, with the likes of Acker Bilk and Terry Lightfoot.

In 1962, he joined Blues Incorporated – actually replacing Rolling Stone Charlie Watts as drummer – and a year later he was asked to join the Graham Bond Trio (soon to become the Graham Bond Organisation) which

also featured Jack Bruce (see **Jack Bruce**) on bass.

In 1966 Baker and Bruce joined forces once again, this time with guitarist Eric Clapton, to form what was hailed as the first 'super-group' – Cream (see **Cream**).

For two years Cream enjoyed mag-

nificent success in Britain and America. They toured extensively, playing to sell-out audiences and clocked up numerous hit singles with 'I Feel Free', 'White Room', 'Badge', 'Strange Brew' and 'Sunshine Of Your Love' ... and a string of hit albums. Then in 1968, at the height of their success, they decided to go their own separate ways, with Baker and Clapton forming Blind Faith, (with Ric Grech and Steve Winwood), which in 1970 spawned the short-lived Ginger Baker's Airforce.

During the 1970s, Ginger diversified his talents. He developed a great passion and interest in black African music and in 1973 opened his own recording studio in Akeja, Nigeria where Paul McCartney and Wings recorded their 'Band On The Run' album. He also fronted (and managed) the Nigerian band Salt, *and* started a trans-Saharan trucking company. Ginger next teamed up with Adrian and Paul Gurvitz to form the Baker-

GINGER BAKER'S first album with The Baker Gurvitz Army

Gurvitz Army, and together they made three albums.

Then, after leaving this band in 1976, Ginger devoted most of his time to playing polo – though he often returned to music when the mood took him. The mood certainly grabbed him again in 1980 when he came out of his self-imposed semi-retirement, to join the contemporary British rock group Hawkwind on an extensive British concert tour. In the spring of 1981, Ginger quit the group suggesting that they were a trifle limited: "I couldn't stand it, they weren't exactly the most musical band in the world." Thereafter he joined forces with Keith Hale (keyboards), Ian Trimmer (sax), Richy Le Gaire (bass) and Billy Jenkins (guitar) for a tour in Italy, and then switched directions again taking up John Lydon's offer to drum for Public Image Limited in April 1981.

THE BAND
Canadian. Male. Vocal Group.
Original line-up: Robbie Robertson (guitar); Richard Manuel (piano); Garth Hudson (organ/sax); Rick Danko (bass); Levon Helm (drums).

It was a professional relationship that lasted through the high-point of rock – that of Bob Dylan and The Band. Yet the group first worked together in Canada in the early 1960s, backing rock 'n' roller Ronnie Hawkins. Dylan met them in Atlantic City, and together, in 1965, produced their first single, 'Can You Crawl Out Of Your Window'. Later several of The Band played on Dylan's 'Blonde On Blonde', album and afterwards toured with him.

One of their most successful recordings together followed in 1968, with their mixture of talents on 'John Wesley Harding'. This was followed by The Band's first release under their own name, 'Music From Big Pink', containing, as it did, the classic 'The Weight', which made the British Top Thirty in September of that year, and was featured in the definitive free-wheeling American-dream movie, 'Easy Rider'. The flip-side was the equally highly-acclaimed 'I Shall Be Released'.

Two years before, the Band moved to Woodstock, in upstate New York, to help Dylan get over his serious motor-cycle accident. And it was in Woodstock, too, that they and Bob Dylan had, arguably their finest hour

THE BAND

THE BAND — 'Music From The Big Pink'

together, in 1969 . . . playing in front of the half-a-million-hoard. A year later, they also played together at the Isle of Wight pop festival in England.

By the middle of 1970, The Band had released their third, highly acclaimed, album, 'Stage Fright', (the second having been entitled simply 'The Band'). And their only other British Top Ten hit, the jaunty 'Rag Mama Rag'.

However, they remained mainly dormant until they appeared at the Watkins Glen Festival (the biggest of them all) in July, 1973.

The following year they emerged to tour with Dylan again – the results going on wax for 'Before The Flood' album. They also provided back-up work on Dylan's 'Planet Waves'. 1975 saw the release of The Band's long-awaited 'Northern Lights Southern Cross' album. Yet by 1976, they collectively felt it was time to call it all a day, and announced they were playing their last live performance, in San Francisco, on Thanksgiving Day. And that was that . . . or was it?

Since then they have, played in studios together, though their career's have headed in a solo direction, with Robbie Robertson turning to production and producing Neil Diamond's 'Beautiful Noise', and 'Love At The Greek' albums.

Helm was closely tied up with the work of Muddy Waters, during the latter '70s, while Danko moved to Arista Records. Richard Manuel also did sessions, notably for Leon Russell.

In the fall of 1980, bassman Rick Danko became more involved with television and film projects . . . and wrote several major scores, including

J.J. BARRIE — *a short stay at the top*

the music for the animated US TV special 'Take Me Out To The Ball Game'. He also attempted to re-vamp and reform The Band for recording purposes, but as he told an American journalist at the time: "It's hard to pin those guys down to anything like a schedule." He's still trying . . .

J. J. BARRIE
Canadian. Male. Singer.

In 1976, J. J. Barrie became one of many dozens of recording artists to have that unfortunate distinction of being labelled one-hit wonders. Yet, for J. J., he joined an elite band – certainly as far as the British charts were concerned – for his one and only hit record, 'No Charge', *topped* the hit parade. Still, it has been his only recording success to date.

He was born Barry Authors in Oshawa, Ontario, Canada, in 1936, and entered showbusiness at fifteen in a comedy double act called Authors and Swinson. "Our act was unique," he recalled. "We were the first variety act to mime to records!"

In 1952, however, Authors and Swinson arrived in England and soon settled into the routine of working the music halls, appearing, with such stars as Max Miller, Rosemary Clooney and Frankie Laine. They also played five seasons at the London Palladium.

For 10 years, the act thrived in Britain – then in 1962 with music halls closing rapidly, Barry decided to return to Canada where he carved a new career for himself in music publishing, management and agency representation. He settled in Toronto, and soon business was booming. Indeed, during the early 1970s he took over the management of Blue Mink and Ocean.

He returned to Britain in 1974 and set up his own recording company, called Power Exchange, through which, he recorded – and released – 'No Charge'. It was Power Exchange's – and J. J. Barrie's – only hit, and neither the Company, nor the singer could repeat that success.

Power Exchange went bankrupt in 1977 and Authors went back to Canada to pick up the threads of his former career on the 'other' side of the showbusiness fence.

He returned to Britain and the

recording studio in 1980 when, together with controversial British soccer manager Brian Clough, he recorded the self-penned songs 'You Can't Win 'Em All'/'It's Only A Game', which were released by MCA Records as a single in the fall of that year.

LEN BARRY
American. Male. Singer.

Len Barry was born Leonard Borisoff on December 6, 1942, in Philadelphia. He studied at Temple University where he met Arnie Satin, Jerry Summers, Danny Brooks and Mike Dennis, and together they formed a vocal harmony group called The Dovells, in 1957, and played at local school hops and dances.

They played together for the next two years and made an unsuccessful single before going their separate ways. However, they reformed in December 1960, and were later signed to a recording contract with Cameo-Parkway in 1961 after passing an audition. Their first single for the new label was 'Bristol Stomp', and it became a million-seller and reached Number 2 in the U.S. chart.

Lead singer Len, later left the group after follow-up singles failed to register as strongly as the first hit, and signed to Decca. His first release 'Lip Sync' was a moderate success, but '1-2-3' which topped the British charts, really established his potential. He consolidated it with his follow-up single 'Like A Baby'.

Len Barry's success was hinged on his high tenor, often falsetto voice –

LEN BARRY — *from teen idol to cabaret singer*

and his hit records carried him through the 1960s and into the '70s with ease. Inspired by soul king James Brown, Len made an easy change from teen-idol to nightclub singer, towards the end of the decade. And today he has consolidated all his success, playing engagements on the American carbaret circuit.

FONTELLA BASS
American. Female. Singer.

A fine vocal range and two massive world-wide hits, established the name and reputation of Fontella Bass in the mid-'60s as one of the leading female singers of soul-pop. The singles – 'Rescue Me' and 'Recovery' – made sure Fontella left her mark.

She was born on August 24, 1942 in St. Louis, Missouri, and at five she was playing piano and singing in the local church choir. Her mother had sung with The Clara Ward Singers and started training her daughter to sing at the age of four. Fontella later became director of the church choir, and an accomplished organist.

She made her first appearance in 1960 in the St Louis 'Gospel Blues Show' where she was discovered by blues star Little Milton – and she later sang and played in his backing band.

Four years later, Milton arranged for a recording contract with Chess and she teamed up with Bobby McClure for her first, and highly acclaimed, single 'Don't Mess Up A Good Thing'.

'Rescue Me' followed, and a lengthy round of tours of both the U.S. and Europe.

The early '70s saw her headlining

FONTELLA BASS — appearing on BBC TV's 'Ready Steady Go'

on both sides of the Atlantic and also saw her marrying jazz trumpeter Lester Bowie. This in turn lead to her becoming more and more involved in jazz. It was in this direction that she had headed by the mid '70s.

And it is in the jazz field that Fontella is still very actively involved today.

THE BAY CITY ROLLERS
British. Male. Vocal/Instrumental Group.
Original line-up: Derek Longmuir (drums); Alan Longmuir (bass); Nobby Clarke (guitar); John Devine (guitar).

Formed in 1967 by Derek and Alan Longmuir at Tynecastle School in Edinburgh, The Bay City Rollers were originally called The Saxons. They changed the name when they left school, and legend has it that they stuck a pin in a map of America, hit Bay City and added the 'Rollers' suffix as an after thought.

They were managed by Tam Paton, a former Edinburgh dance band leader, who organized their local engagements . . . and set about landing a recording contract for the group. It came in 1971 with Bell Records and their first single 'Keep On Dancing', which reached the British Top Ten, was produced by Jonathan King.

But for the next three years, during which time the line-up changed considerably with Paton selecting new members basically for their *teen appeal* and little else, further chart success evaded them, although 'Mañana' was a minor hit.

In 1972, Eric Faulkner (guitar), joined the group – and a year later when Clarke and Devine left, The Rollers were joined by Les McKeown (vocals) and Stuart Wood (guitar). In the spring of 1974, they were back in the Hit Parade with 'Remember (Sha-La-La)'. Roller-mania was just around the corner . . .

From 1974 to 1976, The Bay City Rollers had no equals in international music. They were acclaimed wherever they appeared and given the same treatment by Press and Public alike, as The Beatles had experienced a dozen years previously. Their tours were sell-outs in Britain and America, and unrivalled scenes of wild enthusiasm – screaming, sheer uncon-

THE BAY CITY ROLLERS — with Les Mc-Keown leading the tartan mania

trollable hysteria – were the order of every day!

They had hit records, too: 'Shang-A-Lang' (1974); 'Summerlove Sensation' (1974); 'All Of Me Loves All Of You' (1974); 'Bye Bye Baby' and 'Give A Little Love' (consecutive British chart-toppers in 1975); 'Money Honey' (1975); 'Love Me Like I Love You' (1976); and 'I Only Want To Be With You' (1976). In 1976 'Saturday Night' topped the American Hit Parade. The same year, they left England and launched a major assault on the American market where Roller-mania was rife! But in Britain, their fans deserted them and by 1977 the hit records had dried up.

Earlier in 1976 however, founder member Alan Longmuir had left the group in a blaze of publicity, claiming he was "too old" to be a teenage idol. In fact, he had been sacked . . . for exactly the same reasons! He was replaced by Belfast-born Ian Mitchell, who himself left to form his own group, in 1977. He, in turn, was replaced by

Pat McGlynn before Longmuir was welcomed back to the fold.

Then in November 1978, lead-singer Les McKeown was sacked, following several incidents of wild behavior on tour in hotels, and his confessions in many newspapers of the group's sexual antics with groupies. He returned to Britain and branched out on a solo career with the release of the album – 'All Washed Up'.

McKeown was replaced by South African Duncan Faure.

Since then, The Bay City Rollers have isolated themselves almost totally from the British market, preferring to undertake major tours of Europe, Japan – where they have a massive following – and America, where they are still successful.

"Our British fans have not been very loyal", said Eric Faulkner in a newspaper interview. "People at home seem embarrassed to go out and buy our records."

And Alan Longmuir added: "British fans are fickle".

In March 1980, while on a tour of South Africa, Stuart Wood, Alan Longmuir and Duncan Faure were

arrested and later jailed in Johannesburg, for alleged non-payment of hotel bills (estimated at $10,000) incurred on the tour. They were released after the bills had been hurriedly settled!

HARRY BELAFONTE
American. Male. Singer.

Harry Belafonte was born in New York City on March 1, 1927, and at a young age moved with his family to Jamaica, where he lived for five years. He then returned to New York to attend the George Washington High School, although he never completed his education. In 1944, he joined the U.S. Navy for a two year tour of duty.

After his discharge, while working as a maintenance man, he received two tickets to an American Negro Theater production, which served as his first introduction to legitimate theater. He later became a member of the American Negro Theater with his very close friend, Sidney Poitier, and eventually joined the Drama Workshop.

In one of the Drama Workshop productions, Belafonte's role called

19

HARRY BELAFONTE — still crooning after twenty years

for him to sing one number. Although he thought nothing of it at the time, the singing of that song proved to be important in retrospect some time later. For one night, he was asked to sing at the Royal Roost, a New York night club, and he was signed to an original two-week contract which ran for *five months!*

From this engagement, Belafonte went on to become a successful pop singer, but he was unhappy with this type of work and quit cold, determined to either find his proper niche in showbusiness or get out.

In the interim, however, with two friends he bought a small restaurant in Greenwich Village. The atmosphere was informal, and frequently old friends would drop in. Someone would produce a guitar, and Harry would sing.

It was during these informal performances that drove Belafonte to return to showbusiness – this time as a folk singer.

In 1950, with two guitarists (Millard Thomas and Craig Work) he began to build a repertoire of old and modern folk ballads. Before the end of that year, he was booked into the Village Vanguard night club.

This modest beginning led to a contract with RCA Records *and* his first two motion pictures ('Bright Road' and

the highly successful 'Carmen Jones'). His third film was 'Island In The Sun' in 1957.

In 1955, he became a full-fledged star on Broadway in 'Three For Tonight' and two years later scored a notable success with the million-selling single 'Banana Boat Song'. He followed it up with a million-selling album 'Belafonte Sings The Caribbean' which earned him the nickname 'King Of The Calypso' – *and* two million-selling singles, 'Mama Looka Boo Boo' and 'Mary's Boy Child', which topped the British Hit Parade. In a short space of time, Harry Belafonte had emerged from American night clubs and into the international spotlight.

But besides carving a unique singing and recording career for himself, Harry also diversified his talents once more to take in television series and specials, and major motion pictures including 'The World, The Flesh And The Devil', and 'Odds Against Tomorrow' – made by his own production company, Belafonte Enterprises – and 'The Angel Levine', 'Buck And The Preacher' and 'Uptown Saturday Night'.

Devoted to the continuing fight against injustice, Harry Belafonte became the first member of the entertainment industry to be named as a cultural adviser to the Peace Corps by President Kennedy, working closely with Peace Corps members both in America and abroad. He has been a leading architect of the Civil Rights movement and a strong figure among the responsible voices of purpose and clarity ever since.

Harry Belafonte has continued to tour the world spreading his own kind of gospel and his international trips have presented his art to many cultures in many lands, winning for him the affection and enthusiasm of all people. His appearance in Japan in 1974, was an 'event', playing seven cities, and leading to a return engagement in 1976. He returned to England and Europe for the first time in many years in October 1976, again in 1978, when he appeared in the Royal Variety Show – and 1979.

On the personal side, Belafonte has four children: two girls, Adrienne and Shari by a former marriage; and he and his wife – the former Julie Robinson – are proud parents of a son, David Michael and daughter, Gina.

He and Julie live in a large, comfortable apartment in New York City filled with many paintings, trophies, and records. He is an avid water skier and also enjoys spending his leisure time at his farm in upstate New York.

CAPTAIN BEEFHEART
American. Male.
Singer/Instrumentalist.

At the end of 1980, Don Van Vliet was once more back on the road, touring England, under the name that had won him a cult following in the late '60s, and which had been given to him by his schoolfriend Frank Zappa – *Captain Beefheart*.

He had been born in Glendale, California, in 1941, and formed his first Magic Band 23 years later. It included such musical worthies as Roy Estrada, drummer John French – and top sessions-man, later to turn soloist, Ry Cooder. His first album, 'Safe As Milk', was recorded on the Kama Sutra label, and set the seal for a host of albums

TROUT MASK REPLICA

CAPTAIN BEEFHEART
& HIS MAGIC BAND

CAPTAIN BEEFHEART — *(top) shows his priorities. (Bottom) The 1969 album 'Trout Mask Replica'*

that followed. The LP was Beefheart's forte – certainly not the transient sound of the 45. Over the years, albums would include 'Mirror Man', 'Strictly Personal', the classic 'TROUT Mask Replica', 'Lick My Decals Off, Baby', 'The Spotlight Kid', 'Clear Spot', 'Unconditionally Guaranteed' and 'Blue Jeans And Moonbeams'.

The '70s saw Beefheart retiring from the music business on several occasions, to re-emerge now and again. Legend has it that every time his band – The Magic Band – became competent at playing together, Beefheart disbanded them in favor of a much looser and rawer line-up, and in this direction, he certainly contributed to the imminent rise of 'new wave' music. The decade also saw Beefheart and Zappa arguing regularly. Nonetheless, no history of popular music can be written without reference to the work of either of these two.

Beefheart's music, like his mentor has continued to be inventive and

humorous, though most of it has vee-red into the surreal.

He made a comeback tour in 1980 and played dates in Britain and Europe.

Reviewing one of his sell-out London concerts, James Johnson commented: "Captain Beefheart always stood out as an audible character even when he first emerged during the lunatic period of psychedelic rock. Nearly 15 years later a large cult following remains including new admirers of 'new wave'.

"One may suspect his lyrics are gibberish, even if amusing gibberish, but it is always pleasing to be reminded of the diverse range of eccentrics the rock world is still able to accommodate."

Enough said!

CHUCK BERRY
American. Male. Singer/Instrumentalist/Songwriter.

Over the years, there has been tremendous confusion surrounding the actual birthdate of rock legend Chuck Berry. Most informed sources agree on October 18, 1931, yet some have put the year at 1926, while others have plumped for January 26, 1927. Uncertainty, too, has shrouded his actual birthplace, though most people have settled for St. Louis, Mississippi. Still, San Jose, California runs it a close second.

But . . . what *is* certain, is that Charles Edward Berry has had a profound influence on the history of rock 'n' roll and has proved to be a *great* inspiration to millions, including The Beatles, The Stones and The Who. In short, he has emerged as a legend in his own lifetime. And his self-penned songs – 'Roll Over Beethoven', 'Sweet Little Sixteen', 'Nadine', 'Johnny B. Goode', 'Rock 'n' Roll Music', 'Beautiful Delilah', 'Maybalene', 'Reelin' And A Rockin'', 'Memphis Tennessee', 'Brown Eyed Handsome Man', 'School Days', 'Too Much Monkey Business', 'No Particular Place To Go' and many, many more . . . have all become rock 'n' roll classics. Indeed, the Berry repertoire is one of the most recorded catalogs in rock music.

Chuck Berry started singing at the age of six, in the Antioch Baptist Church choir – and while still a youngster, he taught himself to play guitar. However, at the age of fourteen, he was very much a rebel, and after being convicted of attempted robbery, spent the next three years in a reform school.

Back in circulation in 1947, he took a job at General Motors and later worked as a hairdresser. During his spare-time however, Chuck formed his own trio and played the blues in clubs and at private functions in and around St. Louis, in order to earn extra money to support his wife and two children. At about this time Berry also started to write his own r & b material.

In 1955, he left St. Louis for Chicago where he played with the legendary blues singer Muddy Waters, who was so impressed with the young man's talent that he introduced him to Chess Records. They signed him to a contract and Chuck Berry's first single 'Maybelene' c/w 'Wee Wee Hours' was released. Within weeks it became an American Top Ten hit. Chuck Berry was on the way to superstardom, *and* a place in rock music history.

He spent the next four years touring the States, spreading the gospel of r 'n' b and rock 'n' roll – and recording a stream of songs that became standards. He also featured in many of the rock films of the day, including 'Rock, Rock, Rock', and 'Jazz On A Summer's Day'. So successful was he that he opened his own nightclub in St. Louis, called appropriately Chuck Berry's Band Stand.

However, in 1959 he was charged with violating the American Mann Act, by transporting a minor (a fourteen year old girl) over a State line for immoral purposes. The resulting trial lasted two years and at its end he was found guilty and sentenced to two years imprisonment. The episode not only ruined his marriage, but left his career in tatters.

He was released in 1964 and set about picking up the threads of his livelihood . . . and he did it in brilliant style recording one of the most successful of all his songs – 'Memphis Tennessee'.

Since then, Chuck has continued to consolidate all his early '50s achievements, performing his famous 'duck-walk' all over the world!

CHUCK BERRY compilation

In 1972, he clocked up his first British and American Number 1 hit with the slightly risque 'My Ding-a-ling' – it became his signature tune from then on!

Today, Chuck Berry is looked upon as one of the elder statesmen of rock music, and revered by many aficienados. He is one of a handful of rock 'n' rollers from the 1950s who are still top-of-the-bill stars, and he regularly tours Britain, Europe and America, playing his very own – unique – style of music. Indeed, he was last seen in Britain during 1980, when a short concert tour met with great box-office success.

BLUE MINK
British/American. Male/Female. Vocal/Instrumental Group.

Original line-up: Madeline Bell (vocals); Roger Cook (vocals); Herbie Flowers (bass); Alan Parker (guitar); Roger Coulam (keyboards); Barry Morgan (drums).

Blue Mink was formed in London in 1969 by a group of Britain's top session musicians, with the sole intention of recording an album of instrumental tracks they had written together.

However, when songwriters Roger Cook and Roger Greenaway (who had enjoyed British chart success in 1966 in their own right as David and Jonathan with 'Michelle' and 'Lovers Of The World Unite') came up with the song 'Melting Pot', which duly featured Cook and American Gospel singer Madeline Bell on vocals, the instrumental ideals of the group were abandoned in favor of a much fuller vocal sound. And Cook and Bell were

BLUE MINK — (l-r): Herbie Flowers, Barry Morgan, Madeline Bell, Alan Parker, Roger Cook, Roger Conlam

co-opted as members.

"Originally, Blue Mink was supposed to be a purely studio group, coming together to record and release the odd single and album," says Madeline Bell. "At that time, we were all heavily committed to our own session careers – and we had no intentions of making 'live' appearances. Yet, it didn't quite work out like that in the end."

'Melting Pot' was released in the autumn of 1969 and within weeks reached Number 3 in the British chart. Next followed a barrage of original hits including 'Good Morning Freedom', 'Our World', 'Banner Man', 'Stay With Me', 'By The Devil', and 'Randy'.

"With so many hits to our credit," adds Madeline, "it was inevitable that we would undertake 'live' engagements. So we started off right at the very top, playing a season at London's Talk Of The Town. We then appeared at all the major British cabaret nightspots."

In April 1973, Roger Coulam left the group to concentrate on a return career in sessions, and he was replaced by Ann Odell. Not long afterwards, percussionist Ray Cooper was added to the line-up for the group's American tour which included a sea-

son at the Troubador Club in Los Angeles, where Elton John introduced them on stage.

But . . . in 1975, the group disbanded.

"A lot of things contributed to the group break-up," admits Madeline. "Bad management, frustration – and quite honestly, we'd gone as far as we could go together. We had played at most of the top venues in Britain and appeared extensively on television. We had also had a string of major best-selling singles. However, we all wanted to quit while we were ahead . . . and go our own separate ways."

They did just that, with Roger Cook returning to his songwriting. Today he lives in Nashville, Tennessee and has established himself as one of the most successful British composers of all time! Alan Parker and Barry Morgan – who owned his own recording studio Morgan Studios in London – went back into session work where they have become two of the country's most respected musicians. Herbie Flowers, too, returned to the studio, but later dabbled on his own solo career . . . and then joined the magnificently successful classical-rock band Sky.

For her part, Madeline Bell hit the international cabaret trail as a solo singer and has worked extensively ever since. Today, she is one of the country's leading female vocalists and

besides her extensive cabaret commitments, has managed to retain her session work and regularly graces voice-overs for major British television commercials. In 1981, she started an additional career as a disc jockey for BBC's Radio One.

Ann Odell married, but combines her time as a housewife and session musician, and often works in Madeline Bell's backing group. Ray Cooper meanwhile, has continued to work at his chosen musical trade, performing regularly with Elton John.

MARC BOLAN
British. Male. Singer/Songwriter.

Marc Bolan was born Mark Feld in Hackney, London, on September 30, 1947 – the second son of Simeon Feld – of Jewish/English stock.

In 1962, at the age of fifteen, he was featured in Town magazine as 'the King of the Mods', which led him to follow a career as a male model on leaving school. Young Mark also spent much of his spare time frequenting the London coffee bars as a youth, particularly the Two I's, where Tommy Steele had been discovered singing some years earlier. And he soon became caught up in the whole mod scene.

Two years later, he emigrated to France and lived in Paris for five months with a wizard.

Back in England, he attempted to break into the music industry. He met American producer Jim Econimedes, who guided him to a recording contract with Decca, and his first single 'The Wizard' in 1966. To coincide with the release of the record, Mark changed his name to Marc Bolan. The record wasn't a hit, neither were two follow-up singles – 'Hippy Gumbo' and 'The Third Degree'. Yet, unperturbed, Bolan returned to the recording scene as a member of the group John's Children who managed to have their first single 'Desdemona' banned by the BBC for its semi-obscene lyrics.

In 1968, he left the group and teamed up with Steve Peregrine Took (on percussion) and formed Tyrannosaurus Rex. Originally planned as a five-piece, legend has it that the group

MARC BOLAN'S 1973 album, which marked a decline

folded when the HP company repossessed all their equipment. So Bolan and Took started work as an acoustic duo, with Marc playing a $20 Spanish guitar.

They appeared regularly at the Middle Earth club in London, where they were discovered by BBC Radio One disc jockey John Peel, who featured them almost non-stop on his radio show 'Top Gear' and even helped to get them engagements all over Britain, often working with him on his own road shows. The same year, their Regal Zonophone single 'Deborah' reached the British Top Thirty. The follow up single 'One Inch Rock' was another minor hit, but their album 'My People Were Fair' reached Number 5 in the British LP chart. A year later, after completing their first American tour, Steve Took left – he was found dead in his London appartment in the fall of 1980 from a drugs overdose – to be replaced by Micky Finn.

In 1970, Bolan abbreviated the name of the duo to T-Rex and changed the style of the act to feature electric guitar instead of acoustic. In the fall of

that year, he chalked up an unexpected British Top Five hit single with 'Ride A White Swan', and augmented the sound to include Steve Currie on bass, drummer Bill Legend and guitarist Jack Green. Next followed a whole succession of British hits including 'Hot Love' and 'Get It On', consecutive British chart toppers in 1971; 'Jeepster' – which established Bolan as the 'King of Glam Rock, nicknamed 'The Electric Warrior' (which was the title of his Number 1 album in 1971) – and established T-Rex as one of the most popular groups in Britain. On most of these recordings, he also featured the voices of ex-Turtles singers Mark Volman and Howard Kaylan (see The Turtles).

In 1972, he formed his own record label – The T-Rex Wax Company – which released his single 'Telegram Sam' (his third Number 1). Other chart hits that year included 'Metal Guru' (his fourth Number 1), 'Children Of The Revolution', 'Solid Gold Easy Action', and '20th Century Boy'. 'The Groover' in 1973, however, was to be his last substantial hit, although from 1973 to 1977 he made the lower

MARC BOLAN — the once 'King of Glam Rock'

reaches of the charts on nine more occasions.

1973 also saw him starring in the movie 'Born To Boogie' which was filmed in concert at Wembley and directed by Ringo Starr. And the same year, T-Rex made an unsuccessful tour of the States.

Bolan's reign as a top pop superstar was over.

In 1974, he split from his wife June and a year later suffered a mild heart attack. He also decided to disband T-Rex. It was a bad year!

He told a British rock paper: "I was really over the edge. I'd had nervous breakdowns and gone crazy about five times. I was a near alcoholic for a while. I spent six months in the South of France sitting in the sun all day and drinking brandy. I put on two stone. I was doing my share of drug-taking: I filled my nose. Drinks and drugs are the crutches of the rock world. There's nothing more destructive than being a success in the entertainment industry. It's a killer, no two ways about it.

"At 14 or 15 you get your guitars and start dreaming your dream about becoming the biggest rock star in the world. On the way up, people are only too pleased to give you advice, but nobody ever tells you what to do after you've made it. That's when the dream can turn into a nightmare. Once you've had that first big hit, that's it, everybody knows you, failure would be an embarrassment so you've got to keep it up. That's how the pressure starts, and the more famous and successful you get, the greater the pressure

gets."

He spent 1976 out of the country to become a temporary tax-exile – and in 1977, he attempted a comeback with a lengthy British tour. Joining the re-formed T-Rex on these engagements was his girl friend, Gloria Jones, with whom he was living and who had given birth to his son, Rolan, in 1975.

His career took an upward turn. He landed a personality TV job for Thames Television as an interviewer on the 'Today' program, and later signed a contract with another independent TV station to star in his own music series called 'Marc', which later proved a big success. So much so, that a follow-up series was planned. He never made it.

On September 16, 1977, the car he was travelling in as a passenger, crashed into Barnes Bridge in London, and Marc was killed instantly. The car was being driven by his live-in girl-friend Gloria Jones.

He died four weeks to the day of Elvis Presley's demise . . . and with one show in his successful TV series still to be shown.

THE BONZO DOG (DOO/DAH) BAND
British. Male. Vocal/Instrumental group.
Original line-up: Vivian Stanshall (vocals/trumpet); Neil Innes (guitar/piano); Roger Ruskin-Spear (sax); Rodney Slater (sax); 'Legs' Larry Smith (drums); Vernon-Dudley Bohay-Nowell

(guitar); Martin Stafford (percussion).

The Bonzo Dog (Doo/Dah) Band emerged in the mid-1960s as one of the funniest groups of its kind on the British pop scene. Their act was like a moving cartoon set to music – and besides playing original and satirical material, courtesy of Stanshall and Innes, the band's act also featured a whole array of weird and wonderful machines and dummies, care of Roger Ruskin-Spear.

They were formed in 1966 by art students from various London colleges and started playing together in pubs and clubs all over the city. They were carried along on the wave of success created by The Temperance Seven and New Vaudeville Band (see **The New Vaudeville Band**) in the early days, and adapted their stage act accordingly to feature a heavy bias of nostalgic '20s and '30s material. However, they still retained their biting wit and satire which at times verged on the surreal.

Two not-very-well-received singles on Parlophone followed, before they signed with Liberty Records and cut their debut album – 'Gorilla' in 1967, which contained the classic 'Intro And Outro', a song that virtually summed up the group's zany sense of humor.

In 1968, they enjoyed their only British singles chart success with 'I'm An

Urban Spaceman', which was actually produced by Paul McCartney using the pseudonym Apollo C. Vermouth. The hit record helped to gain them a much wider audience – and they soon became very much in demand for television appearances and landed their own series, which seemed to take the edge off their originality, and certainly drained their material. The strains of their success began to tell. Having to write brand new sketches and routines to satisfy the needs of their television series in record-quick time, proved too much. In 1970 after recording several top-selling albums, including 'The Doughnut In Granny's Greenhouse', 'Tadpoles' and 'Keynham', they disbanded.

Roger Ruskin-Spear went solo with his inane and zany 'Kinetic Wardrobe' one-man-show which featured manic dummies and weird electrical machines set to music, while 'Legs' Larry Smith turned to session work and later performed with Elton John and Eric Clapton. Rodney Slater left showbusiness to work in local government, and Stafford and Bohay-Nowell joined Bob Kerr's Whoopee Band.

Neil Innes went on to establish himself as a musical member of the Monty Python team and worked with Eric Idle on BBC Television's 'Rutland Weekend Television' series. He also wrote and performed all the music for the satirical film send-up of The Bea-

THE BONZO'S — commercial insanity, led by Vivian Stanshall (in shiny jacket)

BOOKER T AND THE MGs — (l-r): Al Jackson, Booker T, Steve Cropper, Don Dunn

tles – 'The Rutles' – in which he played a leading role. And Neil later hosted his own BBC Television series 'The Innes Book Of Records', which is still running.

Vivian Stanshall, meanwhile, formed several abortive groups, before working solo, and has reappeared from time to time on many recording projects most notably on Mike Oldfield's 'Tubular Bells'. He later turned his attention to television and radio, becoming a regular presenter and interviewer.

In 1979, he wrote the zany comedy 'Sir Henry At Rawlinson End', starring Trevor Howard, which enjoyed a huge success in London cinemas during 1980.

Said Viv: "I can't believe it, they must have had some sign outside cinemas saying 'Free Beer Inside' or 'Free Inflatable Women'.

With the success of the movie, Stanshall is preparing a follow up for 1981.

BOOKER T AND THE MGs
American. Male.
Vocal/Instrumental Group.
Original line-up: Booker T. Jones (keyboard); Don Dunn (bass); Steve Cropper (guitar); Al Jackson (drums).

The title of the single was 'Green Onions' and it was originally conceived as a one-off, but in 1962 it was to become a world-wide hit for a group of Stax Records session musicians, who became Booker T and the MGs. And for Booker T. Jones, himself, it was a first gold record – at just 16 years of age!

Born in the Memphis black ghetto in 1944, Jones showed considerable early promise as a musician and was snapped up as a session man by the newly-formed Stax label. But despite the success of 'Green Onions' he was intent on finishing his education by majoring in music at Indiana University. It wasn't until 1966 however – by which time he had also established a reputation as a symphony trombonist – that he decided to return to full time work in pop music.

Because Booker T and the MGs (the MGs, incidentally, standing for 'Memphis Group') was made up of session men, the line-up tended to change, but its most constant members were Jones

himself with Al Jackson, Donald 'Duck' Dunn and Steve Cropper, noted for composing 'In The Midnight Hour' and 'Sitting On The Dock Of The Bay'. (Both Cropper and Dunn were white, thus also giving the group a genuine integrated mix). However, the MGs had worked extensively together on numerous sessions for Stax, backing all the company's major artists including Otis Redding, Carla Thomas, Wilson Pickett and Rufus Thomas.

Despite three more big singles hits in the 1960s with 'Soul Is Limbo', top-lining 'Time Is Tight' and 'Soul Clap '69, the group disbanded in 1972, to reform twice, unsuccessfully, in 1973 and 1977.

Booker had by then started a new recording career with his second wife Priscilla (Rita Coolidge's sister). He also supervised recording sessions for Rita, thus enhancing *her* early reputation.

Cropper, who was later to undertake recording sessions with a number of top names including Jeff Beck, Rod Stewart and Ringo Starr, also became chief recording

PAT BOONE — now a bestselling author of religious books

engineer with Stax. Dunn, who first met Cropper while they were both at school in Memphis and together they formed the Mar-Keys, continued in sessions.

Al Jackson was tragically murdered at his Memphis home in 1975.

PAT BOONE
American. Male. Singer.

Pat Boone can boast an amazing record in America which seems likely will never be beaten. In a four year period from 1955 through to 1958, he had the distinction of always having at least *one* single riding high in the American Hit Parade. And in a career spanning over a quarter of a century, Pat can also boast no less than *thirteen* million-selling singles – with 'Ain't That A Shame' (1955); 'Remember You're Mine' (1956); 'Friendly Persuasion' (1956); 'I Almost Lost My Mind' (an American Number 1 hit in 1956); 'I'll Be Home' (which topped the British charts in 1956);

'April Love' and 'Don't Forbid Me' (Number 1 hits in 1957); 'Why Baby Why' (1957), 'Love Letters In The Sand' (which sold over four million copies and topped the American charts in 1958); 'A Wonderful Time Up There' (1958); 'Cherie I Love You' (1958); 'Moody River' (Number 1 in 1961); and 'Speedy Gonzales' (1961). To date, he has collectively sold over 50,000,000 records world-wide!

He was born Charles Eugene Boone – the great-great-great-great-grandson of pioneer Daniel Boone – in Jacksonville, Florida, on June 1, 1934 and started singing in High School, when a shop-lifting spree for Christmas presents went drastically wrong.

Pat explains: "Just for excitement, a friend and I thought it a great idea to steal Christmas gifts! And we stole several items from local department stores. But I couldn't live with my conscience and confessed everything to my headmaster. He suggested that I earn money to pay back the store by singing. So I began to enjoy singing and realized people enjoyed listening to me. From then on, I became hooked on a singing career."

One of his fellow students at North Texas State College was Roy Orbison, who was spurred on to *his* own singing career following Pat's initial success.

In 1954, Pat sang on the Ted Mack 'Amateur Hour Show' and ended up winning first prize. Next followed a spot on the famous 'Arthur Godfry Talent Scout Show' – the springboard to success for so many major recording artists, although Elvis Presley *failed* the audition to appear in 1954 – which again he won, and as a result, he was signed to a contract with Dot Records.

Then started a prolific recording career for Boone, which for seven years saw him second only in popularity throughout the world to Presley – *and* one of the hottest properties in showbusiness.

Says Pat: "I actually had a six month start on Elvis. We were both Tennessee boys and our careers just see-sawed. In those rock 'n' roll days, Elvis was the pepper and I was the salt. He appealed to the rebels; I appealed to the conformists." Indeed, he was labelled 'Mr. Clean' and 'Mr. Tooth-

paste' by the American media because of his ultra-white, respectable image and reputation.

In 1954, he married his childhood sweetheart Shirley Foley, daughter of Red Foley, the famous Country and Western star, and settled down to family life.

During this time, Pat's recording career went hand-in-hand with one in motion pictures and he made many, after signing his first million dollar contract with 20th Century Fox, including 'April Love', 'State Fair', 'The Main Attraction' and 'Mardis Gras'. And he emerged as the all-American golden boy of showbusiness!

However, in the mid-1960s his career waned slightly. "I tried to change my 'Mr. Clean' image," he says. "I tried electric rock. Beach Boys songs – everything. But I felt I had lost my identity. And I also felt that my wife and I didn't love each other any more. It was when I felt we were apart that we turned to religion. I felt it might cost me my career, but I decided if I was going to make a commitment, I was going to stick by it."

His career however, was safe . . . for with wife Shirley and their daughters Lindy, Cherry, Debby and Laury in tow, they set out to tour America and appear on television as "The Pat Boone Family Show" – which mixed a little religion, a little home-spun philosophy and all of Pat's million-selling hits together. And soon they were in great demand for engagements throughout the States. They also made religious series for television.

In the fall of 1977, Pat's career took yet another upward turn when his daughter Debby enjoyed a massive American hit – the song did nothing in Britain – with the single 'You Light Up My Life', which topped the U.S. Hit Parade for eight weeks to become *the biggest selling record of the past 25 years in America.*

Now billed as Pat and Debby Boone, father and daughter entertained throughout America and starred for seasons in Las Vegas, and on television.

Pat Boone was back on top – and he's stayed there ever since.

He says: "Debby has been just the challenge my career needed. She's stopped me from getting sloppy – and

I'm singing better than I have in a long time.

"I know there are people who will say that Pat Boone is riding on his daughter's coat-tails. To them I say 'Yes, she had a giant hit and I'm very proud of her, but until she's had thirteen million-selling singles – and thirteen Gold Discs – *and* sold fifty million records, I'm not going to get too worried." In recent years Pat has made a name for himself as a best-selling author of no fewer than eight religious books.

In 1980, an album featuring Pat's 'Greatest Hits' was released in the Warwick Record label in Britain . . . with great success.

THE BIG BOPPER
American. Male. Singer.

The Big Bopper was born Jaye P. Richardson on October 24, 1930, in Sabine Pass, Texas, and started entertainig at school, where he became a disc-jockey and played in the school band. At High School, he turned his attentions on writing songs.

In 1955, he was called up for Army service and became a radar instructor. He was discharged in 1956 and then set about establishing himself in the entertainment industry, by attempting to break the world record for a marathon broadcast – which stood at over 122 hours non-stop! He smashed the existing record by a full eight minutes! The attempt received much publicity, and as a result, he was auditioned by the Starrite Publishing Company who were now showing considerable interest in the material he was writing and singing. He was signed to a recording contract, and his first single release was one of his own songs – 'Chantilly Lace' in August 1958 – and it became a major hit in America and Britain, selling a million copies. His follow-up single, 'Big Bopper's Wedding', was also a sizeable hit not long afterwards.

With the success of both records under his belt, Jayepee, as he was called, was asked to join an extensive American concert tour featuring Buddy Holly and Ritchie Valens (see **Ritchie Valens**). Being a big man – in size – he found great difficulty traveling on the tour bus that transported the groups, artists and equipment

JAMES BROWN — fallen on hard times

'Pappa's Got A Brand New Bag', 'I Got You','It's A Man's Man's World', were just a handful. And in 1962 his album 'Live At The Apollo' set a precedent for an r and b/soul artiste by selling more than a million copies. To date, James Brown has recorded 150 plus singles and in excess of 50 albums.

A supreme showman – in 1966 when he visited Britain for the first time, his act was acclaimed one of the most exciting ever seen in the country – Brown was also a leading light in America's Black movement. Indeed, he helped take some of the edge out of the electrifying tension during the infamous American riots of the late 1960s, by putting on a marathon TV show in order to keep people off the streets, and out of trouble.

During the 1970s, James Brown turned slightly away from soul towards the rapidly emerging disco market, without too much success although his 1976 LP 'Body Heat' sold well. And a disastrous venture into his own radio station during the late '70s virtually bankrupted the singer. Indeed, in 1980, a court in Baltimore, Ohio, convicted him of having more than 200,000 dollars-worth of debts.

JACK BRUCE
British. Male.
Singer/Instrumentalist/Songwriter.
Jack Bruce, probably one of the finest bass players in rock music history, was born John Simon Asher Bruce in Glasgow, Scotland, on May 14, 1943 – and on leaving school, won a scholarship to the Royal Scottish Academy of Music.

However, he started his professional career, playing blues with the Graham Bond Trio (later the Graham Bond Organization) with Ginger Baker, and later still played with the celebrated John Mayall's Bluesbreakers, and Manfred Mann.

In 1966, he teamed up once more with Baker (see **Ginger Baker**) and Eric Clapton, to form what was basically the first 'supergroup' – Cream (see **Cream**). Besides playing bass in the group, Bruce also provided the distinctive, wailing vocals that made Cream's sound unique, *and* he was also responsible for writing a lot of the

from gig to gig. Instead, he pursuaded Holly and Valens to take a private plane to the tour's next destination in Fargo, North Dakota – but it never arrived! It crashed, in foul weather, shortly after takeoff and all three stars perished. It was a shattering blow to rock 'n' roll . . .

A year after his death, one of the Big Bopper's compositions 'Running Bear', was taken to the top of the American Hit Parade by his young protege, Johnny Preston, whom he had encouraged to sing, and actually helped to get his first recording contract. It was a lasting epitaph.

JAMES BROWN
American. Male.
Singer/Instrumentalist.
They called him 'Mr. Dynamite' because of his explosive stage per-

formance. They also called him 'the grandfather of soul' because he did more than anyone to establish the music as a force-to-be-reckoned-with throughout the world. But, above all else . . . they called him James Brown.

Born in Pulaski, Tennessee on May 3, 1928, he was brought up in Augusta, Georgia, where he became increasingly influenced by Gospel music.

In the early 1950s Brown formed his own group, The Famous Flames, which, in 1956, had a million-selling hit with 'Please Please Please'. Two years later they also enjoyed outstanding success with 'Try Me'. It was the start of what proved to be a fabulous career for Brown. At one time, he broke every single box-office record at every single black venue in America, such was his popularity. His records, too, sold in millions. 'Out Of Sight',

JACK BRUCE — *virtuoso of the bass*

group's material with Londoner Peter Brown. Indeed, the talented partnership penned the likes of 'SWLABR', 'Tales of Brave Ulysses', 'White Room', 'Sunshine Of Your Love' and 'Take Me Back'. Bruce also picked up other writing credits, both as solo composer and co-writer with Clapton.

When the group broke up in 1968 with Clapton and Baker forming Blind Faith, Jack Bruce went his own way and within a year brought out his first

solo album 'Songs For A Tailor', followed by 'Things We Like'. He also played occasionally with Tony Williams Lifetime. In 1972 he joined Leslie West (guitar) and drummer Corky Laing, to form West, Bruce And Laing, with whom he made two albums. The association lasted until 1973 when he broke away to form the Jack Bruce Band with Mick Taylor (guitar), and Carla Bley (keyboards) which lasted for a further two years.

After being out of the commercial eye for three years, Jack Bruce re-

turned to the recording scene with a vengeance in the autumn of 1980 with the release of an exciting new solo album on Epic. Titled 'I've Always Wanted To Do This', the LP featured such celebrated 'session' side-men as Billy Cobham, Clem Clempson and David Sancious; it certainly helped to re-establish Bruce in his rightful place as one of the world's leading rock stars. In 1981 he recorded with guitarist Robin Trower.

SOLOMON BURKE
American. Male. Singer.

They called him the 'King Of Rock 'n Soul', and by the mid-'60s he was heading the Atlantic label's onslaught onto the soul market.

Solomon Burke was born in 1936 into a deeply religious family in Philadelphia, and soon showed his abilities as a singer. By the age of nine he was the church soloist, and at 10 he was giving sermons. Two years later he was actually the leader of his *own* church – Solomon's Temple. His speaking prowess made his reputation as the 'Wonder-Boy Preacher' and he was soon appearing on radio shows, where he was 'discovered' by a local DJ, who arranged his first record contract.

Solomon had his first hit, albeit a minor one, with 'Christmas Presents From Heaven' – a song he wrote for his grandmother. Three more hits followed, including one he co-wrote with the former heavyweight boxing champion, Joe Louis, before at the age of 22, he was signed up by Atlantic Records.

His first Atlantic release, 'How Many Times' showed promise but had little success. His follow-up, however, 'Just Out Of Reach' in 1961 was one of the top selling r & b singles of the year.

From there his reputation soared, and the '60s saw him at his golden best with such releases as 'Cry To Me', 'Everybody Needs Somebody To Love', 'The Price' and 'Tonight's The Night'. And he proved a great influence on many of the emerging r & b singers of the day including Mick Jagger of The Rolling Stones. There were also a number of top-selling LPs to come from 'King Heavy' as he became known.

Still, by 1968 the hits were becoming more elusive, and he left the Atlantic label and signed for Bell, hoping for a change of luck.

It came in 1974, when he recorded a tribute album to Dr. Martin Luther King. At about the same time he was reunited with Gene Page – who had produced his 1965 hit 'Got To Get You Off My Mind' – and the formula clicked again in his subsequent hits 'Midnight And You' and 'You And Your Baby Blues'.

He continues to work in the States, (he has never had a British Top Twenty single success) though his engagements Stateside are predominantly New York rock clubs. In the fall of 1980, he was one of the attractions to star at Manhatten's Tramps club.

JOHNNY BURNETTE
American. Male. Singer.

Like his friend Elvis Presley, Johnny Burnette, too, came from Memphis, Tennessee, and told interviewers, in the early 1960s, that the city had had a particularly profound effect on his songwriting career.

But there the similarity between him and Presley ends. Burnette was born in March, 1935, and was a late developer in the show business stakes. Although he had been playing the guitar since he was five, he entered show business in his early 20s after working as an Ohio riverboatman, and even as a boxer.

"But lying on the canvas looked like nothingsville to me," he said. And so he opted for a singing and songwriting career, penning several songs for

JOHNNY BURNETTE — killed at the zenith of his career

THE BYRDS — (l-r): Roger McGuinn, Roger Hillman, Gene Clarke, David Crosby

Ricky Nelson, including the million-selling 'Waitin' In School'.

In the Fall of 1960, he had his first big British chart success with 'Dreamin', followed by his biggest success, 'You're Sixteen', co-written with Dick Sherman, which sold more than a million copies, worldwide, and 'Little Boy Sad', 'Girls' and 'Sad Shoes'.

Then at the height of his career, Johnny Burnette was killed in a boating accident in Clear Lake, near San Francisco, California, on August 1, 1964, leaving a wife and two children and his brother Dorsey, by then also an established country singer.

THE BYRDS
American. Male.
Vocal/Instrumental Group.
Original line-up: Jim McGuinn (guitar); David Crosby (guitar); Chris Hillman (bass); Gene Clark (vocals); Mike Clark (drums).

Britain had The Beatles – and the U.S. had The Byrds. *The* top American band – and in their heyday they were unrivalled. They endured for nine years from 1964 to 1973. But their influence continues to be felt, particularly on the West Coast.

Innovation and originality were the hall-marks of this supremely talented band, which sprang from Los Angeles, first as The Jet Set – and later The Beefeaters – before becoming The Byrds, in 1964.

During the nine years of their existence, there were a substantial number of differing line-ups, with members going off in varying directions to form a variety of bands.

David Crosby, had teamed up with Jim McGuinn (he changed his name to Roger in 1968, because of his involvement in the Subud faith), Chris Hillman, Mike Clarke and Gene Clark, in 1964 to form the group. That was the nuts and bolts of the band, but over the years there were numerous changes, which started in 1967 when David Crosby left to join three other talented – or perhaps more accurately, *super*-talented – musicians to form Crosby, Stills, Nash and Young.

This in turn left The Byrds to center around McGuinn, Clark and Chris Hillman.

By then, however, they had enjoyed a string of big hits, which had helped to establish their massive influence, and following.

Their first hit, on CBS, in 1965, was Bob Dylan's 'Mr. Tambourine Man' a world-wide Number 1 followed up with 'All I Really Want To Do', which failed to make the top of the charts because of the success of Sonny and Cher's cover version, and 'Turn, Turn, Turn', written by Pete Seeger.

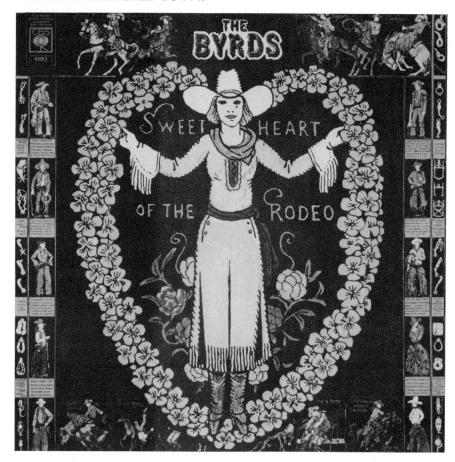

Numerous LPs, too, outlined vast, unexplored tracts of popular music. But it was 'Mr. Tambourine Man' that was to be their classic. It also featured on their first LP, 'The Byrds'.

Through the mid-'60s they reigned supreme. Innovators, they captivated first West Coast audiences, then audiences throughout the U.S., before turning to Britain where they were already developing another cult following.

'The Chimes Of Freedom', another Dylan song, and 'Eight Miles High' (at the time considered a 'drugs' song) only heightened their popularity and their audience increased in leaps and bounds.

In the spring of '67, however, guitarist Gene Clark quit to go solo, because he had developed a morbid fear of flying – and the band once again absorbed new members, including Gram Parsons (from the International Submarine Band) who later left in protest against a projected South African tour, and Clarence White.

As time progressed, The Byrds seemed to be losing something of their flair, with McGuinn expressing

concern that the band seemed to be going totally into a country music direction.

It was a low point in The Byrds' career, but fate took a hand with the film 'Easy Rider'. The group were featured on the soundtrack, and produced 'Ballad Of Easy Rider'. Their popularity returned and, it wasn't long before they were charting again, with 'Chestnut Mare'.

However, in 1973, The Byrds got together for a final fling, with Clarence White (on guitar), McGuinn (guitar), Hillman (bass) and Joe Lala (drums). And so they ended their career together . . . although McGuinn – who *owned* the name 'The Byrds' – constant throughout, was always ready to reform the outfit right into the mid-'70s.

Hillman had quit in 1969 to form the Flying Burrito Brothers another West Coast cult band – with fellow Byrds Mike Clarke and Gram Parsons, although he later returned to the fold. Later still, he joined Manassas before turning to sessions.

Drummer Clarke stayed with The

Burrittos until 1974, and then joined Firefall. Parsons, too, stayed with the group, but died mysteriously in 1973, the same year that Clarence White, who had joined The Kentucky Colonels, was killed by a drunken hit-and-run driver.

There were other components of Byrds' line-ups. Although retrospectively the band might appear stylized from the point of view of live appearances, their impact was great, echoing still along numerous avenues of popular music. Albums – all gems – include, 'Preflyte', 'Mr. Tambourine Man', 'Turn! Turn! Turn!', 'Fifth Dimension', 'The Notorious Byrd Brothers', 'Sweetheart Of The Rodeo', 'Dr Byrds And Mr Hyde', 'The Ballad Of Easy Rider', 'Untitled', 'Byrdmaniax', 'Farther Along', 'Younger Than Yesterday', 'Byrds' and a number of compilations.

Meanwhile, as The Byrds were fading, original member David Crosby, was still enjoying the limelight as part of Crosby, Stills, Nash And Young . . .

The basis of that outfit was formed in 1968 when Crosby left The Byrds and was preparing to go solo. At a jam session at John Sebastian's Los Angeles home, he teamed up with Stephen Stills, who had just left Buffalo Springfield, and Graham Nash, of the top British pop band, The Hollies. Neil Young joined later that year.

These four immensely talented artists stayed together, on and off, until 1974, during which time they made four albums. 'Crosby, Stills And Nash', 'Deja Vu', 'Four Way Street', and the compilation, 'So Far Theirs', were rare talents, and it was this mixture which gave them such extraordinary impact. In 1978 they reformed to make 'CNS'.

Stills had become a talented multi-instrumentalist by his late teens. A more obscure fact about him is that, in the mid-'60s, he auditioned for The Monkees, before forming Buffalo Springfield. Buffalo split in '68, and Stills was offered Al Kooper's place in Blood Sweat And Tears. He turned it down in favor of playing guitar for his girlfriend Judy Collins on sessions – and bass on Joni Mitchell's first album.

With his reputation growing, he became part of Crosby, Stills And Nash, but was later to spend some time in England, playing with top musicians such as Eric Clapton, Jimi Hendrix and John Sebastian, and generally widening his musical horizons. 1971 saw him developing a band that would become Manassas, which featured, among other members, Hillman and Joe Lala. In 1973 Stephen Stills married French singer Veronique Sanson and moved to Colorado, but a year later, Crosby, Stills, Nash And Young reformed for a world tour. It was designed as a one-off, and afterwards, its members again went their separate ways, with Stills – composer of the haunting '4+20', on 'Deja Vu' – going back to his solo career. Later he teamed once more with Neil Young. An extremely talented instrumentalist, he enjoyed his peak in the early '70s. His 'Suite: Judy Blue Eyes' (written about Judy Collins) was CSN's first U.S. hit single.

Canadian Young – in fact an epileptic and diabetic – was a very different matter. He had been a fan of Stills for some time and drove across America in a hearse to find him. Together they formed Buffalo Springfield . . . although, strictly speaking, he was working illegally because he didn't have the proper permits.

But no matter. His work on behalf of Crosby, Stills, Nash And Young was prolific, but his solo work during the '70s, while it showed considerable talent, also underscored a more melancholic side to his personality. His 'After The Gold Rush' is a classic.

Graham Nash grew up in Manchester, and there met Allan Clarke, with whom he formed The Hollies (see **The Hollies**). In the mid-'60s they were one of Britain's most popular homegrown bands, but Nash decided to depart from this lucrative set-up in 1968 fearing that the band was not progressing in the right direction. Alternatively, it has been suggested that he had outgrown this 'pop' approach. He became friendly with David Crosby and Stephen Stills – and together they formed Crosby, Stills And Nash.

Later in the '70s, Nash, who had by then well and truly settled in California, recorded a couple of solo albums, although neither were well viewed critically. His energies, by then, had gone into production and writing,

although in '75 he teamed up again with Crosby to make 'Wind On The Water'. Crosby, too, by then showing preference to go in a solo direction.

In 1979, two of the original Byrds, Chris Hillman and Roger McGuinn played a moderately successful series of concerts in London.

EDDIE CALVERT
British. Male. Instrumentalist.

In 1954, Eddie Calvert made musical history – and chalked up two unique 'firsts' in his career – when his trumpet instrumental version of a German tune, 'O Mein Papa', topped the British Hit Parade for five weeks and later registered strongly in America. The record sold over three million copies internationally to become the *first* instrumental record ever to reach this incredible number of sales. As a result, Eddie Calvert became the *first* British instrumentalist to win a Gold Disc in America.

He went on to enjoy magnificent recording success with such singles as 'Stranger In Paradise', 'John And Julie', 'Zambesi', 'Mandy' and 'Little

EDDIE CALVERT — 'The Man with the Golden Trumpet'

Serenade', and established himself as one of the biggest stars in Britain during the 1950s, nicknamed 'The Man With The Golden Trumpet'.

Eddie was born on March 15, 1922, in Preston, Lancashire, and was taught to play trumpet at the age of eight by his father, who played cornet in the local brass band. The young Eddie followed his father into the band – The Preston Town Silver Band – two years later at the age of eleven.

After national service as a despatch rider in the Army, from which he was discharged following a serious crash, he joined Billy Ternant's Band with whom he broadcast extensively. In 1945, he played with Geraldo And His Orchestra . . . and for the next two years toured Europe for ENSA, before branching out on his own and forming his first band in London for night club appearances.

In 1951, he started recording for Melodisc and a year later turned to engagements on the variety stage and radio. In 1953, he recorded 'O Mein Papa', the number that was to take him to international stardom.

He followed it up two years later with another British chart-topper – 'Cherry Pink And Apple Blossom White'.

Through the 1950s and '60s, Eddie Calvert enjoyed spectacular success, touring the world to entertain audiences in theater seasons and cabaret engagements with his golden trumpet. He appeared at major venues across the globe, while domestically he headlined bills at the London Palladium and in major summer seasons.

At the end of the '60s, however, he left Britain for South Africa where he was appointed entertainment liason officer between the Bantu tribe and the South African Government.

He died from a heart attack in Johannesburg, in 1978.

CANNED HEAT
American. Male.
Vocal/Instrumental Group.
Original line-up: Bob Hite (vocals); Alan Wilson (guitar); Henry Vestine (guitar); Larry Taylor (bass); Adolpho De La Parra (drums).

There was a feel of beery '60s pop festivals, and an infectious, bouncing enthusiasm about Canned Heat, who

CANNED HEAT — fronted by Bob Hite, who died of a heart attack in April 1981

emerged as a jug band, out of Los Angeles, in the middle of that decade, led by Bob 'The Bear' Hite.

Hite's first group, which featured a future Heat drummer Frank Cook, was a jug band. But former record store manager Hite, had always had a preference towards the blues, and it was in this direction the band had drifted by 1966, when Vestine – a former member of Frank Zappa's Mothers Of Invention – and Taylor, joined.

In 1967, the band released their first album, 'Canned Heat'. But they reached the real take-off point of their career later that year, after appearing at the Monterey Jazz & Blues Festival. The following year, Wilson's 'On The Road Again' became the group's first

hit single, but then Vestine left to form his own band – although he later returned to Heat. His place was taken by Detroit guitarist Harvey Mandel.

It happened to coincide with the start of Heat's two-year boom, during which time they had three more big hit singles, 'Going Up The Country', 'Let's Work Together' (their only million-seller) and 'Sugar Bee'. In 1969 they appeared at the Woodstock Festival.

Then tragedy struck! Having spent much of 1970 in Europe, the band returned to the U.S., and later that summer, guitarist Al Wilson was found dead in Bob Hite's garden, in Topanga Canyon, Los Angeles.

It was a blow that shattered the band – and they never recovered.

Between 1970 and 1975, the line-up changed considerably. There were seemingly endless comings and goings. Mandell, for example, who joined in 1970 stayed for a year before

first joining John Mayall and then later forming his own instrumental outfit, Pure Food And Drug Act. In 1974 he formed a new band, which, interestingly, toured Europe *supporting* Canned Heat.

The following two years saw him closely linked with the Rolling Stones, and he was tipped to replace Mick Taylor, although nothing materialized and the job went to Ronnie Wood. Nonetheless, Mandel remains a highly influential guitarist and continues to work regularly.

Meanwhile, the Canned Heat line-up continued to change, with Vestine, by 1971, having returned to the fold only to quit again four years later. Other noted personnel included Mexican bass player Antonio De La Barreda, Joel Scott Hill and James Shane.

Still by the mid 1970s the group centered on Hite, his younger brother – guitarist/vocalist Richard Hite – and Vestine, though the excitement, had left them.

And during the mid 1970s they were still going, but without the originality of their earlier days.

Sadly in April 1981, Bob Hite died of a heart attack, aged 38 years.

DAVID CASSIDY
American. Male. Singer.

Hysterical girls sobbed and screamed whenever he appeared: David Cassidy was the biggest teen sensation since The Beatles. But the difference was that *his* act was specifically contrived to tug at the teenies' heartstrings, which resulted in Cassidy making a fortune, and afterwards proclaiming it had all been a nightmare.

Born the son of actor Jack Cassidy and actress Evelyn Ward, in New York on April 12, 1950, he started to make his mark as a teen hero in the weekly 'Partridge Family' clean-cut television show, having by then moved to Hollywood when his parents divorced. However, prior to this television exposure, his lead vocals on 'I Think I Love You' (fronting the Partridge Family) had become a five million-plus seller, in 1970.

David enjoyed his heyday when still in his early 20s, appearing in the Partridge Family and later as a solo artiste. But by the mid-'70s that edge was vanishing fast. Nonetheless, he had been an enormous phenomena, approached only by The Osmonds and The Bay City Rollers.

As a solo artist, between April 1972 and October 1973 he had two British chart topping singles with 'How Can I Be Sure?' and 'Daydreamer'/'The Puppy Song'. In addition he had a string of chart hits including 'Could It Be Forever?', 'Rock Me Baby', 'If I Didn't Care', 'Darlin' and 'I Write The Songs'.

During this time David Cassidy toured the U.S. and Europe extensively and was always greeted by screaming teenyboppers. It was Beatle-mania all over again!

Early in 1974, a fan died at one of his London concerts, and David had a re-think of his career. And later tried to switch his bopper image to an older age group in the hope of appealing to adult audiences. In the event, it didn't really work, and in 1977, his young fans received their final blow, when he married actress Kay Lenz, and retired from showbusiness to live in Hawaii.

Kay, who appeared in television's 'Rich Man, Poor Man' later revealed that her husband was a total insomniac, haunted by the tensions of his former stardom. He – for his part – admitted that being a teen idol had been a living hell.

"I had become a freak attraction to the kids. My world was a hideous fantasy", he said. "The people who manipulated me, the agents and the record companies, made me into a monster that teeny boppers could go crazy at and scream over. I didn't have a life anymore. I hated to get up each day because I despised myself!"

The final straw in his teen idol career had been the tragedy of the 14-year-old – who had been crushed to death at a London concert. "It will haunt me till the day I die," he said.

CHUBBY CHECKER
American. Male. Singer.

It was The Twist – and it was the dance craze of the early 1960s (before hippy, hippy shakes had taken over) that swept the world. And it thrust a former chicken packer from Philadelphia into the limelight, under the name of Chubby Checker.

Born Ernest Evans on October 3, 1941, Chubby Checker started singing in High School . . . and in his spare time worked in the chicken market owned by Henry Colt. Chubby was always singing as he went about his part-time chicken-packing job, and Holt was so impressed with his vocal ability, that he became his manager and contacted Kal Mann at Cameo-Parkway Records, who in turn signed him to a long contract. His first single 'The Class' was released in 1959. For the release of that first record, Ernest Evans had assumed the highly contrived stage name of Chubby Checker. He adopted the name because he bore a striking resemblance to Fats Domino – Chubby=Fats; Checker=Domino!

But he rose to spectacular success shortly afterwards when he recorded the massive-selling 'The Twist' single, which came about purely by accident. And it was a case of Chubby being in the right place at exactly the right time.

In 1958, Hank Ballard had cut the original version of 'The Twist' and when the dance craze swept across America in 1960, his record was re-released. Ballard was set to appear on the top-rated 'American Bandstand' show, singing his latest re-release, but for some unknown reason he never made it. Instead, Chubby Checker took his place, sang 'The Twist' on air and caused a tremendous reaction from viewers. So much so, that Cameo-Parkway decided to release the song as a single. It went on to sell a million and launched Checker's career.

He gained momentum shortly afterwards when the Church came out *against* the new craze, condemning it as immoral. The resulting publicity only increased record sales. And re-

CHUBBY CHECKER — *on his first visit to Britain*

spectability was to come for The Twist in 1961, with reports that it had been danced at the White House by Democrat politicians including President John Kennedy and his wife Jackie.

From then on it was plain sailing all the way for Chubby Checker. His subsequent releases 'Let's Twist Again', 'Slow Twistin', 'Dancing Party', 'Limbo Rock' – and with Bobby Rydell – 'Teach Me To Twist' and 'Jingle Bell Rock' were all outstanding hits . . . and he enjoyed a phenomenal reign at the top of the showbusiness tree.

In 1964, he married former Miss World, Dutch beauty Catherine Lodder, but by then his record career was waning. He tried to launch a succession of new dance crazes linked to his record releases like 'Pony Time', 'The Fly' and 'Let's Do The Freddie', but without too much success, and he drifted into the inevitable American nightclub circuit.

He resurfaced in 1973 when he was featured in the rock movie 'Let The Good Times Roll', but by then Chubby's good times had already rolled by. However, The Twist craze was set on a brand new course – temporarily – in 1975 when the re-released 'Let's Twist Again' made the British and American charts. But by then, an attempted comeback by Chubby had failed.

He took up health food and jogging to keep in shape for another comeback attempt . . . but it never came on the scale he was hoping. And now he appears on the club circuit, notably on America's West Coast.

LOU CHRISTIE
American. Male.
Singer/Songwriter.

Lou Christie was born Geno Lugee Sacco in Glen Willard, Pennsylvania, on February 19, 1943 and won a scholarship at Moon Township High School, where he studied music and singing.

In 1963, after moving to New York, he landed regular work as a session singer, and provided back-up vocals on numerous recordings. After each session, he pestered the producers and engineers for a recording test – and eventually Roulette Records relented, auditioned him, and signed him to a contract. His first release was

LOU CHRISTIE — stayed at the top for five years

the self-penned 'The Gypsy Cried' which became a million-selling single. He followed it up with, 'Two Faces Have I'. Next came two years Army service before he returned to the charts again with yet another self-written song 'Lightning Strikes' which made Number 1 in America and sold over 2,000,000 copies. 'Rhapsody In The Rain' was a hit the same year, but ran into trouble over the sexual nature of the lyrics.

A bleak spell followed and Lou's career took a back seat until 1969 when he chalked up two more massive hits with 'I'm Gonna Make You Mine', and 'She Sold Me Magic'.

His chart career went into decline during the next decade, but Lou is still very active on the recording scene – writing, recording and producing. And he still performs occasionally, too, for night club audiences in America.

He made a major comeback at the launching of the 'new' Peppermint Lounge in New York, to celebrate its opening in November 1980.

THE DAVE CLARK FIVE
British. Male.
Vocal/Instrumental Group.

Original line-up: Dave Clark (drums); Mike Smith (organ); Denis Payton (sax); Lenny Davidson (guitar); Rick Huxley (bass).

The Dave Clark Five are currently one of the hottest properties in America – ten years after they split up. Indeed, like The Beatles, they have been offered huge sums for them to get together and undertake U.S. concert engagements. Their hit records, and there were many, change hands for three and four times their face-value . . . and they have built up a huge cult following. But there is unlikely to be a return to performing for the group.

Says Dave: "We've turned down several big money tours of America. And if we got back together we could certainly earn a few bob, but it's always a mistake to go back.

"Mike Smith is still making records and plays many sessions. Denis Payton is a successful Estate Agent in Devon. Rick Huxley has his own Electrical business and Lenny Davidson owns several antique shops".

And Dave himself, combines his time producing records, writing and occasionally recording, when the mood takes him. He also has ambitions of making movies – and a few years ago enrolled for a course at London's Central School of Music And Drama.

The Dave Clark Five was formed in the North London suburb of Tottenham in 1960 – and started playing together in a local ballroom. They were signed to a recording contract with Pye's Piccadilly label, but without success, and they decided to remain semi-professional and *not* to give up their day jobs which included stuntman and film extra (Dave); finance correspondent (Mike); clerk (Lenny); electronical engineering (Denis); and lighting engineer (Rick).

Their engagements increased, however, and in 1963 they actually played at Buckingham Palace.

In October of that year, they switched labels to Columbia and recorded 'Do You Love Me', which reached Number 30 in the British charts, but was over-shadowed by Brian Poole's version. A month later, though, they topped the British Hit Parade with 'Glad All Over', which reached Number 6 in America.

It was the start of an exceptionally successful career for the group, for they were immediately offered a contract for tours by impresario Harold Davidson which guaranteed them at least $200,000 a year.

In 1964, with four more hits under their belt – 'Bits And Pieces', 'Can't You See That She's Mine', 'Thinking Of You Baby' and 'Anyway You Want It' – they embarked on a phenomenal tour of America, which set the seal of their success. At one time, they were second only in popularity to The Beatles.

1965 saw more tours and even more hit records – 'Everybody Knows'; 'Reelin' And Rockin'; 'Come Home'; 'Over And Over' and 'Catch Us If You Can', from the film of the same name, which marked the group's movie debut that year.

And so it continued . . . with major American and British tours, and more hits – including 'Red Balloon' (1968); 'Good Old Rock 'n' Roll' (1969) and 'Everybody Get Together' (1970) – until 1970, when they decided to call it a day, and go their own separate ways. However, in 1978 a compilation album of their 'greatest hits', released under the title of 'Twenty Five Thumping Great Hits', put them back at the top of the British LP chart . . . and added to their fortunes. But there was still no going back.

Said Dave: "I got as far as I wanted to go in pop. I didn't want to recapture the past.

"I was always the Manager of the group in our heyday – I didn't depend on other people. Even though we were young, we had the sense to look after our money. I always think it's a bit sad when you see people who were big stars in their time, back singing in little clubs. There are singers who should have made a fortune in the '60s but came out with nothing.

"We were all pretty shrewd with our money. We didn't go throwing it around because we knew the bubble would burst someday. I waited until 1967 to buy my own place – a penthouse in Mayfair. I still live there."

PETULA CLARK — *a British institution*

PETULA CLARK
British. Female. Singer.

Petula Clark is one of the few artists to make the change-over from child star to adult entertainer without any problems whatsoever, and *without* losing any of her former popularity. Indeed, as she grew older, and emerged as one of the foremost singers in international music – her success and reputation increased.

That's not all . . . she is also one of just a handful of British entertainers who have ever headlined cabaret seasons in the lucrative night spots of Las Vegas.

She was born Petula Sally Olwen Clark on November 15, 1932, in Epsom, Surrey, and began her show-business career at the age of seven. At nine, she was performing regularly on radio – and she appeared in over 500 shows for the Forces during World War II.

During her teens, Petula appeared in more than twenty major films, including 'A Medal For A General', 'Strawberry Road', 'London Town', 'The Card', 'Here Come The Huggetts' and 'Vote For Huggett', and she also

sang on radio and television extensively.

She enjoyed her first hit single in 1954 with 'The Little Shoemaker' on Polygon Records, which reached Number 17 in Britain. Next followed 'Majorca'. A year later, she switched labels and joined Pye and scored with her first single for the new company – 'Suddenly There's A Valley'.

It was during the latter days of the 1950s that she established herself as a major star in Britain and internationally, a position she has consolidated ever since.

In 1961, she topped the British chart for the first time, with 'Sailor', followed by her first million-seller 'Romeo'. And next came a magnificent run in the International Hit Parade stakes with 'Monsieur', which topped the German chart in 1962; 'Chariot' (a French chart-topper in the same year); and British hits – 'My Friend The Sun', 'Ya Ya Twist', 'Casanova', 'Downtown', (an American chart-topper in 1964), 'I Know A Place', 'My Love' and 'I Couldn't Live Without Your Love'.

In 1961, she married Claud Wolff, who at that time was publicity director for Vogue Records in France. He became her manager and for a while the couple made their home in Paris. Almost immediately Petula started to establish herself in the French market – and within a year had emerged as the country's leading female singer, with a string of hits to her credit. She repeated that success all over Europe.

For the next few years, while starting her family, Petula Clark still managed to amass a tremendous recording track list, scoring with such songs as 'This Is My Song' – another British Number 1, in 1967; 'Don't Sleep In The Subway', 'The Other Man's Grass', 'Kiss Me Goodbye' and 'The Song of Love'. She also returned to movies and starred in several including – 'Goodbye Mr. Chips', and 'Finian's Rainbow'.

During the early '70s, she combined the roles of singing superstar and housewife-and-mother perfectly, and regularly headlined lengthy tours of Britain, Europe and America – where she was a major attraction in Vegas.

Then, in 1977, she went into retirement and rarely worked, apart from the occasional television or charity

show appearance. Instead, she spent most of her time with her family in their homes in London, Megeve, or Geneva.

"In the last three years I've hardly worked," she said in the fall of 1980. "But now I've got a band together and I'm going back on the road again in the New Year. I want to know if I've still got something to offer.

"After all, I've never really had to work at my career like other top artistes and I'm lucky to have done so well. I have had a lovely family life."

However, in December 1980, it was announced that Petula would star as 'Maria' in a spectacular revival production of the hit musical 'The Sound of Music', to be staged in London at the Apollo Victoria Theatre, in August 1981 – her first-ever appearance in a *stage* musical.

JIMMY CLIFF — *has inspired countless reggae bands*

JIMMY CLIFF
Jamaican. Male. Singer.

Success for Jimmy Cliff didn't come easily. In fact it's something he's been working at since he left his home in St. Catherine, Jamaica, in 1962 – at the age of 14 – to go to Kingston in search of fame and fortune in music.

He was born James Chambers in Somerton, Jamaica in 1948, and enjoyed his first local record success with 'Daisy Got Me Crazy'. Next followed a succession of ska records including 'I'm Sorry', 'Hurricane Hattie', 'Dearest Beverley', 'Make It Up' and 'King Of Kings', which all sold moderately well in his native country.

After a government-sponsored tour of America with Byron Lee and The

Dragonaires in 1965, he moved to Britain where producer Chris Blackwell signed him to Island Records. He soon built up a large fan following in the country, after what seemed like endless rounds of engagements in ska and reggae clubs. His initial single release 'Give And Take' failed to chart, still it did become an enormous discotheque success. But with 'Wonderful World, Beautiful People', two years later, he began to make an impression on a wider record buying public. It reached the Top Ten in Britain and was followed by the less successful 'Vietnam', before his next hit with Cat Stevens' 'Wild World'.

In the early '70s, he starred in the reggae movie, 'The Harder They Come', which hoisted him to international stardom. It gained a cult following all over the world and Jimmy was able to spread his own kind of 'word' about the plight of black people everywhere.

Since then, he has continued to perform his reggae gospel – and still plays to packed audiences. Currently with WEA Records, his last classic release of major importance was 'No Woman, No Cry'.

Jimmy, who still lives in Somerton, St. James, has spent the recent years touring what he calls "the Third World" with extensive concert engagements in South America and South Africa.

Today, he looks upon himself as a "musical messenger".

He says of his world travels: "I have always been a humanitarian in that view. Within the whole masonic work there, 'cause the singers and players of instruments is doing a masonic job, I man work as the shepherd. The shepherd have two things to do: The shepherd open the gate and see that everyone go through, and then closes it. That has been my work. That has been the history of my work".

JOE COCKER
British. Male. Singer.

When Joe Cocker hit the chart jackpot in the fall of 1968, topping the Hit Parade in Britain with his dynamic, gutsy version of The Beatles' 'With A Little Help From My Friends' – everyone believed he was an overnight star, made in true Hollywood tradition. Nothing could have been further from the truth. Joe had spent nine years prior to his chart success, playing night after night in the tough Northern clubs and pubs, without ever making headlines.

He was born John Robert Cocker on May 20, 1944, in Sheffield, Yorkshire, and joined his first local group, The Cavaliers – for whom he played drums – at the age of fifteen. After leaving Sheffield Central Technical School, he joined the East Midlands Gas Board as a fitter, yet continued with his group activities with the band now re-named Vince Arnold And The Avengers.

One day in 1963, he heard that record producer Mike Leander was auditioning a rival group in Sheffield. So he gatecrashed the session, with his own group, muscled in on the audition himself . . . and performed for Leander. The producer was impressed and signed Vince Arnold And The Avengers to a record contract.

Joe, was given leave of absence from the Gas Board, to try his luck in the pop world . . . and the group's first single, 'I'll Cry Instead' – a cover of a Beatles' album track – was released shortly afterwards. It failed to make any kind of impact, and totally disillusioned with showbusiness, Joe returned to his former trade as a fitter and then set about rethinking his whole musical career.

Determined to succeed, he decided to put together the ultimate group, from local musicians, to play a much more gutsy brand of music. He called it The Grease Band, featuring Henry McCullough on guitar; Kenny Slade on drums; Alan Spenner on guitar; Chris Stainton on bass; and Tommy Eyre on keyboards.

The Grease Band, fronted by Cocker, spent the next four years working semi-professionally in the North of England until at last, they were signed to EMI Records, and released their first single 'Marjorine' in the spring of '68, which reached 48 in the British Top Fifty. Joe's second single with the group was 'With A Little Help From My Friends' and it went to the very top of the chart, registering strongly in America.

He toured the States in 1969, and played at Woodstock, where he met Leon Russell who in turn produced Cocker's next single success 'Delta Lady' – it made the British Top Ten. A year later, he was back on the road in

JOE COCKER — appearing at one of London's infamous Crystal Palace Garden Parties

the States as part of Russell's massive rock package Mad Dogs And Englishmen, and back, too, in the chart with another single – 'The Letter'. But it was during this tour that rumors abounded about Joe's drugs problem, which he vehemently denied. However, he returned to Britain and drifted into semi-retirement.

In 1972, he made a disastrous comeback with a world tour, taking in Britain, America and Australia, where he was arrested on a drugs charge and eventually deported from the country. Back home, and *again* back in isolation, he set about re-thinking his career once more. He emerged in 1974 with a new album – 'I Can Stand A Little Rain' – and a new tour of America where in 1975 he scored a Top Ten hit with 'You Are So Beautiful'. But for the next few years, his career and private life were dogged with problems . . . *drinks* and *drugs*, and *financial troubles* to plague him.

In the face of such heavy odds, Joe Cocker became a recluse, living off former glories on the West Coast of America.

Another comeback was attempted in the fall of 1980 with a massive British tour, including a series of London concerts which played to sell out success . . . but so nearly met with total disaster when Joe refused to appear on stage until his manager had been paid every penny of the fee, reputed to be in excess of $12,000, in *cash*.

Said Joe, trying to explain away the financial problems that were dogging his career: "I don't care about money – but that's why my life is so confused. I can't appear in Britain as *Joe Cocker*, I have to do it under some kind of company name because of my financial problems. I'm relieved to have a great manager who stops me getting involved in details like collecting money."

A sad state of affairs for one of the great characters in rock music, and after that particular London concert a journalist, reviewing the show, said that Joe's passion for the bottle had "earned him a grace and physique of a bearded dolphin!"

Later, the comeback concert tour of Britain was cancelled.

ARTHUR CONLEY — the prótege of Otis Redding

ARTHUR CONLEY
American. Male. Singer.

A protege of the late, great, Otis Redding, (see **Otis Redding**), Arthur Conley is best remembered for his 1967 Top Ten hit, 'Sweet Soul Music'.

Born on January 14, 1946, he was raised in Atlanta, Georgia, where he started his musical career singing in local clubs.

A spell singing in the Southern States followed before he met Otis Redding in Baltimore in 1965, and played him a demo-tape of his singing 'I'm A Lonely Stranger'.

Otis was very impressed by Arthur's vocal ability and helped to land a recording contract with his own Jotis label. He later produced all of Conley's early releases for the label.

In 1967 Redding and Conley adapted the old Sam Cooke classic 'Yeah Man' into 'Sweet Soul Music' – and Arthur was on the way to instant stardom.

There followed a successful tour, but Redding's tragic death on December 10, 1967, in a plane crash, seemed to affect Conley's life and career. A few successful singles, including 'Funky Street' and 'People Sure Act Funny' followed, and, in 1971, he switched record labels, hoping somehow for a repeat of 'Sweet Soul Music'. That was not to be, and Conley

totally faded in the '70s.

However, he still performs in clubs all over America and Europe hoping for a revival in his fortunes!

JESS CONRAD
British. Male. Singer.

Jess Conrad became a singer by accident. An aspiring actor, he had landed a small part in the British comedy film 'Further Up The Creek' in 1959, and on its completion, he decided to learn his trade thoroughly by appearing in local repertory theater. So, with this in mind, he applied for, and later joined, the Hornchurch Repertory Company in Essex, England.

It was while appearing with the company that television producer Daphne Shadwell saw him and signed him to play 'Barney' in the play 'Rock-a-bye Barney', about a rock 'n' roll singer.

The show was a big success and for the first time, Jess was called upon to sing on stage, which prompted Jack Good to sign him to appear in his hit TV show 'Wham!'. As a result of his appearances on television, Jess was later signed to a recording contract and scored his first British chart success in 1960 with 'Cherry Pie', followed by 'Mystery Girl' in 1961, and 'Pretty Jenny' a year later – all minor hits. In 1978, however, 'Cherry Pie' had the dubious distinction of being featured on a compilation LP as one of several of "the worst pop songs" ever recorded. Another Conrad single, 'This Pullover' was also on that album!

Jess combined his singing career with acting for the next few years, and during the 1960s he starred in several feature films including 'The Boys' and 'Aliki', followed by successful appearances on television in plays like 'The Flipside Man' and 'The Paradise Suite' . . . *and* summer season and pantomime engagements throughout Britain.

He also appeared in the West End in the hit musical 'Pip' . . . and toured the country throughout the '70s in the rock musicals 'Godspell' and 'Joseph And The Amazing Technicolour Dream-coat'.

Born Gerald James in South London in February 1940, Jess Conrad, however, has never deserted his rock 'n' roll roots and regularly appears – when his acting commitments allow – in clubs and cabaret venues all over Britain with his Hollywood Rock Machine band.

During the Christmas season 1980/81, he returned to London's West End stage to re-create his role of 'Joseph' in the Lloyd-Webber/Rice musical 'Joseph And The Amazing Technicolour Dreamcoat' which played a successful season at the Vaudeville Theatre.

RUSS CONWAY
British. Male. Instrumentalist.

Born Trevor Stanford on September 2, 1927 in Bristol, England, Russ Conway, started playing piano as a youngster, though it was at singing that he excelled. So much so that much later he won a scholarship to join the choir of the famous Bristol Cathedral School.

At fourteen he left school and trained to become a solicitor's clerk. Then, in 1942, he was summoned for national service, and joined the Royal Navy. The years of war that followed for Russ were climaxed by the award of a Distinguished Service Medal during operations in the Aegean Sea and Mediterranean.

After the war, Russ served with the Merchant Navy for short spells, and then in 1955, finally decided to follow a professional music career, and set about earning his living by playing piano in London nightclubs. In one

RUSS CONWAY — *continues to tinkle the ivories*

such club, he was discovered by record producer Norman Newell, who signed him to Columbia Records as his audition pianist.

Russ later branched out on his own to become accompanist for such leading stars of the day as Lita Rosa, Denis Lotis, Dorothy Squires, Joan Regan and Gracie Fields.

In 1957, he clocked up his first hit record with the instrumental 'Party Pops' – a compilation single of several sing-a-long melodies. It was followed in 1958, by another single in similar vein, entitled, appropriately enough, 'More Party Pops'. A year later, he topped the British hit parade with 'Side Saddle', which he followed up a few months later with his second chart-topper – 'Roulette'. And by the time hit parade success had deserted him in 1963, Russ Conway had notched up no less than twenty chart singles. Only The Shadows and Duane Eddy have had more instrumental hits to their credit in Britain.

During the late '50s and '60s, Russ turned more and more towards the variety stage, enjoying magnificent success on tours all over Britain – topping the bill several times at the London Palladium – and throughout the world. He also appeared extensively on television.

Today, he continues to perform in theater and cabaret seasons not only in Britain but in Australia and South Africa.

SAM COOKE
American. Male. Singer.

Hailed by one British music writer as "the father of soul music as we know it today", Sam Cooke had a powerful influence on many of his soul contemporaries, including Aretha Franklyn, Smokey Robinson, Johnny Nash, Marvin Gaye and Otis Redding. Rod Stewart has called him "my favourite singer" and recorded two Cooke standards – 'Bring It On Home To Me' and 'Twistin' The Night Away'.

Sam Cooke was born one of eight children in Chicago on January 22, 1931, into a strong church-going family. His father was a local minister.

His early musical influence was Gospel music and with one of his brothers and two sisters, he was featured singing in a church group at the

age of nine under the collective name of The Singing Children. Then as a teenager he sang with another Gospel group The Highway QC's . . . and in 1950, he joined The Soul Stirrers, with whom he sang and recorded, for the next six years.

It was during his spell with The Stirrers that Sam Cooke started to build up a huge fan following for himself – being the focal point of the group – and it was inevitable that he would soon branch out on his own solo career. Indeed, he had always had an ambition to move away from the Gospel music played by his group, to cover more contemporary pop, rock 'n' roll and r & b. When Speciality Records later released some of Cooke's early recordings in their own right, they were forced to use the pseudonym Dale Cooke. But it didn't take long before the real identity of *Dale* Cooke was discovered and it led to Sam being asked to leave The Soul Stirrers.

In 1956 his solo career was guided by Little Richard's manager Bumps Blackwell, who bought out his contract from Speciality and signed him to the Keen label. During this time, he recorded the single 'You Send Me', written by his brother Charles. It went on to sell over two million copies and top the national Hit Parade. It also registered his first hit in Britain.

Sam Cooke was launched on the road to soul super stardom. At the same time 'You Send Me' was in the chart, his old recording company Speciality, re-released an earlier Sam Cooke single 'I'll Come Running Back To You', on the strength of his new found fame. This record, too, sold a million copies.

Cooke was with Keen Records for four years and in that time he enjoyed several more hit singles including 'Wonderful World', and 'Only Sixteen'. He joined RCA Victor in 1960. But prior to his change of labels, he also formed his *own* record company, in association with one J. Alexander, called Sar Records. It was one of the first black-owned record labels and recorded such Gospel artistes as The Valentinos, Johnny Taylor – a former member of The Highway QC's; and The Sims Twins.

However, it was as a recording

artiste for RCA that Sam Cooke established himself as one of *the* major soul singers in the world – and a dynamic performer. In four years, he sold nearly 20 million records with a barrage of international hits. 'Chain Gang', 'Sad Mood', 'Cupid', 'Twistin' The Night Away', 'Bring It On Home To Me', 'Ain't That Good News', 'Tennessee Waltz', 'That's Where It's At', 'Another Saturday Night' and 'Shake', were all among the best-sellers. He also combined his time touring in concerts and appearing in the nightclubs of Las Vegas, where he was in great demand. From 1960 to 1964, he established himself as one of soul's genuine superstars!

On December 11, 1964, he was shot three times at close range by a woman, he was allegedly trying to rape in a Los Angeles motel. He was killed instantly. The court later returned a verdict of justifiable homicide, claiming the woman shot in self-defense.

FLOYD CRAMER
American. Male. Instrumentalist.

Floyd Cramer is today one of the most respected men in country music and almost a permanent fixture at the Nashville Grand Ole Opry alongside his great friend Chet Atkins.

His distinctive style of piano playing, which he humorously calls – "a

FLOYD CRAMER — *responsible for the 'Dallas' theme tune*

whole tone slur" – has endeared him to millions of fans all over the world and dominated the country scene for twenty years. To the majority of aficienados, Floyd Cramer is quite simply the best country pianist in the world.

He was born in Shreveport, Louisianna on October 27, 1933, and started playing piano at the age of five. During his teens, he played with various local groups, before joining the successful and celebrated 'Louisianna Hayride Show'.

In 1955, he was virtually discovered by Chet Atkins who took him to Nashville, the home of country music. And it was in the Tennessee city that he really made his musical mark and was soon featured extensively on sessions, working with the likes of Jim Reeves and The Browns. However, it was his work with Elvis Presley on record that really established him.

Floyd was soon recording on his own and in 1960 his first single 'Last Date' sold over a million copies and reached the Number 2 slot in the U.S. chart. A year later, he topped the British Hit Parade with 'On The Rebound'.

Since then, of course, Floyd like his mentor Chet Atkins, has continued to work in Nashville bringing his own particular sound and style to hundreds of recording sessions.

In recent years, however, Cramer came back to the recording scene with a vengeance after recording the theme tune to the top television series 'Dallas'.

CREAM
British. Male. Vocal/Instrumental Group.

Original line-up: Jack Bruce (bass); Ginger Baker (drums); Eric Clapton (guitar).

The first supergroup of the '60s, Cream were formed in 1966 by Jack Bruce (formerly with the Graham Bond Organisation, John Mayall and Manfred Mann), Ginger Baker (ex-Graham Bond Organisation) and Eric Clapton, from John Mayall's Blues-

CREAM — *(l-r): Ginger Baker, Eric Clapton, Jack Bruce*

CREAM — The classic psychedelic album cover

breakers and the Yardbirds. For more than two years they enjoyed a magnificent sequence of successes, particularly in America.

Besides undertaking extensive, sell-out tours of Britain and the States, Cream also clocked up several hit singles including 'I Feel Free', 'Strange Brew', 'Anyone For Tennis', 'Sunshine Of Your Love', 'White Room' and 'Badge' . . . and a clutch of hit albums.

Cream were noted for their virtuoso performances on stage (by the 'cream' of British musicians) of many blues standards, yet their albums bristled with original material from the pen of Clapton and Bruce. It also threw up the talented song-writing partnership of Jack Bruce and Pete Brown, responsible for among other numbers, 'White Room' and 'Sunshine Of Your Love'.

The band split in 1968 after performing a noted farewell concert – which spawned a 'Goodbye' album and 'Farewell' TV movie – at the Royal Albert Hall in London. Clapton and Baker (see **Ginger Baker**), later formed Blind Faith, while Bruce (see **Jack Bruce**) went solo.

CREEDENCE CLEARWATER REVIVAL
American. Male.
Vocal/Instrumental Group.
Original line-up: John Fogerty (vocals/guitar); Doug Clifford (drums); Tom Fogerty (bass); Stu Cook (piano).

They arrived on the crest of the West Coast wave, as the American music industry turned to San Francisco in 1968, to look to both the future and to the immediate profits. Originally called The Blue Velvets and later, The Golliwogs, the four-man band adopted the name Creedence Clearwater Revival in 1967, and the following year shook the entire industry with their debut 'Creedence Clearwater Revival' album.

The group were all born in the San Francisco Bay area and initially banded together as Tommy Fogerty and the Blue Velvets, playing teenage clubs and various Army, Navy and Airforce Military bases. But after signing with Fantasy Records, they changed their name to The Golliwogs, in an attempt to combat the British beat boom.

1967 saw the foursome turning professional, and becoming the contrively named Creedence Clearwater Revival – and then their premier album. Between then and 1972, they recorded a host of first-class singles and albums – pushing the band to the forefront of international popular music.

Hit albums included 'Willy And The Poor Boys', 'Cosmo's Factory' and 'Green River'. And top singles included the classic chart-topping 'Proud Mary' and 'Bad Moon Rising', 'Green River', 'Down On The Corner', 'Travellin' Band', 'Up Around The Bend', 'Long As I Can See The Light', 'Have You Ever Seen The Rain' and 'Sweet Hitch Hiker'.

It has been suggested that John Fogerty, who fronted the group, felt he had something to prove in his music. But in so doing, perhaps, he missed the point that his band had achieved a broader popularity than most of their rivals, particularly in the singles' field.

Brother Tom, however, left the band at the turn of the 1970s, and embarked on a solo career and has since recorded five solo albums, before forming his own group Ruby. This left John Fogerty, Clifford and Cook, who performed as a threesome, until 1972, when they disbanded – still very much at the top of their profession.

Cook and Clifford went on to join the Don Harrison Band. John Fogerty embarked on a distinguished solo career, initially recording the 'Blue Ridge Rangers' album. Yet while this appeared to be the work of a band, it was, in fact, an entirely solo effort, with Fogerty playing all the instruments, singing, arranging and producing the whole package himself. He followed it with two U.S. hit singles, 'Jambalaya' and 'Heart Of Stone'.

Curiously he tends to work hard, but sporadically. Nonetheless, he's one of America's top rock performers and composers, with an understanding of his market few of his contemporaries can equal. Greater things are yet to come . . .

CREEDENCE — (l-r): Tom Fogerty, Stu Cook, Doug Clifford, John Fogerty

In November 1980, former rhythm guitarist Tom Fogerty married Tricia Clapper in the East Bay suburb of San Francisco. To mark the occasion, Tom persuaded brother John Fogerty, Doug Clifford and Stu Cook to come together once more – eight years after Creedence had disbanded – to play at his wedding reception. The impromptu jam session lasted over an hour, with the group running through *all* their old hits.

THE CRYSTALS
American. Female. Vocal Group.
Original line-up: DeeDee Kennibrew; Pat Wright; Barbara Alston; Dolores 'La La' Brooks; Mary Thomas.

The Crystals were formed in 1961 as a semi-professional singing group, by five Brooklyn, New York, schoolgirls . . . all eager to make a name for themselves as pop stars. They certainly made history, by becoming the first group signed to the newly formed Philles Record label, run by Phil Spector and Lester Sills.

It was Spector who became the group's mentor and inspiration, and he produced all their subsequent

THE CRYSTALS — *the girls from Brooklyn*

singles, which started that year with 'There's No Other' – an American Top Twenty hit.

However, it was a mere lull before the storm of outstanding chart success for the girls. Their follow-up single 'Uptown' reached the U.S. Top Ten; while their third release 'He's A Rebel', written by the rapidly emerging singing star Gene Pitney (see **Gene Pitney**), went to the very top of

the American Hit Parade in the fall of 1962. It also marked their first success in Britain and heralded the advent of the famous Phil Spector 'sound' which was to be developed fully with The Ronettes and Righteous Brothers. What people didn't know at that time, though, was that the original Crystals were not featured on 'He's A Rebel', but a session group from Los Angeles, fronted by Darlene Love, replaced them and this 'manufactured' group also recorded the follow-up single 'He's Sure The Boy I Love'. When they recorded 'Da Doo Ron Ron' in 1963, Darlene Love failed to turn up for the session and the newly signed Cherilyn Sakisian La Pier – later to become known as Cher (see **Sonny and Cher**) – stepped in and took her place.

Mary Thomas had left the group in 1962 and The Crystals continued to work as a four-piece group. They clocked up their biggest success 'Then He Kissed Me' in 1964. The same year, Phil Spector dropped the group from his label in order to concentrate on their successors The Ronettes, and The Crystals moved to United Artists Records where they failed to recreate their initial success, and later split up.

45

BOBBY DARIN
American. Male. Singer.

Bobby Darin was born Walden Robert Cassotto on May 14, 1936, in the Bronx area of New York and was raised by his mother, a former professional entertainer. His father had died a few months before his birth.

An excellent scholar and musician – he could play piano, drums, bass, guitar and vibes proficiently while still a youngster – Darin won a scholarship to study science in college. And it was while completing his education, however, that he started singing and playing piano in New York supper clubs.

In 1956, he was signed to Decca Records and released 'My First Love', a song he had co-written with a friend Don Kirshner, who later discovered The Monkees. Two years later, he wrote and recorded 'Splish Splash', which brought him international stardom. The record enjoyed outstanding chart success on both sides of the Atlantic . . . and he followed it up with an avalanche of hit singles: 'Queen Of The Hop', 'Dream Lover', 'Mac The Knife' – which topped the American and British charts in 1959 – 'Beyond The Sea', 'Clementine', 'Bill Bailey', 'Lazy River' and 'Nature Boy'.

Besides establishing himself as a major recording artist – he had thirty-seven hits in the American Top Hundred – Bobby also emerged as a star of television and movies, having signed a long contract with Paramount. And his film credits included 'Too Late Blues', 'Pepe', 'Come September', 'Hell Is For Heroes' and many more. He also became one of the highest paid and most in-demand nightclub entertainers in America!

During the early 1960s, however, his fortunes fluctuated. He was diversifying his talents too far and refused to specialize. He did return to the chart reckoning on many occasions though, and scored with three major hit singles at this time: 'Multiplication' (1961); 'Things' (1962); and 'If I Were A Carpenter' (1966). But he never quite consolidated his earlier success, though his TV and cabaret commitments increased.

He died of a heart attack in Lebanon Hospital, Hollywood, on December 20, 1973, after suffering from heart disease since the age of eight when he was struck by a severe attack of rheumatic fever.

DAVE DEE, DOZY, BEAKY, MICK AND TICH
British. Male.
Vocal/Instrumental Group.
Original line-up: Dave Harman (Dave Dee — vocals); Trevor Davies (Dozy — bass); John Dymond (Beaky — guitar); Michael Wilson (Mick — drums); Ian Amey (Tich — guitar).

Formed in the early 1960s in Wiltshire, Dave Dee, Dozy, Beaky, Mick and Tich started out life as Dave Dee and the Bostons, under which name they released several unsuccessful singles.

In 1965, on the verge of disbanding through lack of any real success, the group were persuaded by managers Alan Blaikely and Ken Howard to record one final number. 'You Make It Move', proved the group's salvation and gave them their first British hit, albeit in the lower reaches of the Top Thirty. However, it was a vital stepping stone . . . and from 1965 to 1969, they enjoyed a further dozen hit singles all written by Howard and Blaikely: 'Hold Tight' (1966); 'Hideaway' (1966); 'Bend It' (1966), 'Save Me' (1966), 'Touch Me Touch Me' (1967), 'Okay' (1967), 'Zabadak' (1967), 'Legend Of Xanadu' (their only Number 1, in 1968), 'Last Night In Soho' (1968), 'Wreck Of The Antionette' (1968), 'Don Juan' (1969) and 'Snake In The Grass' (1969).

Despite their chart success in Britain and a large fan following – they were one of the first groups to utilize comedy on stage – the group failed to establish themselves in America. In 1969 Dave Dee left the group to concentrate on his own solo career, which embraced singing and acting, and in March 1970 he notched up his only hit single 'My Woman's Man'. Three years later, he joined Atlantic Records as head of A & R in their London head-

*BOBBY DARIN — **died in Hollywood in 1973***

D,D,D,B&T — (l-r): Dave Dee, Dozy, Mick, Tich and Beaky

quarters, and in 1980, he quit the company to form his own record label – Double-D Records.

Meanwhile, the rest of the group, now called D,B,M&T, continued to perform and as such they, too, enjoyed moderate chart success in the summer of 1970 with 'Mr President'.

They have continued to play together ever since.

JIMMY DEAN
American. Male. Singer.

Jimmy Dean was born Seth Ward in Plainview, Texas, on August 10, 1928 and enjoyed a massive British and American hit in 1961 with 'Big Bad John'. Legend has it that Jimmy actually wrote the song while traveling on an aircraft to Nashville where he was on his way for a recording session. It became his only major international success.

The record went on to top both the British and American charts and sell over two million copies, bringing for 'The Long Tall Texan' immediate success, which culminated on his own weekly ABC television program 'The Jimmy Dean Show'. He also took over from the perennial compere to host the ever popular 'Merv Griffin Show' on many occasions.

It was in 1948, after his discharge from national service with the Air Force that Jimmy formed his own group The Texas Wildcats in Washington where they landed appearances on the WTOP-TV station's morning show. In 1952 the group were signed for a lengthy tour of American bases in the Caribbean. And for the next dozen or so years, he toured America playing the cabaret and supper clubs, and appeared on television in his own shows for CBS-TV.

Jimmy never managed to follow up his massive hit successfully, although he had several minor hits – 'Cajun Queen', 'Dear Ivan', 'PT 109', 'Little Black Book', the country chart-topper 'The First Thing Every Morning' and 'I.O.U.' in 1976 – and his television series kept his name very much in the frame of popularity. When the show was eventually taken off the air, Dean turned his own brand of country music into a major attraction on the American nightclub circuit, where he's still going strong today.

JOEY DEE AND THE STARLITERS
American. Male.
Vocal/Instrumental Group.

Original line-up: Joey Dee (vocals); Carlton Latimor (organ); Larry Vernieri (vocals); Dave Brigati (vocals); Willie Davis (drums).

Joey Dee was born Joseph Dinicola in Passaic, New Jersey on June 11, 1940 and started the famous Starliters in 1958. For the next year they worked in clubs around the New York area . . . and in 1960 landed a residency at the celebrated Peppermint lounge in the city. The nightclub became outstandingly successful and famous during the early '60s as the home of The Twist.

In their time at the venue The Starliters' sound was regularly augmented with several up-and-coming groups and singers including The Ronettes.

Signed to the Roulette label, Joey Dee and The Starliters enjoyed a multi-million singles success in 1962 with 'Peppermint Twist' which topped the U.S. chart for three weeks – it also registered their one and only hit in Britain. The same year, they embarked on several tours of America, and later appeared in 'twist' movies – 'Hey Let's Twist' and 'Vive Le Twist'.

They chalked up another hit single in 1962 with 'Shout' and enjoyed outstanding success with their album 'Doing The Twist At The Peppermint Lounge'. But after the dance craze started to fade towards the end of 1962, Joey Dee's career went with it.

Still, he'd made a small fortune from The Twist and later opened a coin shop in Miami, Florida, which he runs today.

He was tempted out of retirement in November 1980, to sing at the opening of the 'new' Peppermint Lounge in New York . . . where it had all begun 20 years before!

DELANEY AND BONNIE
American. Male/Female.
Vocal/Instrumentalists.

They first met in Los Angeles and were married within seven days of that meeting, in 1967. That was the start of the Delaney Bramlett (born in Pontococ, Mississippi, in 1940) and Bonnie Lynn (born in Granite City, Illinois, in 1941) duo – Delaney And Bonnie. They were the first white act to sign for the Stax/Volt label, with their distinctive gospel/rock style and worked with Booker T and the MG's on sessions.

Both had had a substantial background in rock music before they met. Delaney with The Shindigs, a duo he formed with Joey Cooper; and Bonnie as one of Ike and Tina Turner's Ikettes.

Soon after their marriage, they began playing publicly together, backed by anyone who'd turn up to play – hence the idea being born of The Delaney And Bonnie And Friends act.

By this time too, there had been a couple of label switches, which saw them ending up with Atco. Meanwhile Delaney and Bonnie were attracting the interest of a number of top liners in the rock world, including ex-Traffic guitarist Dave Mason. They also worked with Leon Russell, Bobby Whitlock, Jim Keltner, Duane Allman,

Rita Coolidge . . . and many more. For the 1969 U.S. Blind Faith tour, Delaney And Bonnie And Friends – always basically a loose amalgam – joined the bill. The same year saw their only British chart single success with 'Comin' Home'.

During subsequent tours they played with George Harrison, Eric Clapton, and The Plastic Ono Band gaining momentum and enhancing their reputation all the time.

But the bubble burst in 1972, when they split – privately *and* professionally . . . and divorced.

Subsequently, both pursued solo careers and recorded solo albums. Delaney later went into retirement, to emerge in 1977 for the Delaney And Friends Class Reunion Album. Yet as solo artistes, they did not match their earlier (joint) success.

Both have continued to record separately – and work regularly on sessions.

BO DIDDLEY
American. Male.
Singer/Instrumentalist/Songwriter.

Bo Diddley, along with Chuck Berry (see **Chuck Berry**), was one of the most influential figures in the development of rock 'n' roll. Certainly he inspired numerous rock groups, including The Rolling Stones, The Yardbirds, Manfred Mann, The Pretty

DELANEY AND BONNIE — (l-r at front): Bonnie, Delaney with guests, Eric Clapton and George Harrison

Things – who took their name from one of his best-known songs – and The Animals.

He was born Ellas McDaniel on December 30, 1928 in McComb, Mississippi and at the age of five, moved with his family to Chicago. At seven, he started to play the violin – and later taught himself to play guitar.

As a teenager in high school, Bo formed his first group, The Langley Avenue Jive Cats and on graduating, he created another band featuring the talents of Frank Kirkland (drums), Billy Boy Arnold (harmonica), Jerome Green (maraccas) and his half-sister 'The Duchess' on guitar. The group progressed to playing the blues in the night clubs in Chicago.

Bo soon found that he couldn't make too much money from his music, so to supplement his income, he took part time employment as a construction worker.

He says: "I also boxed – light-heavyweight. When I was at school, kids started calling me Bo (it means bad boy) Diddley, so when I fought, I used that name. It was ideal for the

BO DIDDLEY — with one of his famous odd-shaped guitars

stage too."

However, in 1955 he auditioned for Checker Records, a subsidiary of Chess, whose stable included top-lining black blues singers Howlin' Wolf, Muddy Waters, Little Walter and John Lee Hooker. His first single 'Bo Diddley' was issued the same year and made his reputation. Actually it was originally called 'Uncle John' but the head of the record company insisted he change the title.

Bo brought a new excitement and a new sound to records: — a pulsating jungle beat, heavy bass and the incessant shuffling rhythm of maraccas, a style which was immortalized much later on The Stones' 'Not Fade Away'. It was the Diddley trade mark, much copied by his contemporaries. Bo Diddley also pioneered the use of the electric guitar on blues numbers, he experimented with techniques and sound, and became the first r 'n' b artist to exploit the use of a total electric sound on record. He was noted, too, for his array of weird, wonderful and brightly colored guitars, which

were self-designed and often self-made. His favorites were a bright red, oblong-shaped axe one covered entirely in fur and another covered in bright purple carpet.

"I couldn't afford to buy an electric guitar when I first started playing," he says. "I knew the sound I wanted, so I figured out how I could make it. I'd take an accoustic guitar and add bits of old radios and things like that. That's how it started!"

Although he only clocked up three minor hit records – 'Say Man', 'Pretty Thing' and 'Hey Good Looking' – Bo Diddley was responsible for writing many r 'n' b classics including 'Roadrunner', 'I'm A Man', 'Who Do You Love' and 'You Can't Judge A Book By Looking At The Cover', which were all covered by major recording artists during the 1960s and early 1970s.

Bo Diddley's performing career was given a tremendous shot in the arm in 1972 when he appeared in Richard Nader's rock 'n' roll revival show and was later featured in the movie 'Let The Good Times Roll'. In

1976, he recorded a new album 'Twentieth Anniversary Of Rock' for RCA, featuring such celebrated sidemen as Joe Cocker, Billy Joel, Roger McGuinn and Keith Moon. Two years later, he undertook a successful British tour with another legendary rock 'n' roller from the 1950s – Carl Perkins.

DION — his career took an upturn after a meeting with Phil Spector

DION
American. Male.
Singer/Songwriter.

Born in the Bronx area of New York on July 18, 1939, Dion Dimucci was hailed as one of the finest singers of the 1960s. Yet he never quite lived up to his reputation.

He started his singing career with a group called The Timberlanes, in the mid-1950s. With them he recorded one single – 'The Chosen Few'.

However, it wasn't until 1957, fronting The Belmonts, that he hit the recording jackpot, via a series of what became classic rock 'n' roll singles: 'Where Or When', 'Wonder Why', 'Lonely Teenager' and 'Teenager In Love' – his first British hit in 1959. It was in 1961 that he topped the American chart with the million-selling 'Runaround Sue', hastily followed by other smash successes including 'The Wanderer', 'Donna The Prima Donna' and 'Ruby Baby'.

During the mid-'60s, Dion turned away from music. He drifted towards drugs, and at one time had a very serious drugs problem, which he eventu-

ally kicked. In 1968 he returned to the U.S. charts with 'Abraham, Martin And John' heralding something of a metamorphosis of his career . . . and he settled down to sing more folk-oriented music. During the early 1970s, he became regarded as one of America's most respected singer/songwriters.

In 1973, he re-formed The Belmonts for a reunion concert at Madison Square Garden which was recorded for the live album 'Reunion'. Two years later, he joined forces with Phil Spector, who produced his hit single 'Born To Be With You', and set about transforming his career once more.

FATS DOMINO
American. Male.
Singer/Instrumentalist.

From his first professional appearance at the age of fourteen in 1942 at the celebrated Hideaway Club in New Orleans, until today, the work of Fats Domino has been characterized and dominated by his pounding piano style. (He had been taught to play piano by his Uncle Harry). And by the age of twenty-one Fats had capitalized on his unique style to make his first million-seller, 'The Fat Man'.

He was born Antoine Domino in New Orleans, on February 26, 1928 – and in 1948 became a member of The Billy Diamond Dance Band, before being signed up for Imperial Records for whom he recorded 'The Fat Man'.

With the success of his single Fats and his group – The Fats Domino Band – toured America extensively and gained outstanding acclaim. And throughout the 1950s he churned out a stream of classic rock 'n' roll hits including 'Blueberry Hill' – which reissued, re-entered the British chart in 1976 – 'Ain't It A Shame', 'Poor Me', 'Please Leave Me' and 'All By Myself', which from 1954 to 1959 all sold between an incredible three and five million copies!

The 1960s, however, saw Fats reduce his recording work load, and go into semi-retirement, although he was still a widely popular nightclub act. In 1963, though, he had a massive British and American hit with 'Red Sails In The Sunset'. It wasn't, oddly enough, until 1967 that he first came to Britain, when Brian Epstein brought him over for London concerts.

Meanwhile, critics were saying that he had lost some of his originality, but by 1970 his work had once again come to the fore, amid restated interest in the origins of rock 'n' roll. In 1972 he appeared in the movie 'Let The Good Times Roll'.

These days, Fats does far less concert work, preferring to spend his time with his wife – by whom he has had eight children – at their New Orleans home. He still, however, appears in cabaret in Las Vegas, from time to time, hailed, quite rightly, as one of the living legends of rock 'n' roll.

LONNIE DONEGAN
British. Male.
Singer/Instrumentalist.

Lonnie Donegan rose to international prominence as one of the founding fathers of a new wave of music that swept through the world – albeit for just a few short years – during the mid-1950s. Skiffle.

He was born Anthony Donegan of Irish/Scottish parentage in Glasgow, Scotland, on April 29, 1931, and started to take an active interest in music as a teenager, teaching himself to play guitar. Lonnie was fascinated by American blues, and Dixieland.

In 1949, while serving in the British Army in Vienna, he spent his spare time entertaining his fellow servicemen, and on demobilization formed his own folk-oriented group and turned professional. Not long after its formation, the group appeared in London with the American blues singer Lonnie Johnson, from whom Donegan adopted his professional stage name. But when the group later failed to break through to any kind of lasting success, Lonnie Donegan disbanded the outfit and joined the Ken Colyer Jazz Band – which was later taken over by Chris Barber – playing guitar and banjo.

In 1954, still very much an active member of the renamed Chris Barber Band, Lonnie recorded several numbers for Decca Records, one of which

FATS DOMINO — creator of a stream of rock 'n' roll standards

LONNIE DONEGAN — his songs have become folklore in the UK

became the first-ever record to *enter* the British hit parade at Number 1), 'Have A Drink On Me' (1961) and 'Pick A Bale Of Cotton' (1962). For seven years, he enjoyed great success. He even fronted his own record label for Pye – 'Lonnie Donegan Presents . . .'

Yet, during those heady days of chart success, Lonnie Donegan started to branch out in showbusiness and diversify his talents, he was not content to sit back and rest on the laurels of his success. As early as 1957, Lonnie appeared on the variety stage, starring in pantomimes and summer seasons, establishing himself as an all-round entertainer. He had a ready-made market.

Throughout the 1960s and early 1970s, Lonnie Donegan's career thrived. He enjoyed success in concert and cabaret in Britain, and undertook seasons in Canada and America – where he regularly played Las Vegas. Then in 1976, he suffered three major heart-attacks in rapid succession which curtailed his performing, and he later made his home in California.

However, two years later, he was back in the recording studio at the suggestion of Paul McCartney, to make a new album called 'Putting On The Style', which was a contemporary reworking of many of Lonnie's former hits. The album featured some of the biggest recording names in rock music as side-men – Elton John, Brian May, Leo Sayer, Ringo Starr, Ron Wood, Rory Gallagher and Adam Faith, who produced the set.

The same year, he was back touring Britain with a new group, and in 1979 he featured at the celebrated annual International Festival of Country Music at London's Wembley Arena.

DONOVAN
British. Male. Singer/Songwriter.

It was inevitable really that when Donovan first appeared on British television in 1965 – to become a resident performer on the ITV pop/rock show 'Ready Steady Go' – he would be hailed as Britain's answer to Bob Dylan. Dressed in denim (topped by a denim hat), with a harmonica harness around his neck – and an acoustic guitar strapped to his side, he summed up the fashionable ideal of the lone protest singer of the mid-

was 'Rock Island Line'. It was released a year later, and within weeks became a fantastic success in Britain . . . and America. It was totally unexpected, but on its strength Lonnie Donegan left the Barber band and once again formed his own group.

'Rock Island Line' sold more than three million copies world-wide, but Lonnie received just $7, as a session fee, for making the record.

He followed up his initial hit record with a vast array of hits, often adapting old folk and blues songs into the new wave skiffle, among them, 'Lost John' (1956), 'Bring A Little Water Sylvie' (1956), 'Don't You Rock Me Daddy-O' (1957), 'Cumberland Gap' and 'Gamblin' Man/Putting On The Style' (both number one hits in 1957), 'Does Your Chewing Gum Lose Its Flavour' (1959), 'Battle Of New Orleans' (1959), 'My Old Man's A Dustman' (which in 1960

'Cosmic Wheels'.

He was born Donovan Phillip Leitch in Glasgow on May 10, 1943 – and during the early 1970s, based himself in America where he wrote and composed the music for his own theatrical stage show '7-Tease' in 1974. He recorded the concept album in Nashville . . . and then virtually disappeared from the limelight.

He says: "I didn't actually disappear, I just took stock. I actually wasn't doing the kind of things that were in the commercial eye. I suppose it was like I'd been away from the scene, but really I hadn't at all. I took time off to have a look at all the things around me that were going on. *And* – to enjoy my young family.

"When I started out in the business I was very green and very cynical . . . but I've come to terms with it now."

Married with two daughters, Oriole and Astrella (his wife Linda also has a son Julian by the late Rolling Stone Brian Jones), Donovan today lives with his family in Windsor and combines his time writing his own kind of songs . . . and performing.

*DONOVAN — **surveying the cosmos in an early promo shot***

1960s.

If Donovan's approach to music verged at times on the ethereal it did not deny him commercial success, for he was highly profitable as a recording artist. Between 1963 and 1968, he enjoyed seven British Top Ten hits with 'Catch The Wind', 'Colours', 'Sunshine Superman' – his only Number 1 chart success in America in 1966 – 'Mellow Yellow', 'There Is A Mountain', 'Jennifer Juniper' and 'Hurdy Gurdy Man'. And a hatful of hit albums. The last single, though, came at a time when Donovan purists considered was lyrically and musically the most successful period of his career with the release of the album 'A Gift From A Flower To A Garden'.

In 1969, he collaborated with Jeff Beck to produce the hit single 'Barabajagal', and then almost dropped out of the limelight and into semi-retirement in Ireland. He re-surfaced a year later, as composer of the film score for 'If It's Tuesday, It Must Be Belgium'. In 1972, he appeared in the musical film 'The Pied Piper', for which he also penned the soundtrack, and in 1973, he completed the score for another major picture – 'Brother Sun, Sister Moon'. It was the same year, he released his successful (if a trifle risqué) album,

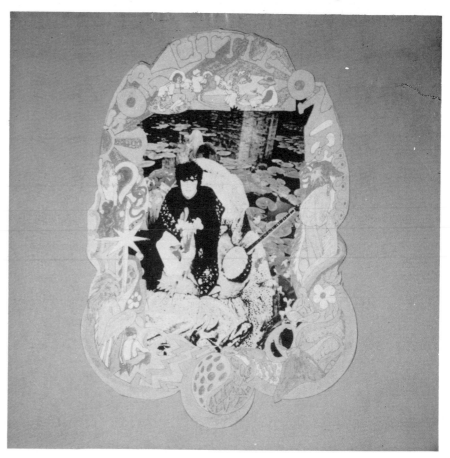

A colorful figure, his was a combination of many of the ideas of philosophy and music fashionable in the mid-1960s. Yet, his musical treatments remain an enduring testimony to that era.

Donovan made a successful comeback to performing in 1980 with appearances at the Edinburgh Festival in his native Scotland, followed by a tour of Germany and France. At Christmas he starred alongside Billy Connolly and Ralph McTell in a special concert – in aid of children's charities – at the London Palladium. And during 1981, his comeback was complete when he undertook a major concert tour of Britain . . . and released a brand new album.

THE DOORS
American. Male.
Vocal/Instrumental Group.
Original line-up: Jim Morrison

(vocals); Ray Monzarek (keyboards); John Densmore (drums); Bobby Krieger (bass).

If ever one member emerged to represent what this band was all about, it was Jim Morrison, in his relationship with The Doors. Born December 8, 1943, in Melbourne, Florida, the son of a rear-admiral, his teens saw him rebelling vigorously against his authoritarian background. Yet at the same time he was an intellectual, with an extremely broad knowledge in the Arts. And so, in the midst of this educated anarchy, he was created the 'Lizard King', the man who was to front, and effectively hold together one of *the* most influential of American rock bands.

In 1964, at UCLA, where he was studying film technique, Morrison met keyboards virtuoso Ray Monzarek, who had received extensive classical music training in his home town, Chicago. This was the basis of The Doors, who alighted on their name from William Blake's: *"There are things that are known, and things that are unknown; in between the doors,"* and from the title of Aldous Huxley's book on drug experiments, "The Doors of Perception".

The two augmented the embryonic band with Bobby Krieger and John Densmore, both from Los Angeles. And The Doors had got themselves together.

The next step was to find success, but in this capacity they had little initial luck, until The London Fog, in Sunset Strip, hired them for a run. They remained there for four months gaining acclaim from the underground, and eventually getting sacked. After a few more difficult months, they signed for Electra Records. Their first release being 'The Doors' album, in 1967, which blew the lid off everything, and rocketed them to international acclaim and prominence. It sold a million copies!

The album showed Morrison's preoccupation with sex and death, themes that would become so central

THE DOORS — *the 1968 album 'Strange Days'*

to The Doors. It also contained the Krieger classic, 'Light My Fire', which was to prove an enormous hit for them as a single on both sides of the Atlantic, and later for José Feliciano. This was followed by two more hugely successful LPs, 'Strange Days' and 'Waiting For The Sun'. The latter contained another massive-selling hit single, 'Hello I Love You'.

Morrison's stage performance had continued to grow in stature as he became increasingly wrapped up in his belief, and his vision of rock-star-as-performer. Leather-clad and lewdly suggestive, he *was* the 'Lizard King'. The stage fireworks became better and better, and the Morrison image further projected itself into the corners of rock audiences.

The Doors were also very much involved with soft drugs. There was even an attempt to record an LP while under the influence of LSD. For the most part, their use actually seemed to *highten* their performances.

As the '60s drew to a close, they were the most celebrated rock band in America.

Lyrically, they had tuned into some of the most bizarre aspects of American culture, while at the same time projecting themselves – and bludgeoning their audiences – with huge sound systems.

Then, at a Miami concert in April, 1969, in the wake of a couple of other scrapes with the law, Morrison was charged with committing indecent exposure on stage. Perhaps even the most devoted fans felt that something like this was inevitable.

Morrison, who for years had been a dedicated high-liver, denied the charge. But it cost the band dearly. Their manager, Bill Siddens, reckoned subsequently cancelled dates lost The Doors $1,000,000. It also meant the band cut down on live appearances, although two new LPs, 'Morrison Hotel/Hard Rock Cafe' and the equally celebrated 'L.A. Woman', did extremely well.

It was time for Morrison to take stock. His great interest was making

films, and he embarked on a couple of projects, but by the end of 1970, weakened by excess, he decided to retire – though it's unsure whether he intended this to be a permanent measure.

However, he and his wife went to live in Paris, where he could write poetry.

The band, though, continued to work and rehearse, hoping for his return – he never did – and in early 1971 struck well into the U.S. Top Twenty with 'Love Her Madly'.

On July 3, 1971, Morrison died, in his bath, of a heart attack, and along with Jimi Hendrix and Janis Joplin he became one of the most-missed figures of the '70s.

But The Doors, themselves continued to work, with 'Riders On The Storm' becoming a chart success later that year. Two more albums, 'Other Voices' and 'Full Circle' followed, but in time the band had to acknowledge the strain of Morrison's absence. They were exhausted, and, in 1973, split up for good.

Since then, Ray Monzarek tried to reform the band, but didn't quite make it. Two solo albums, 'The Golden Scarab' and 'The Whole Thing Started With Rock 'N' Roll' didn't quite make it either.

Krieger and Densmore went into record production, then formed the Butts Band. In '77 Krieger became heavily involved in jazz and released the album 'Bobby Krieger And Friends'.

None of them recaptured past glories.

But as Rolling Stone's Billy Altman put it: "Brash, courageous, intelligent, adventurous and exciting. The Doors were all of this – and more. Of all the groups to emerge from the West Coast in the late '60s, only The Doors succeeded in getting their often-disturbing messages across to the core of America, through both hit albums and singles. And the fact that they could do so without compromising their stance or their act makes the accomplishment that much more incredible".

Footnote: A re-released 'Riders On The Storm' re-entered the British charts in March, 1976.

LEE DORSEY
American. Male. Singer.

New Orleans was the birthplace – on Christmas Eve 1924 – of Lee Dorsey. And it's a city that has continued to hold considerable fascination for him, to such an extent that, in the early 1970s he decided to return to live and work there. Today, he's very active on the music scene there!

Perhaps remembered best for his single 'Holy Cow', which enjoyed considerable success on both sides of the Atlantic in 1966, Lee had first emerged on the American music scene in 1961, with 'Ya Ya', followed up by 'Do-Re-Mi'. Four years later, the former boxer-turned-singer enjoyed hits with 'Get Out Of My Life Woman', 'Confusion', 'Working In The Coalmine' and 'Holy Cow'.

The latter part of the 1960s, however, were not so kind to him, and despite having switched to the Polydor label for an album, 'Yes We Can' in 1970, he did not repeat his earlier recording success.

*LEE DORSEY — **boxer turned singer.***

THE DRIFTERS
American. Male. Vocal Group.
Original line-up: Clyde McPhatter; Gerhart Thrasher; Andrew Thrasher; Willie Ferbee.

One of the perennial vocal groups in pop music history – and one of the most successful of all time, despite undergoing numerous changes of line-up, The Drifters were formed as a Gospel group in 1953, in Harlem, New York . . . and the same year turned professional.

Their first single release in June of that year was 'Gone', featuring Clyde McPhatter on lead-vocals who was formerly with the group Billy Ward And The Dominoes. Indeed, in those early days, the group recorded under the name of Clyde McPhatter And The Drifters.

They had their first chart success in August of that year with 'Money Honey', by which time Bill Pinkney had replaced Willie Ferbee. It was the start of a fabulous success which a year later saw them score four more chart singles – 'Lucille', 'Such A Night', 'Honey Love' and 'Bip Bam'. When McPhatter was summoned for Army service in 1955, the lead-singer berth was taken over by Johnny Moore, and the group enjoyed another success with 'Ruby Baby' (a big hit for Dion And The Belmonts in the early 1960s).

The following year Moore, too, was drafted, and the group worked with a succession of lead singers until 1958 when they disbanded.

However, The Drifters' manager, George Treadwell, who owned the group name, was determined to keep it alive . . . So he formed a new group using members of a black Harlem outfit called The Five Crowns, featuring James Clark, Wilber Paul, Claud Clark, John Clark and Dock Green, and re-christened them. Next he added the dynamic vocal talents of a young singer to front the group – Ben E. King.

And during this period, The 'new' Drifters enjoyed magnificent success with such international hits as 'Save The Last Dance For Me', 'There Goes My Baby', 'This Magic Moment', 'Dance With Me' and 'True Love, True Love'. When King left, to go solo, Rudy Lewis took over on lead, and recorded 'Up On The Roof', 'On Broadway', 'Some Kind Of Wonderful', and 'Sweets For My Sweet'. On several of these recordings, The Drifters were joined by a female back-up group which featured Dionne and Dee Dee Warwick, Doris Troy and Billy Davis.

When Rudy Lewis died in 1963, Johnny Moore – who had returned to the group the same year – took over as lead vocalist and was highlighted on such hits as 'Under The Boardwalk', 'At The Club', 'Saturday Night At The Movies', and 'Come On Over To My Place.'

Then, during the second half of the '60s, the group faded from view – and several 'lookalike' outfits emerged calling themselves 'The Original Drifters', 'Bill Pinkney And The Originals' and several more. And *they* all found success on American and European tours, trading in on the name.

However, in 1967 when manager George Treadwell died, his wife Fayrene took over their management and took steps to reform and revitalise the group. They resurfaced the same year and the third phase of The Drifters' career took shape.

They returned to chart success with two re-released singles 'At The Club' and 'Come On Over To My Place' in 1972. The following year Bill Fredericks took over as lead-singer on 'Like Sister And Brother', before handing back the reins once more to Johnny Moore who fronted the subsequent hit singles 'Kissin' In The Back Row', 'Down On The Beach Tonight', 'There Goes My First Love', 'Can I Take You Home Little Girl', 'Hello Happiness' and 'You're More Than A Number In My Little Red Book'.

During this time, they established themselves as one of the most successful groups of all time, in great demand for live appearances in concert and cabaret, all over the world.

The success story has continued.

Today, The Drifters work steadily across the globe, with twelve weeks a year appearing in cabaret in Las Vegas; nine weeks in Lake Tahoe; and regular seasons in Bermuda and Australia.

However, it is in Britain where they have virtually made their home-base, and they have created their own special niche on the domestic cabaret circuits.

In 1980, their single 'Pour Your Little Heart Out' was featured on the soundtrack for the movie 'The Bitch'. The same year, Johnny Moore – the longest serving member of the group, parted company to go solo. He rejoined them once more in the spring of 1981 to complete a line-up of Moore, Clyde Brown, Lewis Price and Ray Lewis.

DUANE EDDY
American. Male. Instrumentalist.

Duane Eddy – 'the twang's the thang' – was born in Corning, New York on April 26, 1938 . . . and was brought up in Phoenix, Arizona.

He learnt to play guitar at the tender age of five and was soon taking an active interest in music. At fifteen, he started playing with various local groups. In 1957, he joined a group led by jazz guitarist Al Casey, and at the same time took lessons from Jim Wybele.

Duane's musical career began to take shape, however, and in 1958 he was discovered by a local disc jockey called Lee Hazelwood, who later helped to develop his distinctive twangy guitar sound – which was created by tuning a normal 6-string guitar down an octave. It became Eddy's trademark, along with the raucous saxophone solos, courtesy of Steve Douglas and Jim Horn, and manic rebel shouts from Ben De Moto, featured on his early London singles.

It was also in 1958 that Duane Eddy had his first international hit success with 'Rebel Rouser', produced by Hazelwood. His debut single, though, 'Movin' 'N' Groovin' ', was a minor U.S. hit . . . yet in his first year as a recording artist, he sold more than three million records – making recording history for an instrumentalist – with such hits as 'Cannonball', 'Peter Gunn', 'Yep', 'Forty Miles Of Bad Road' and 'Some Kinda Earthquake' . . . all guitar classics! To date, he has sold more than 30 million records from nearly 25 single successes. In Britain alone, he has clocked up 21 hits.

Besides a spectacular recording career, Duane Eddy branched out into acting – he was featured in several movies, including 'A Thunder Of Drums', 'The Wild Westerner', 'Because They're Young', and 'The Savage Seven' – *and* composing. More than half the numbers he recorded were self-penned and he was made an honorary member of Washington State in 1961 for writing the title tune for the film 'Ring Of Fire'.

Today, Duane continues to work on sessions in America and he still returns to the concert stage whenever he can. In 1977 he signed a new recording deal with Warner Brothers, and during 1980 he undertook a comprehensive British and European tour.

DUANE EDDY — the 'twang' was the 'thang'

EVERLY BROTHERS
American. Male. Vocal duo.

The Everly Brothers – Don and Phil – were one of the most successful vocal duos in pop music during the latter days of the 1950s and early 1960s, clocking up no less than *eighteen* million selling singles. They also had a marked effect on the development of rock 'n' roll all over the world. And hit singles like 'Bye Bye Love', 'Wake Up Little Susie', 'Bird Dog', 'Lucille', and 'Walk Right Back' went on to become rock 'n' roll classics.

Born in Brownie, Kentucky (Donald Isaac on February 1, 1937; Phil on January 19, 1939) the sons of famous Country and Western singing stars Ike and Margaret Everly, Don and Phil started their own singing careers at an early age on their parents' Kentucky Radio show in 1945, and later appeared on stage as part of their parents' act. Indeed, for the next dozen years or so, they toured America together, although the young boys took a winter break each year to catch up on their education. When Don and Phil finally graduated from high school, Ike and Margaret decided it was time to call it a day and retire from showbusiness, leaving the stage free for their sons.

In 1956, The Everly Brothers were signed to Columbia, but met with little success. Still, their early career took off a year later when Wesley Rose became their manager and signed them to the Cadence label, and asked Chet Atkins to produce them. Their first single 'Bye Bye Love' sold a million . . . and next followed a spectacular run of hit singles for the label, all of which featured the boys' velvet harmonies, highlighted to perfection on 'All I have To Do Is Dream', their first British chart-topper in 1958. In 1960, they joined Warner Brothers Records. Yet despite a change of label, the hits continued to flow including the monster-selling 'Cathy's Clown' which topped the U.S. charts for five weeks, (and the British Hit Parade for nine weeks) in 1960. For the next five years, they enjoyed spectacular recording success in Britain and America with a string of classic hits like 'Walk Right Back' and 'Temptation'.

In 1963, while on tour of Britain, Don

EVERLY BROTHERS — (l-r): Phil and Don

Everly suffered a nervous breakdown – and Phil was forced to carry on alone. It marked a major turning point in their career. From then on they gradually went their own separate ways. Yet, they still managed to hit the chart jackpot again in 1965 with 'The Price Of Love'.

During the latter days of the '60s, the Everly Brothers returned to their country roots and enjoyed great acclaim with a series of best-selling albums. At the turn of the '70s, they undertook two successful tours of Britain together in 1971 and '72. But a year later, Don Everly announced that the Brothers' last appearance together would be at the John Wayne Theater of Knotts Berry Farm in Buena Park, California.

"I've quit," he said. "I'm tired of being an Everly Brother."

At the resulting concert, the boys – way below their performing best – were pulled off stage by the promoter Bill Hollingshead. Phil Everly smashed his guitar and walked off stage. His brother, Don, decided to finish the show on his own – but it marked the end of an era, and the finale to one of the most successful singing partnerships of all time. Both brothers decided to go their own solo ways.

Said Phil: "I was never content to think of myself as merely half of *something*, always as an individual. The main reason we went our separate ways in 1973 was that we figured we had done all we could together. It was time to strike out on our own – and see what we had to offer as individuals."

With the break up behind him, Don returned to Nashville, Tennessee, to carve a career for himself in the country field, and he has since made several successful solo albums including 'Brother Juke Box'. He returned to performing again in 1977, making his debut at the International Festival of Country Music at Wembley in England. And he has been a regular performer there ever since, besides occasionally going out on tour in America.

Phil, meanwhile, has stayed in California, writing and recording his own songs.

He says: "I've tasted stardom, I'm in the history books. Nobody can take that away from me.

FABIAN
American. Male. Singer.

Despite being hailed by one music journalist as "the worst pop star in the world", Fabian managed to chalk up several major record successes during his singing career, including the million-selling single 'Tiger' in 1959. And he established himself as one of America's most popular teen idols . . . with his devastating good looks.

Born Fabiano Forte in Philadelphia on February 6, 1943, he attended the same boys club as his neighborhood friends Frankie Avalon (see **Frankie Avalon**) and Bobby Rydell. All three had budding ambitions to become famous singers.

In 1957, Fabian was introduced to Bob Marcucci and Peter de Angelis, who headed Chancellor Records in Philadelphia, and after taking singing lessons, he was signed to a recording contract. De Angelis figured that with Fabian's good looks and just a moderate voice, he was destined for major success. He was proved right!

De Angelis recounted the story: "We were talking to Frankie Avalon and he said he knew a fifteen-year-old kid at Southern High who looked like a cross between Elvis and Ricky Nelson. So Bob went over to take a look.

FABIAN — The looks were enough

He was so pretty, we just knew he had to be a commercial proposition, so we signed him and taught him a few things vocally. But he never really did go much on singing."

His first single release in 1958 was 'Lillie Lou' which failed miserably in the chart, yet his follow-ups 'I'm A Man' and 'Turn Me Loose' established him as a major attraction. Shrewd guidance by Marcucci and de Angelis, brilliant packaging and publicity helped to keep the wheels of success in motion. Appearances on the top TV program 'American Bandstand' certainly helped, too, to further his cause. The girls went wild and "the worst pop star in the world" was becoming a teenage heart-throb. In 1959 he recorded his only million-selling single 'Tiger'. The same year, his career took a dramatic turn, when he was signed to make his first movie – 'Hound Dog Man' – the title song from which was a major international hit. Other films followed in rapid succession including 'High Time', 'North To Alaska' and 'The Longest Day'.

Since then, Fabian has continued to make his career in movies and his credits have also included 'Five Weeks In A Balloon', 'Fireball 500', 'A Bullet For A Pretty Boy', 'The Day The Lord Got Busted' and 'Disco Fever'. He has combined a successful picture career with one on television, having starred in the celebrated 'Bus Stop' series in the 1960s, and today he is a regular in television movies, one of the most interesting – 'Katie: Portrait Of A Centerfold' being made in 1978.

After 1970, he reverted back to his original name of Fabian Forte, the name he works under today.

MARIANNE FAITHFULL
British. Female. Singer.

As rock 'n' roll threw up its heroes of the sixties and early seventies, so it did its casualties. Brian Jones, Jim Morrison, Janis Joplin and Jimi Hendrix in particular fell victim to its peculiar pressures.

Some faces came into the business and stayed. Some arrived and disappeared with equal speed. Many others hung around the periphery, although in this fringe position they were rarely in the place to which the spotlight shifted.

Marianne Faithfull

INCLUDING

AS TEARS GO BY   COME STAY WITH ME

MONO LL 3423   LONDON

The one exception to this was Marianne Faithfull who seemed, somehow, to combine all of this – *success, failure, victim* and *victor* of public acclaim. Her's was a butterfly's frailty, endearing to the fashionable, but variously taking its toll on her.

To suggest that she was musically significant would be untrue. But her striking good looks, and outspokenness, particularly on sexual matters guaranteed Press and public attention. But more than that . . . was her

varying relationships with the Rolling Stones.

The daughter of an Austrian baroness, Marianne – who was born in London on December 29, 1946 – was a 17-year-old convent schoolgirl in Reading, Berkshire, when she first met Stones' manager Andrew Loog Oldham at a London party. She became his girlfriend and when he discovered that she could actually sing, as well, he signed her up for management. In 1964 she recorded the Mick

MARIANNE FAITHFULL — her first album, produced when she was eighteen years old

Jagger/Keith Richard song 'As Tears Go By', although at the time it charted she was still at school. Her Top Ten career, however, was short-lived. Between then and July 1965 she made only three more records that squeezed into the best-selling end of the charts.

However, during this time she was

MARIANNE FAITHFULL — *The face of the '60s*

gaining popularity, and touring with such groups as Freddie and the Dreamers and The Four Pennies. In her personal life, she had married art gallery boss John Dunbar, though the marriage was short lived and she later moved in with Mick Jagger.

So she established her position, giving at the time a series of interviews liberally spiced with salacious reflections. She admitted in one, for example having slept with three of the Rolling Stones before opting for Mick. Another contained her desire to make a sex film, to include frank love sequences with Jagger. To add to this was even more speculation among the pop-conscious as to the colorful goings-on in her private life.

Then came her 'Girl On A Motorcycle' movie featuring frequent scenes of nudity, with Penthouse magazine carrying a spread of the film's more risque stills.

But by the 1970s interest in Miss Faithfull had waned, and Mick and the Stones had gone their own way. Marianne, however, hung on. She turned to acting and often appeared on the West End stage in Chekhov and Shakespeare . . . though her private life was still littered with drugs and attempted suicide bids.

An attempted comeback in 1979 didn't work out, though momentarily the Press once again became interested in her, if only for nostalgia's sake. But two singles failed to re-establish her, and an LP, 'Broken English', ran into difficulties through its use of 'obscene' language.

Her's though, was the story of an era. Beautiful on the one hand, rebellious and amoral on the other.

GEORGIE FAME
British. Male.
Singer/Instrumentalist.

Georgie Fame is *still* generally considered to be one of the leading rhythm-and-blues artists in Britain today, by aficienados of the music nearly twenty years after he first rose to national prominence . . . an amazing testimony to his standing in the business.

He was born Clive Powell in Leigh, Lancashire, England, on June 26, 1943, and started his first group – The Dominoes – at the age of thirteen. The young Clive always wanted to become a professional musician, but on leaving school, he had to settle for a more mundane way of life and started work in a local cotton mill. However, what spare time he had on his hands, he spent playing piano and organ with various local groups.

During his first holiday from work, he joined Rory Blackwell's Band and started playing engagements on the British Holiday Camp circuit . . . and before long he achieved his ambition, and turned professional.

In 1961, he joined Billy Fury's backing group, The Blue Flames – and a year later, after leaving the rock 'n' roll idol, the group landed what turned out to be a three-year residency, playing jazz and r and b at London's Flamingo Club.

Then in 1964, he topped the British Hit Parade with 'Yeh Yeh' which was followed by a whole succession of hits – 'In The Meantime', 'Get Away', (his second British chart-topper, in 1966), 'Sunny', 'Sitting In The Park', and 'The Ballad Of Bonnie And Clyde' – his third Number 1, in 1967. In 1968, he toured Europe singing with the legendary Count Basie Orchestra.

During the early 1970s, Georgie Fame teamed up with Alan Price (see **The Animals**) and together they fronted their own BBC Television series and chalked up a hit single in 1971 with 'Rosetta', besides making forays into concert and cabaret engagements.

They parted company in 1973 and Georgie re-formed The Blue Flames in 1974 for club and recording work.

Since then, he has combined his time working in the recording studio by performing and writing television jingles for British TV, most notably for Maxwell House coffee.

In 1979, with The Blue Flames in tow once again, he undertook his first extensive British concert tour for several years, which met with only moderate success at the box office.

FIFTH DIMENSION
American. Male/Female.
Vocal Group.
Original line-up: Florence La Rue; Marilyn McCoo; Billy Davis Junior; Lamont McLemore; Ron Townson.

The Fifth Dimension was without doubt one of the most successful vocal groups in pop music at the turn of the 1970s, with a string of international hit records including 'Up, Up And Away', 'Magic Garden', 'Stoned Love Picnic', 'Let The Sunshine In'/'Acquarius' and 'Wedding Bell Blues' to their credit.

The group was formed in Los Angeles by Florence La Rue and Lamont McLemore who, together with McCoo, Davis and Townson, worked under various names in those early days, including The Versatiles and The Hi-Fi's. Billed as The Vocals, they toured with (and backed) the legendary Ray Charles. And it was while touring as part of the Ray Charles

Revue, that they met Marc Gordon who later became their manager.

Gordon introduced the group to Soul City Records, whose owner Johnny Rivers signed them up and determined they should be called Fifth Dimension. Their first single 'Go Where You Wanna Go' reached the U.S. Top Ten and a follow up release 'Up, Up And Away' – which virtually launched the songwriting career of Jim Webb – sold over a million copies . . . and, with their subsequent hit singles and albums, established themselves in the international arena at the tail end of the 1960s. The hits continued well into the 1970s, too, particularly in America where they scored with 'Love Lives', 'Angels And Rhythms' and 'Portrait'.

In 1969, Florence La Rue married manager Gordon, and the same year, group members Billy Davis Junior and Marilyn McCoo also hit the wedding trail.

Yet, despite Gold Discs on both sides of the Atlantic and a large international fan following the group's recording career went into decline in the mid-1970s, and they eventually disbanded. A reunion in 1975 failed miserably.

However, husband-and-wife team Marilyn McCoo and Billy Davis Junior reappeared eighteen months later with an international hit – 'You Don't Have To Be A Star', and they have continued to work together ever since.

WAYNE FONTANA
British. Male. Singer.

Wayne Fontana was born Glynn Ellis in Manchester on October 28, 1945. He started his musical career at school with a skiffle group called The Velfins, and later formed a pop-cum-rock 'n' roll outfit, called The Jets, with whom he toured the pubs and clubs of Greater Manchester.

In 1963, the group was spotted playing in Manchester's Oasis Club and asked to undertake an audition for Philips/Fontana Records at the venue the following evening in front of a live audience. The chance was too good to turn down, but the next evening only Wayne (who took his stage name from the Fontana Records label) and the bass player, Bob Lang, turned up to perform! So faced with an extreme dilemma – and in sheer desperation – Wayne actually chose two of his musician friends from out of the audience who had turned up to lend moral support. And with Eric Stewart (on guitar) and Ric Rothwell (on drums) they managed to weave together enough material to pass the audition, impress the record company, *and* land the lucrative contract. But then the problems arose because the group had no name! However, stimulated by a recent horror movie that was doing the rounds of local cinemas, they adapted its title and became known as The Mindbenders.

Their debut single released on Fontana a few months later, was a cover version of Bo Diddley's 'Roadrunner', which enjoyed moderate success. A year and two more singles later, though, they finally hit the chart jackpot with a cover of Major Lance's American hit 'Um Um Um Um Um Um', which reached Number 2 in Britain. And in 1965, their single 'Game Of Love' went on to top the British and American charts. During the same year, Wayne's backing group The Mindbenders cut the single 'Groovy Kind Of Love' in their own right, and when the record made the British Top Three, in the fall of that year, they decided to branch out on their own, leaving Wayne to concentrate on a solo career.

The Mindbenders enjoyed considerable success on their own over the following months, including two more hit singles – though they could never

WAYNE FONTANA AND THE MINDBENDERS — (l-r): Wayne Fontana, Eric Stewart, Ric Rothwell, Bob Lang

hope to consolidate their initial chart success. And, after appearing in the movie 'To Sir With Love', they decided to call it a day and disbanded. Eric Stewart later formed the group Hotlegs, with whom he clocked up a massive Top Three single success in Britain in 1970 with 'Neanderthal Man'. They later became known as 10CC.

Wayne Fontana, meanwhile, made the chart again with four singles from 1965 to 1966, the most successful of which was 'Pamela Pamela' reaching Number 11 in 1966.

Today, like so many of his contemporaries, Wayne spends his time touring in concert, but the mainstay of his work is on the British cabaret circuit. However, he frequently tours America, working with rock 'n' roll revival shows, where he has retained a large fan following.

In the summer of 1979, he undertook an extensive 'Sounds Of The Sixties' tour of Britain with Gerry And The Pacemakers (see **Gerry and the Pacemakers**) and The Swinging Blue Jeans (see **The Swinging Blue Jeans**).

THE FOUNDATIONS
British. Male. Vocal/Instrumental Group.
Original line-up: Peter Macbeth (bass); Alan Warner (guitar); Clem Curtis (vocals); Eric Allandale (trombone); Tony Gomez (organ); Pat Burke (sax); Mike Elliot (sax); Tim Harris (drums).

In many ways it was the soft sell 'pop' sound of the late 1960s. The Foundations made records that were reasonably uncomplicated musically, and downright basic lyrically. It was an undemanding formula, a sort of English soul, but it was outstandingly successful.

Formed in 1966 by eight young men who met regularly in a London coffee bar and decided they wanted to make the same kind of music together, the group started rehearsing in a rented basement in London's Bayswater area. They later landed a residency at The Butterfly Club in Westbourne Park. It was here that they were discovered by record dealer Barry Class, who became their manager and introduced them to hit songwriter Tony Macauley, who in turn signed them to Pye Records.

Their first release, 'Baby Now That I've Found You,' written and produced by Tony Macauley, was a British Number 1 hit and a million seller, and they followed it up with the Mike D'Abo song 'Build Me Up Buttercup', in 1968. Other hits included 'Back On My Feet Again', 'Any Old Time', and 'In The Bad, Bad Old Days'.

1968, however, saw the band's fortunes begin to fade. Curtis and Elliott left, to be replaced by Colin Young. Yet the aspect of the pop boom which had made The Foundations a success was over, and although they kept together for another two years, they were unable to command the attention they had once enjoyed.

They finally split in 1970. Though today the name incidentally is *still* carried on by a band with a totally different line-up, who regularly perform British club and cabaret engagements.

CONNIE FRANCIS
American. Female. Singer.
Constance Franconero was born in Newark, New Jersey, on December 12, 1938, of Italian descent. She made her performing debut at the age of five, singing 'O Sole Mio' at a school concert, and at twelve won a TV talent contest, playing the accordion!

After High School she turned professional at 18, singing in cocktail lounges, with the help of an identity card which falsified her age! Soon after, she landed a contract with MGM Records.

Despite this apparent upswing in

THE FOUNDATIONS — (l-r): Tim Harris, Pat Burke, Mike Elliot, Eric Allandale, Tony Gomez, Clem Curtis, Alan Warner, Peter McBeth

her career, she was discouraged by initial lack of success, and embarked on a four-year radio and television course at New York University.

In a last-ditch bid to save her career, her father – a former docker – suggested she record an up-tempo version of the classic 'Who's Sorry Now?'. It was an immediate success, and by November 1957 had earned her a million seller.

She didn't look back, and between 1957 and 1966 recorded a string of hit singles including 'I'm Sorry I Made You Cry', 'Carolina Moon', 'Stupid Cupid', 'Lipstick On Your Collar', 'Mama', 'Everybody's Somebody's Fool', 'Breakin' In A Brand New Broken Heart', 'I'm Gonna Be Warm This Winter' and 'Jealous Heart' . . . to emerge as the world's leading female vocalist.

Towards the end of the '60s, however, Connie Francis, who reached the pinnacle of her popularity when she was still in her teens, was beginning to fade from the forefront of entertainment, although she was still a popular nightclub attraction.

At the height of her popularity, she had become involved with another teen star, Bobby Darin, whom everyone expected her to marry. The romance, however, was short-lived.

By 1965, when she had a big hit with 'My Child' she had already been married once and divorced. This, and another subsequent divorce, she blamed on her strict upbringing.

"Although I was in showbusiness, I guess the sexual revolution just passed me by," she said years later.

In 1974, she staged a comeback, and shortly afterwards had a miscarriage – her third. Her third husband – travel boss Joe Garzilli – suggested she return to work to help get over it.

But tragedy struck.

The night after her comeback concert she was raped at knifepoint in her New York hotel room and she later sued the hotel's owners for negligence and was awarded $3,055,000 in damages.

The rape left her deeply scarred, mentally. Connie became a recluse, and also underwent two-and-a-half years of psychiatric treatment.

Bravely, however, she emerged once again in 1978, and came to London to record an LP of her former hits given an updated treatment – only for tragedy to strike once again: she was robbed of $50,000-worth of jewellery, while she stayed at a West End hotel.

It was just another episode in a long line of jinxes.

In 1964, she fled a Mexico City hotel, in just her night dress, in the midst of an earthquake. But the manager of the nightclub where she had been appearing, pursued her to Miami with threats of legal action if she didn't return to complete her *contract*!

Then in 1967, $85,000-worth of her clothes and jewelery was stolen from a friend's car in New York.

Nonetheless, as journalist Nancy Wills wrote in the Daily Mail in August, 1978: "Between 1958 and 1963, Connie Francis was the biggest female recording star around. In her day, Connie was as big as Donna Summer, Linda Ronstadt and Olivia Newton-John combined."

FREDDIE AND THE DREAMERS
British. Male. Vocal/Instrumental Group.
Original line-up: Freddie Garrity (vocals); Peter Birrell (bass); Roy Crewsdon (guitar); Berni Dwyer (drums); Derek Quinn (guitar).

Freddie and The Dreamers were one of the few British recording groups during the early 1960s to feature comedy extensively in their act – and right from the start of their career, lead singer Freddie Garrity was nicknamed 'The Clown Prince Of Pop'. Yet, despite their zany appearance on stage and television, the group managed to enjoy outstanding chart success in Britain and America with a succession of bubble-gum hits: 'If You Gotta Make A Fool Of Somebody' (1963), 'I'm Telling You Now' (1963, which two years later topped the American chart), 'You Were Made For Me' (1963), 'I Understand' (1964) . . . and several more minor successes.

The group was formed in Manchester in 1960 and former milkman Freddie Garrity joined them a year later. They rose to national prominence two years later after passing a BBC audition which led to a recording contract with Columbia Records. The group's debut single – a cover version of a James Ray hit – 'If You've Gotta Make A Fool Of Somebody', reached the Number 3 slot in Britain.

For the next three years, they enjoyed great success, headlining concert tours all over the world, and after their American Number 1 in 1965, the group's hit single 'Do The Freddie' – which did absolutely nothing in Britain – actually started a new dance craze in the States, and Freddie And The Dreamers were in great demand. Incidentally 'Do The Freddie' was covered for America by Chubby Checker (see **Chubby Checker**).

Yet, when chart success started to recede, they moved away from the pop stage and more towards variety, and they enjoyed success in summer shows and pantomimes. The group split up in 1972 while Freddie Garrity and Peter Birrell moved into television to host their own children's series 'The Little Big Time'. The group reformed by public demand in 1976, with a brand new line-up, and together they undertook tours of Australia and North America.

Today, however, Freddie And The Dreamers have returned to the British cabaret clubs, although they do occasionally appear on major domestic television shows. Freddie Garrity is still very much in demand for summer season appearances . . . and he has established himself as one of the biggest attractions in British pantomime. A great favorite with children.

BOBBIE GENTRY
American. Female.
Singer/Songwriter.

A former Las Vegas nightclub dancer, Bobbie Gentry leapt to the forefront of popular music in the autumn of 1967, with her self-penned and curious 'Ode To Billy Joe'. It was as if she had come from nowhere to storm the charts, and as a result earned herself *two* Gold records, one for the single, another for the album of the same name.

The same year she won 3 Grammy Awards – for Best Solo Female Per-

BOBBIE GENTRY — *inspired the movie 'Ode to Billy Joe'*

formance; Best Contemporary Rock 'n' Roll Vocal Performance and Best New Artiste.

She rapidly gained a following and began the rounds of U.S. TV and radio appearances. She also had her own British television series during the early '70s.

Her next big hit was 'I'll Never Fall In Love Again', which reached Number 1 in Britain in August 1969. This, particularly, underlined her popularity in the U.K. A few months later, Bobbie – who had been born Roberta Streeter of Portuguese descent in Chickasaw County, Mississippi, on July 27, 1944 – teamed up with country favorite Glen Campbell, and jointly they recorded the hit 'All I Have To Do Is Dream'.

1970 saw her next, but last, British single success with 'Raindrops Keep Fallin' On My Head'. But this in no way signalled the end of her popularity. She worked consistently throughout the '70s performing live, and for television audiences, world-wide.

The 1976 film version of her 'Ode To Billie Joe' hit – which was made by

Max Baer, and told the story of Billy Joe Macallister's suicide from Tallahatchie Bridge – revived her somewhat flagging fortunes. And Bobbie stepped *back* into the limelight of Las Vegas and Reno nightclubs, where she remains a big cabaret attraction today. The wheel of fortune, had turned full circle for the former childhood singer and guitarist.

GERRY AND THE PACEMAKERS
British. Male. Vocal/Instrumental
Group.
Original line-up: Gerry Marsden (guitarist/vocals); Freddie Marsden (drums); Les Chadwick (bass); Les Maguire (piano).

Liverpool's Gerry And The Pacemakers became the second group in 1962, to be signed by Brian Epstein, after he had virtually discovered The Beatles. And their careers ran parallel in the early '60s.

Like their famous contemporaries, Gerry Marsden and his group had built up a large fan following on Merseyside, and were regular headliners at the celebrated Cavern Club. And like The Beatles, they, too, had spent many months before appearing at the famous Star Club in Hamburg.

In 1963, the Epstein magic worked again when Gerry And The Pacemakers emerged from the shadows of their stable companions, to top the British Hit Parade with their debut single 'How Do You Do It' which also did magnificently well in America. In actual fact, the song – written by Mitch Murray – had been destined for The Beatles to record as *their* first single, until producer George Martin saw more potential in the group's own composition 'Love Me Do'.

Gerry And The Pacemakers followed up their initial success by topping the British chart again with both their subsequent single releases, 'I Like It' and 'You'll Never Walk Alone' – from the musical 'Carousel' which was quickly adopted by supporters of Liverpool soccer club as their very own football anthem. And for the next three years the group enjoyed exceptional chart success with further hits: 'I'm The One', 'Don't Let The Sun Catch You Crying', 'It's Gonna Be Alright' and 'Ferry Across The Mersey', the

title song from the group's movie debut in 1965.

They split up in 1968 and Gerry Marsden attempted to establish himself as a solo singer in his own right. However, single releases 'Please Let Them Be' and 'Gilbert Green' failed miserably in the chart stakes. The same year, though, he was chosen to take over the leading male role from Joe Brown in the highly successful West End musical 'Charlie Girl', to star alongside the legendary Anna Neagle. He proved a shrewd choice and remained with the show for over five years, before leaving to host a children's series on commercial television in Britain.

In 1975, he re-formed the Pacemakers to headline a triumphant 'Mersey Beat' revival tour of America, which played to sensational business across the States, before he returned to Britain to resume his solo career. In 1979, he re-formed the group yet again for a successful 'Sounds Of The Sixties' tour of Britain.

Today, Gerry has diversified his talents to take in summer seasons, and pantomimes – in 1977 he starred in the pantomime 'Jack And The Beanstalk' in Liverpool for the first time in his fifteen year career – though the mainstay of his appearances are on the British cabaret circuit, where he has proved a great attraction.

GARY GLITTER — *forced back into action through bankruptcy*

GARY GLITTER
British. Male. Singer.

Gary Glitter's rise to success in the pop world during the early 1970s, when he was hailed 'The King Of Glam Rock', was very much a case of 'if at first you don't succeed try, try, try again . . .' Because Gary certainly *tried*. Before he finally made the breakthrough from obscurity to recording success in 1972 (in Britain at least), when his single 'Rock 'N' Roll Parts One and Two' just failed to top the chart Gary had made several assaults on the charts working under a string of different stage names.

He was born Paul Francis Gadd in Banbury, Oxfordshire, on May 8, 1944, and at the age of fourteen he formed a guitar trio with two schoolfriends and together they worked in London's Safari Club. Two years later, he released his first single 'Alone In The Night' under the name of Paul Raven, and for the next few years, toured with the British rock 'n' rollers of the day; Cliff Richard, Tommy Steele and Billy Fury. Shortly after, he recorded 'Tower Of Strength', which became a Number 1 chart success for Frankie Vaughan. Gary's version sank without trace!

During 1965, he met writer/producer Mike Leander – who later became his manager – while working for a short spell as program associate on the ITV pop show 'Ready Steady Go'. Leander employed him as a member of a group he was forming to back The Bachelors on tour, and immediately the schedule was completed, Gary took over as lead singer, and as Paul Raven And The Boston Sound, the band toured Britain and Europe.

Two years later, he appeared on the concept album for MCA of 'Jesus Christ Superstar' and in 1968 – under the name Paul Munday – he released the single 'Musical Man'. Once again, it sank without trace!

It was in 1971 that he and Mike Leander virtually 'manufactured' Gary Glitter, for the release of the single 'Rock 'N' Roll Parts One And Two', in an attempt to jump on the rapidly emerging 'glam rock' bandwagon.

The record *wasn't* an instant hit. It took four months to chart, and later just fell short of the coveted Number 1 slot. Yet from then on, it was success all the way for Gary with an incredible run of hit singles: 'I Didn't Know I Loved You Till I Saw You Rock 'N' Roll', 'Do You Wanna Touch Me?' 'Hello, Hello I'm Back Again', 'I'm The Leader Of The Gang' and 'I Love You Love Me', consecutive Number 1 hits in 1973. 'Remember Me This Way', 'Always Yours' (his third Number 1 chart success); 'Oh Yes You're Beautiful', 'Love Like You And Me', 'You Belong To Me', and many, more. . . .

Gary Glitter was noted for his flamboyant stage clothes – often wearing gold and silver lurex outfits that got more outrageous as the hits went by. Then there was his exciting and dynamic stage act, which used every gimmick in the business. It was pure unadulterated showbiz razzamatazz – showmanship at its most contrived. For Gary, however, it was *always* an act, and he performed it all with tongue stuck very firmly in his cheek.

In 1976, after clocking up thirteen consecutive hits, he decided to retire from showbusiness "for personal reasons" in a blaze of publicity after becoming engaged to 22 year old Mary Medalee. Neither the engagement or his retirement lasted very long . . . lack of money and mounting debts saw to that. Within a few months, he was back on the scene, making an inevitable comeback on the British cabaret circuit, revelling in the recent nostalgia of his former chart hits.

Then in October 1980, he was summoned before a London Bankruptcy Court with debts of more than $400,000 – $375,000 of which was owed to the Inland Revenue.

Said Gary: "My trouble was not enough glitter on stage and too much of it off stage. Too much high living and extravagance. I also lost a lot of money on my tours. Still . . . I'll be back, what's $400,000 among friends? I'll pay everybody off as soon as I can!"

Earlier in the year, Gary attempted to raise some of the money by selling his bizarre and extravagant stage costumes at one of the most unusual auctions ever to take place at Sotherby's. However, the sale raised a mere fraction of the money he had hoped and he subsequently made a number of comeback concerts in London, in which he failed to make the years roll back.

BOBBY GOLDSBORO
American. Male. Singer/Songwriter.

The sentimental 'Honey' with its life

BOBBY GOLDSBORO — still in demand after seventeen years

and death lyrics, was the song that virtually made Bobby Goldsboro an international household name, when it topped the American chart in April, 1968 and reached Number 2 in Britain. But ironically, he had already enjoyed outstanding success in the States with *three* million-sellers from 1964 to 1968: 'See The Funny Little Clown' (1964), 'Little Things' (1965) and 'It's Too Late' (1966).

He was born on January 18, 1941, in Maryanna, Florida, and during his teens his family moved to Dotham, Alabama, where Bobby studied at Aburn University. He learned to play guitar and on graduation played with various local outfits, before joining Roy Orbison's group in 1962.

He started writing songs with Orbison, who later encouraged him to go solo and try his luck as a singer. Not long afterwards he joined Laurie Records. Later still he was signed to United Artists and made 'See The Funny Little Clown'.

With the success of 'Honey', however (the record was re-released in 1975 reaching the Number 2 slot again in Britain), Bobby Goldsboro became a world star – and regularly toured internationally, appearing on television and in concert engagements.

In 1973 he charted once more with 'Summer (The First Time)', followed by 'Hello Summertime' – which was used as a movie and television commercial for Coca Cola . . . with suitably changed words.

His success has continued ever since through nearly two decades and numerous musical changes. He is still very actively involved in music – writing songs, producing and recording. And he is very much in demand for television shows, and live appearances particularly on the American cabaret circuit.

LESLEY GORE
American. Female. Singer/Songwriter.

Education isn't a bad thing, after all, but in the case of Lesley Gore's career, it probably spelled ruination.

Born Tenafly, New Jersey in May 1946, the daughter of a wealthy swimsuit manufacturer, her early singing voice showed considerable promise. At 16, she was snapped up by Mercury

LESLEY GORE — penned the lyrics for the movie 'Fame' after ten years in the shadows

Records, and in 1963 was hailed as a major star when she had two big hits on both sides of the Atlantic with 'It's My Party' which topped the U.S. charts, and 'Judy's Turn To Cry'. And for the next few years she had a string of successes, notably in America, with further singles, including 'Sunshine, Lollipops and Rainbows', and albums, snapped up by teenagers, who identified with her and her material.

But, despite this success she was determined to finish her education, by gaining her Bachelor of Arts degree from Sarah Lawrence College in Bronxville, New Jersey. The year she entered the college – 1965 – she cut right back on live appearances.

When she finally emerged, and felt it was time to re-establish herself, it was arguably too late. Live appearances in 1970/71 didn't much impress the critics and her second career floundered. She did, however, sign a new contract with Motown Records in 1972 – though two years later switched to A & M.

Lesley later turned to songwriting and in 1980 enjoyed great success, having penned several of the lyrics for the movie 'Fame', directed by Alan Parker. Most of the music for the film was composed by her brother Michael.

GRAND FUNK RAILROAD — at a Hyde Park free concert in London

GRAND FUNK RAILROAD
American. Male.
Vocal/Instrumental Group.
Original line-up: Mark Farner (guitar/vocals); Don Brewer (drums); Mel Schacher (bass).

Volume alone is not sufficient to keep an act in the public eye. But, in the case of Grand Funk Railroad, decibels spelt dollars, and, at the turn of the '70s, they had acquired for themselves the niche of being America's top-rated heavy metal band, a place to be occupied later by the even more bizarre Kiss.

The group hailed from Flint, Michigan in 1969 and started life as a trio, although they were joined in 1972 by keyboard player Craig Frost.

Emerging from various local bands, Grand Funk attracted the attention of former Detroit DJ Terry Knight and it was he who virtually hustled Farner, Schacher and Brewer on to the road to fame and fortune . . . and later became their manager and mentor.

Until Capital signed them, record companies had fought shy of the band. Critics hated them – but the young record buyers loved them. They saw the value in a band who could produce an album track entitled 'T.N.U.C.' (reverse it) on their debut album, 'On Time'.

And 'Loud, white noise,' as it was called, enjoyed a terrific following,

particularly in the U.S.

By 1970, Grand Funk had established themselves as one of America's leading bands – their concerts were a sell-out. Yet perhaps the strength of the band's appeal lay in the aggression of their music, stemming as it did from origins in the highly-industrialized Michigan.

In 1976, the group made 'Born To Die' which they planned as a farewell album, although they did stay together to do sessions with Frank Zappa on 'Good Singin', 'Good Playin' later that year.

DOBIE GREY — 'Drift Away' was the big hit and he did just that afterwards

DOBIE GRAY
American. Male.
Singer/Songwriter.

It was in 1973 that the 'I want to get lost in your rock 'n' roll' lyrics of 'Drift Away' gave 31-year-old Dobie Gray his first American Number 1, eight years after his first British and American success with 'The In Crowd'.

The singer/songwriter, born in Brookshire, Texas, in 1942, was one of eight children. He headed for Los Angeles in his early 20s and soon landed a job with Sonny Bono – of Sonny and Cher fame – at Specialty Records.

'Look At Me', and 'The In Crowd' followed soon after, but later he found difficulty getting the right material.

Gray, himself one of eight children, shifted his career to acting, and even appeared in the New York cast of "Hair". But he also continued to put his voice to good use with the group Pollution, and made demo tapes for singer/songwriter Paul Williams.

'Drift Away' was his most spectacular success which was written by Paul Williams' brother, Mentor. Much of Gray's work at that time was in the Country field in Nashville – unusual for a Black singer.

In 1975 he switched record labels to Capricorn, hoping to find a repeat of 'Drift Away's' success, but without too much luck.

BILL HALEY
American. Male.
Singer/Instrumentalist.

On April 12th, 1954, Bill Haley and his group The Comets recorded the song that was to become the anthem of rock 'n' roll – 'Rock Around The Clock' – at Pythian Temple, New York . . . though the song had actually been released earlier by Sonny Dae and had failed to register. In reality, Haley's version didn't exactly set the world on fire either at that time . . . It was only a year or so later, when it was used as soundtrack music for the movie 'Blackboard Jungle' that it became a hit. And Haley suddenly found himself acclaimed the creator of rock 'n' roll. Since then, 'Rock Around The Clock' – which topped the British chart in 1955 – has been re-released at regular intervals all over the world, (normally to coincide with a Bill Haley tour), and has sold in excess of 20,000,000 copies!

Bill Haley was born William John Clifton Haley on July 6, 1925, and started his musical career playing guitar in various local country and western groups, though without much success. A six-year spell working on a radio station in Pensylvania followed, and it was here that he became aware of the influence Black music was playing on listeners. He soon realized its great potential.

During his spare time, Bill continued to play country and western, though occasionally, he introduced elements of the Black music that fascinated him so much. He experimented with the music as often as he could, working in new treatments into his stage act with his group The Saddlemen.

Until then, Haley had released several singles, but had yet to find a winning formula for recording success. So he decided to take his musical experiments a stage further, combining the best of the Black r 'n' b, with the best of country. It proved the fore-

BILL HALEY — with the everpresent kiss curl

runner of rock 'n' roll . . .

The Saddlemen later changed their name to The Comets, and this change brought about a substantial alteration in their fortunes. In 1951, they enjoyed moderate success with 'Rock The Joint', followed by 'Crazy Man Crazy' in 1953 – a self-penned song, inspired by the language Haley heard students using at the colleges he played. This became the first rock 'n' roll hit. Two years later, 'Rock Around The Clock' hailed the birth of a brand new age, and a brand new music. When the movie 'Rock Around The Clock', featuring Haley and The Comets, was released in cinemas all over the world, it caused riots, chaos and devastation. In Britain alone, teddy boys jived and bopped in the aisles . . . *and* wrecked numerous cinemas in their exhuberance. Bill Haley had arrived at last.

In his later years he lived a life of quiet seclusion in his Rio Grande Valley home emerging occasionally to tour with the Comets.

However, in the fall of 1980 an extensive British and European concert schedule was hurriedly cancelled when Bill was stricken with a mystery disease and confined to his home. In November he was admitted to a Los Angeles hospital with reports circulating of a suspected brain tumor and on February 9, 1981 the reluctant hero of rock and roll passed away.

TIM HARDIN
American. Male.
Singer/Songwriter.

Music trends come and go. And performers whose influence has lasted a whole decade count themselves lucky – they are very few and far between. Tim Hardin, born into a musical family, in Eugene, Oregon, on September 13, 1940, and a descendant of the famous outlaw John Wesley Hardin, was one such figure. Although himself an accomplished singer and performer, he is perhaps best known as a songwriter.

At the start of the 1960s, he settled in Cambridge, Massachusetts, following a two-year spell in the Far East with the U.S. Marines. And he soon built up a substantial following among folk fans, during the heyday of the solo singer/guitarist.

TIM HARDIN — found dead in a Los Angeles appartment in 1980

In 1966, Bobby Darin had a huge hit with Tim's classic 'If I Were A Carpenter' – a song which was later to give Johnny Cash and his wife June Carter a gold single, and The Four Tops a massive British and American hit in 1968.

Meanwhile, Tim Hardin's own career was growing. In the late 1960s he moved to Woodstock and became a firm friend of Bob Dylan and the Band. It has been suggested that he – in part at least – inspired Dylan's John Wesley Harding album. Dylan adding the 'g'! By this time, too, he had also penned the classic 'Lady Came From Baltimore'. 'Reason To Believe' had yet to be recorded by a host of performers, most notably Rod Stewart on his 'Every Picture Tells A Story' album.

The late 1960s and early 1970s saw Tim Hardin recording much of his own work, but by then his career was beginning to slide although he enjoyed moderate success with a handful of albums including 'Tim Hardin I' and 'Tim Hardin II' (for Vine); 'Bird On A Wire' and 'Nine' (for CBS).

He rarely performed and his career seemed dogged by ill-health. There were also reports and rumors of drink and drugs addiction.

In 1974, however, he quit America and moved to Britain where he took up residency in the South of England with his family, and often appeared on the British club circuit with fellow folk singer Tim Rose. His health, too, started to improve.

He remained in England for just over a year before returning to Los Angeles, where for the next five years he lived almost as a recluse, in virtual obscurity. He *did* venture out occasionally to perform, though the mainstay of his income during this time came from past record and writing royalties.

Friends and colleagues also talked of a long battle spent trying to beat the drugs and the booze!

On December 29, 1980, he was found dead from a heart attack in his Los Angeles apartment. And the career of Tim Hardin, which promised so much, but never quite realized its full potential, came to an abrupt and tragic end.

GEORGE HARRISON
British. Male. Singer/Songwriter.

George Harrison today is a very contented man, with a mad passion for motor-racing – he's a regular patron at Formula One circuits all over the world, and his single 'Faster' was inspired by his good friends from the racing world, Jackie Stewart and Nicki Lauder – *and* gardening!

He lives with his Mexican wife Olivia and their young son Dhani, at Henley-On-Thames, in Oxfordshire, England, enjoying life to the full again following several years of severe depression – brought on by the break up of his first marriage to Patti Boyd – and ill-health, courtesy of heavy bouts of drinking.

He was born on February 25, 1943 in Wavertree, Liverpool, and started playing guitar at the age of fourteen. His mother bought him his first guitar for just $6.00 and he joined the group that was to become known as The Beatles, in 1958.

When the group finally called it a day in 1969, George had already paved the way for his own solo career, having recorded two albums – 'Wonderwall' in 1968, from the film of the same name, and the dire 'Electronic Sounds' in 1969. When the split finally

GEORGE HARRISON — has provided the backing for a number of movies

came about, Harrison went out on his own to produce and record a highly original triple album called 'All Things Must Pass' in 1970, featuring the hit single 'My Sweet Lord' which topped the British and American charts in 1971. The same year, he organized the massive, and breathtakingly successful, Bangladesh concert at Madison Square Gardens in New York, which featured some of his many friends, including Ringo Starr (see **Ringo Starr**), Eric Clapton, Bob Dylan, Billy Preston, Badfinger (see **Badfinger**), and his own spiritual mentor, Ravi Shankar (see **Ravi Shankar**). All the proceeds raised by the concert and subsequent album ('Concert For Bangladesh') – which ran into many

millions – went to the famine relief fund for the troubled country. George also scored in the singles charts with – 'Bangladesh' – taken from the hit album. He enjoyed single success again in January 1973 with 'Give Me Love (Give Me Peace On Earth)'.

However, during the following years, George's career *and* life suffered several major setbacks. In 1974, his wife Patti left him for his best friend Eric Clapton, and he turned to excessive drinking to combat his depression. The same year, he launched his own record label, Dark Horse, but it wasn't the success George had hoped for. A few months later, he was the subject of a lengthy lawsuit which claimed that his hit single 'My Sweet

Lord', was a direct copy of The Chiffons' early '60s hit, 'He's So Fine'. The result of the proceedings saw him paying out a hefty sum of money in royalties to the plaintiff.

Since then, though, things have certainly looked up again for the youngest former-Beatle. He remarried and settled once more in Britain and when his wife Olivia presented him with a son – George was delighted; his happiness was complete.

For many years now, George Harrison has been a great fan and devotee of the cult humor presented by the Monty Python team on television. Indeed, during 1978 he regularly appeared on TV with Python star Eric Idle in his 'Rutland Weekend Television' series. He was featured, with great success, too, in the TV movie 'The Rutles' – a gentle send-up of The Beatles and all they stood for!

In 1979, as a direct result of his friendship with the zany team, George put up a substantial amount of money from his own business interests and resources, to help finance the Monty Python movie 'Life of Brian', after the massive EMI company had withdrawn backing. It was a shrewd move, for 'Life Of Brian' became a massive box-office success in Britain and America. He followed this up by injecting substantial quantities of cash into two other movie projects 'The Long Good Friday' and 'The Time Bandits'. He also produced in 1980 a leather bound volume of his own writing, on sale for a mere $350 each.

NOEL HARRISON
British. Male. Singer.

Whether being born in the shadow of a famous parent is a considerable advantage or a great disadvantage is debatable. But for Noel Harrison it meant, at all costs, that he simply couldn't do anything that might in the least be seen as copying his celebrated father, actor Rex Harrison. And possibly for that reason, Noel – an accomplished guitarist – embarked on a singing career. He had only one major hit, 'Windmills Of Your Mind', from the film, 'The Thomas Crown Affair', reaching the British Top Ten in February, 1969.

By this time though, Noel Harrison

NOEL HARRISON — *one major hit and he disappeared*

had gained a considerable following on the British college and club circuit, coming as he did, at the height of the mid-'60s folk music boom. But although his musical career was looking promising – he had a second minor hit with the haunting 'A Young Girl' – he was drawn towards acting. It was inevitable, coming from his background.

During 1966/67, he featured extensively in the television series 'Girl From UNCLE' and later took Tommy Steele's role in a touring production of 'Half A Sixpence' and several more major stage roles.

In 1972, at 38, he married 25-year-old Margaret Benson at Kensington Register Office, London. His previous marriage, to model Sara Tufnell, had ended the year before.

Throughout the '70s he concentrated his career entirely on the theater.

BOBBY HELMS
American. Male. Singer/Songwriter.

Hailed by Cashbox magazine as "the Number One Country Singer Of

1957", Bobby Helms had become a hard-bitten showbusiness trouper by the time he had reached the tender age of thirteen, and was regularly featured singing on station WWTV in his hometown of Bloomington, Indiana. Indeed, such was his success and great potential, that the Grand Ole Opry actually flew him to Nashville each month to appear on their Saturday night show.

He was born on August 15, 1933 and soon established himself as a child star and a major attraction in the American country music scene. During the late 1950s, he clocked up several notable American chart singles with 'Fraulein', 'My Special Angel' – a million seller in 1957 – 'Schoolboy Crush' (the first record Cliff Richard ever recorded!) and 'Just A Little Lonesome', while in Britain he scored with 'No Other Baby' and 'Jacqueline'. But his biggest hit of all came in 1958 when he recorded the massive-selling 'Jingle Bell Rock' ... which took five years to become a million-seller.

Then, riding on the crest of a wave of success and on the verge of a brilliant career, Bobby disappeared from the music scene and into self-exile and retirement, though throughout the 1960s his name cropped up from time to time on obscure record labels like Harmony, Little Darlin' and Creton. However, he has continued to write songs, though without too much success. Obviously, he is hoping to recapture the triumph of his monster hit 'Jingle Bell Rock', which is re-released almost annually.

THE HOLLIES
British. Male.
Vocal/Instrumental Group.

Original line-up: Allan Clarke (vocals); Graham Nash (guitar); Eric Haydock (bass); Don Rathbone (drums); Tony Hicks (guitar).

The Hollies were formed in Manchester in 1962 by Allan Clarke and Graham Nash, who had previously worked together in a vocal/guitar duo called The Guystones. The original group line-up included members of two of Manchester's top groups – The Deltas and The Dolphins – and legend has it, that they took their name from the holly tree.

As The Deltas, the group were playing a local engagement one Christmas Eve when, in dire need of a new name, someone spotted the seasonal decorations hanging from the ceiling and suggested *The Hollies*. The name stuck!

They enjoyed tremendous success playing in and around the clubs and dance halls of the Manchester area during 1962 and with the sudden emergence of Merseybeat at the turn of the year, The Hollies were signed to a recording contract with Parlophone to become record stable-mates of The Beatles. Their first single – 'Ain't That Just Like Me' – was a re-working of the old Coasters' hit. It was a moderate success. But the group played it safe and covered another Coasters' song – 'Searchin'' – as their follow-up. It reached Number 12 in the British chart. Their third release, 'Stay', in the

THE HOLLIES — (l-r): Allan Clark, Bernie Calvert, Bobby Elliott, Terry Sylvester, Tony Hicks

fall of 1963 made the Top Ten to establish them as a major group to challenge the dominance of the Liverpool bands.

Meanwhile, drummer Don Rathbone had left the group to join Shane Fenton And The Fentones (see **Alvin Stardust**), and he was replaced by former-Fentone drummer Bobby Elliott. Still, for the next three years, with such hits as 'Just One Look', 'Here I Go Again', 'We're Through', 'Yes I Will', 'I'm Alive' – their only British chart-topper, in 1965 – 'Look Through Any Window', 'If I Needed Someone' and 'I Can't Let Go', The Hollies became one of Britain's most successful and consistent groups. And the *only* one to offer any kind of challenge to the supremacy of The Beatles and Stones. They regularly scored in the international charts too, – and toured the world, particularly America, where they developed a tremendous fan following.

In 1966, following a massively suc-

cessful sell-out U.S. tour, Eric Haydock was taken ill and left the group, emerging shortly afterwards with his own band. His replacement was the former-Dolphins bass-man Bernie Calvert. Yet, despite a major change of line-up, the hits continued to roll off the Hollies' conveyor belt of success through to 1968. And they scored with some of the all-time classic pop singles – 'Bus Stop', 'Stop, Stop, Stop', 'On A Carousel', 'King Midas In Reverse', 'Jennifer Eccles' and 'Listen To Me' – which all showed off to perfection The Hollies' magnificent vocal harmonies, and the unique voice of Graham Nash. Indeed, it was the superb harmonies that helped establish the group all over the world. They were one of a handful of groups to have their own unmistakable, instantly recognizable sound.

1968, however, saw the departure of one of the vital forces within the group – Graham Nash. Unhappy at the direction in which the group's recordings were heading (and particularly upset at the decision to record the 'Hollies Sing Dylan' album), Nash was also disappointed at the lack of success of 'King Midas In Reverse' – it was a change of style that just hadn't come off. So after recording 'Jennifer Eccles', he left the group, saying that he wanted to make records that "say something". He did just that in his own way and re-surfaced shortly afterwards in America as a member of Crosby, Stills And Nash (see **The Byrds**).

Graham Nash's replacement in the line-up was the former-Swinging Blue Jeans guitarist Terry Sylvester, an old friend of the group, and he sang on all their subsequent hit records which included the singles 'Sorry Suzanne', 'He Ain't Heavy He's My Brother', 'I Can't Tell The Bottom From The Top', 'Gasoline Alley Bred', 'Hey Willy', 'The Baby', 'Long Cool Woman In A Black Dress', 'The Day That Curly Billy Shot Crazy Sam McGhee' and 'The Air That I Breathe'.

Founder-member Allan Clarke was the next to leave, in 1971, to embark on a solo singing career. And indeed, he made several singles and albums in his own right. Yet, for a while the group continued with Swedish singer Michael Rickfors – who sang on 'The

Baby' – fronting The Hollies. However, Clarke returned in 1972 when 'Long Cool Woman', a song he had recorded with the group before leaving went on to top the American Hit Parade the same year. He has been a vital member ever since.

One of the most polished and professional groups in the business, The Hollies have carved a unique place for themselves in the annals of popular music. Indeed, at one time during 1976, they had clocked up more hit singles in Britain than any other group in history, including The Beatles, achieving a massive 290 weeks in the chart with 27 singles alone.

Since then, although the hit singles ran out by 1974 – their albums are still regularly among the British best-sellers – The Hollies have continued to add to their amazing reputation, which today sees them as one of the most respected groups around. And *still* very much at the top of their profession.

Says Terry Sylvester: "The great thing about being in The Hollies is that there is total freedom for all of us to diversify our talents in other directions. We operate a very democratic system, and there are no ties. For six months of the year, we are all very much committed to recording and touring all over the world, particularly in the States. It's a very tough schedule. But for the remaining six months, we go our separate ways to do the things *we* want to do as individuals.

"I'm a very active person and I like to be involved in recording. Quite honestly, there are a lot of songs which come on the market that I'd love to sing, which wouldn't necessarily suit the style of The Hollies. Some of my own songs for instance. I suppose it's natural that I want my own artistic freedom on record, so I have become involved in a solo recording career of my own and have had several singles released."

"It's nothing new for The Hollies. Allan Clarke also records on his own, and like me has had a few singles released and several albums. Tony Hicks is very heavily involved in record production and writing, and Bobby and Bernie write and often sit in on session. But the great thing is, that

none of our individual projects affect the group adversely. On the contrary, they stimulate The Hollies. When we meet up again after a period away from each other, we are all full of new ideas, new techniques to explore. In that way, it can only help the group as a whole to progress. I think that is why we have been so successful for so long; and why we will continue to do so for many, many years to come."

MARY HOPKIN
British. Female. Singer.

Mary Hopkin was born on May 3, 1950 in Pontardawe, Glamorgan, South Wales and started singing at the age of four.

While majoring in music, art and English at the local grammar school, and studying singing at Cardiff College of Music and Drama, she earned extra pocket money performing in local working men's clubs. And soon there followed appearances in various television folk music programs . . . and for a time, she made many successful recordings in Welsh, for Cambrian Records.

In 1968, she appeared on British television's 'Opportunity Knocks' show, where she was seen by top model Twiggy, who was captivated by her pure voice and charming talent. Twiggy in turn, raved about the

MARY HOPKIN — *out of the limelight since 'Those Were The Days'*

young Welsh girl to Paul McCartney, who, equally impressed, signed her to a recording contract with the newly-formed Beatles' company Apple. Her first single for the label was a reworking of the old Limeliters hit 'Those Were The Days' (from the Russian folk song 'Darogoi Dlimmoyo'), which McCartney produced. Within weeks of its release, in August 1965, the song went on to top the British Hit Parade for six weeks, followed by a month-long stint at the top of the charts in America. It also topped Hit Parades all over the world, selling a massive eight million copies.

Mary followed up her first chart success with a handful of best-sellers, including 'Goodbye' (in 1969, specially written for her by Paul McCartney), which reached Number 2 in Britain, and 'Temma Harbour' in 1970. With each success, came offers for films, and musicals and Mary soon found herself touring the world.

In 1970, she represented Britain in The Eurovision Song Contest, singing 'Knock Knock Who's There', which finished second in the contest – and the same year, she starred alongside Tommy Steele in the stage pantomime 'Dick Whittington' at the London Pal-

WHATEVER HAPPENED TO . . .?

ladium. The following year, she appeared with David Essex in 'Cinderella' in Manchester.

Not long afterwards, she married record producer Tony Visconti and left showbusiness to start a family, although she has continued to sing and write songs. Indeed, during her self-imposed exile from the business, she guested on many albums singing back-up vocals for Ralph McTell, David Bowie and Thin Lizzy. She did, however, make a brief return to the singles market in 1976 with 'If You Loved Me', which reached the British Top Thirty.

Today, Mary Hopkin lives with her two children – Jessie and Delaney, she is parted from her husband – in the village of Wargrave in Berkshire, and continues to write songs.

At Christmas 1980, she starred in 'Rock Nativity' which was presented for a season at the Hexagon Theatre in Reading . . . and plans a major comeback in 1981.

JOHNNY HORTON
American. Male. Singer.

Johnny Horton – hailed as the 'singing fisherman' for his expert ability as an angler – was on the verge of outstanding success as a country singer at the start of the 1960s, when tragedy struck. He was killed in a car crash on November 5, 1960 just close to Milano, Texas . . . and a spectacular was over almost as soon as it began.

Johnny Horton was born on April 30, 1929, in Tyler, Texas, and grew up in East Texas, where he sang in local clubs, and often appeared on radio. He was discovered by Tillman Franks who later became his manager and guided him to a recording contract during the middle '50s. His first record release was 'I'm A Honky Tonk Man'.

Tillman masterminded his career and soon realized that Horton's big voice was used to its best advantage on story-book songs . . . and by the end of the decade, he had steered him to his biggest chart successes with 'Springtime In Alaska', 'Sink The Bismark' and the monster-selling 'Battle Of New Orleans' in 1959, covered in Britain by Lonnie Donegan .

After his death, he had a British hit in 1961 with the title track from the smash-hit movie 'North To Alaska'.

FRANK IFIELD
British. Male. Singer.

In January 1963, Frank Ifield became the first British recording artiste-ever to score three Number 1 hits in the British charts with consecutive single releases: 'I Remember You', 'Lovesick Blues', and 'The Wayward Wind'. And for the next three years, he became one of the most popular singers in the country, consolidating all his recording success with further hits, 'Nobody's Darling But Mine', 'Confessin', 'Mule Train' and 'Don't Blame Me'.

He was born Frank Edward Ifield in Coventry, England on November 30 1937, and at the age of nine emigrated with his parents to Australia where the family settled in Sydney. At the age of 15 after winning a radio talent show, Frank left school and went into showbusiness professionally. Within two years, he was appearing regularly on Australian radio.

In 1956, when television was launched on the continent, Frank Ifield became the first artist to have his own TV series – 'Campfire Favourites' – and he also enjoyed recording suc-

FRANK IFIELD — still smooth

cess with a hit single 'Whiplash', the title song from the hit television series.

Then in 1959, after enjoying tremendous success in his adopted country – where he was established as one of the continent's most popular stars – Frank decided to return home to England in an effort to break through there. It took him precisely twelve months. Almost immediately, he was signed to a recording contract and in February 1960, he clocked up his first hit with 'Lucky Devil'. Two years later, he hit the jackpot with 'I Remember You'.

During the halcyon days of the 1960s, Frank Ifield toured the world, headlining concert and cabaret bills. And, when the hit records faded, he turned more towards the variety stage, and appeared in summer shows and pantomime, including stints at the London Palladium.

And of course, he has continued to carve out a brand new career for himself in Britain on the domestic cabaret circuit.

He often returns to his country roots and in 1981 starred at the International Festival of Country Music at Wembley, England.

THE ISLEY BROTHERS
American. Male. Vocal Group.
Original line-up: Ronald Isley; Rudolph Isley; O'Kelly Isley.

For over twenty years, The Isley

Brothers have been at the top of popular music in America and Britain. The years roll on . . . but the Isleys continue to reign supreme, in a class of their own and almost as big today as they were when they made their first hit record – 'Shout' – in 1959, a million-seller.

They were born in Cincinatti, Ohio – O'Kelly on December 25, 1937; Rudolph on April 1, 1939; and Ronald on May 21, 1941 – and started singing together at an early age. They were discovered in 1959 singing at the Howard Theater in Washington DC, and signed to RCA Victor. 'Shout' which they wrote themselves, was their debut single for the label.

Three years, a change of label to WAND, and several moderate hits later they recorded the classic 'Twist And Shout', which sold a million, and was later recorded by numerous other groups including The Beatles.

In 1965, The Isleys signed for Tamla Motown and soon afterwards moved to England where they had built up an enormous following. Their first Motown release was another classic 'This Old Heart Of Mine', followed by 'I Guess I'll Always Love You' and 'Behind The Painted Smile'.

But by 1969, they were back in America, and on their own label T-NECK. They were heading into the rock field, too, having been joined by brothers Ernie and Marvin Isley, and their cousin Chris Jasper. They chalked up another million-seller the same year with 'It's Your Thing', followed by 'Put Yourself In My Place'. It was ten years since their first success – and constantly original, the group began experimenting with synthesisers and broadening their rock base.

They moved into the '70s with a new confidence and were soon back among the charts with several classic singles – 'That Lady', 'Highway Of My Life', 'Summer Breeze', 'Harvest For The World', 'Fight The Power' and 'Take Me To The Next Phase'.

One of the most original bands in the history of pop, The Isleys have virtually become an institution – and a hit making one at that. Still going strong and ever on the look out for new ideas, the '80s should prove as productive *and* successful as the '60s and '70s for The Isley Brothers.

TOMMY JAMES AND THE SHONDELLES
American.
Male. Vocal/Instrumental Group.
Original line-up: Tommy James (vocals); Joe Kessler (guitar); George Magura (sax/bass/organ); Mike Vale (bass/piano); Ronnie Rosman (keyboards); Vinnie Pietropaoli (drums).

No discotheque in 1968 was complete without a copy of Tommy James and the Shondells' 'Mony Mony', a Number 1 hit in Britain in the summer of that year.

The Shondells first appeared in 1964, with a cover version of the Raindrops' 'Hanky Panky' which topped the American chart in 1966. But by the mid-'60s, they had established themselves as one of America's leading groups with a succession of hits to

JAN AND DEAN — (from l-r)

TOMMY JAMES — the pressure of stardom took its toll

their credit including the U.S. Number 1 hit 'Crystal Blue Persuasion', 'Ball Of Fire', 'I Think We Are Alone Now', 'Mirage', 'Crimson And Clover' and 'Sweet Cherry Wine'. There were also a number of highly successful LPs,

and the result was that the group's appeal – by then it was essentially bubblegum – made them much in demand. Too much in demand, in fact.

For some time James – born Dayton, Ohio, on April 29, 1947 – had been using drugs as a cushioning effect against over-work, and eventually, one night in Alabama, he collapsed. Doctors feared he would never recover, but miraculously he did . . . although it spelt the end for the Shondells after 19 American hits in a row. They went on briefly to become Hog Heaven.

James, for his part, headed for the seclusion of his farm in upstate, New York, for a total rest cure. It worked, and in time he started writing songs again, with Bob King. The early '70s saw him record a number of U.S. successes, including 'Cat's Eye In The Window', 'Nothing To Hide' and, 'Draggin' The Line'.

And today, he continues to write and record his own songs, though without the pressures he experienced as a superstar.

JAN AND DEAN
American. Male. Vocal Duo.

It was the early '60s, and everything was sun and fun, and sand and sea in Southern California . . . And the surfing sound was all around. Two acts best summed up the period – The Beach Boys, who have been together ever since, and Jan and Dean. Jan Berry (born on April 3, 1941) and Dean Torrence, (born on March 10, 1940) both came from Los Angeles, went to high school together . . . where they started singing in the locker room after gym classes.

At college – Jan went to the University of Southern California studying commercial art; Dean went to the University of California on a medical course – they started singing more seriously together, aided and encouraged by friends, including future Beach Boys member Bruce Johnston. The two cut three records for Arwin – 'Baby Talk', 'There's A Girl' and 'Clementine', but continued with their education, until they had their first big breakthrough, in 1961, with 'Heart And Soul', on the Challenge label, a hit on both sides of the Atlantic.

The comparison between their music and that of the Beach Boys is obvious, but their work was related, rather than being in competition. Indeed, Jan sang lead on the 'Beach Boys' Party' hit 'Barbara Ann', and in turn Brian Wilson often worked on Jan and Dean recordings.

During the early '60s they enjoyed a moderate hit with 'Linda', followed by their million-selling single 'Surf City' in 1963, and several more big hits followed, including 'Honolulu Lulu', 'Drag City', 'Dead Man's Curve', 'Ride The White Surf' and 'The Little Old Lady From Pasadena', while 'New Girl In School' enjoyed some airplay two years later.

Tragedy struck in 1966, when during the filming of the movie 'Easy Come, Easy Go' Jan was involved in a serious car smash, damaging himself permanently, physically and mentally, in the process. He was totally paralyzed for over a year.

Dean tried to continue a solo career, but it didn't work out, and a reunion gig in 1973 failed miserably. They haven't worked together since.

Jan is now totally out of the music business, but Dean – a qualified doctor – runs a Hollywood studio, designing posters and LP covers.

And he still surfs . . .

EDEN KANE
British. Male. Singer.

Eden Kane was born Richard Graham Sarstedt on March 29, 1942, in Delhi, India, where his father managed a gigantic tea plantation near Darjeeling.

At the age of ten, he returned to England with his family and went to school in Surrey, where he became increasingly interested in music and formed his first group.

He was discovered singing in a talent contest in London by producers Michael Barclay and Philip Waddilove, who signed him up to a management contract. And he later signed a record deal with Pye for whom he released his first single 'Hot Chocolate Crazy' in 1960. It wasn't a hit!

In 1961, he switched labels to Decca and recorded the song that was to

EDEN KANE — success in the USA remained elusive

make him a star – 'Well I Ask You' – which topped the British Hit Parade in the summer of that year. He followed it up with 'Get Lost', 'Forget Me Not' and 'I Don't Know Why' – and at the same time toured Britain playing theater engagements with such other stars of the day as Billy Fury and Marty Wilde.

He recorded his last big British hit – 'Boys Cry' – in 1964 which reached Number 8 in the chart, and then set about establishing a name and career for himself in Australia, where he became one of the biggest stars on the continent.

In 1970, he moved to America hoping to repeat his Australian success and make a name Stateside. However, in May of that year, he married U.S. journalist Charlene Groman – a millionairess – in Los Angeles, where he lives today. Eden, though, never quite broke through to success in America.

He returned to England briefly in 1976 to record an album with his brothers, Peter – who had a British Number 1 hit with 'Where Do You Go To My Lovely' in 1969 – and Robin (who enjoyed chart success in '76 with 'My Resistance Is Low') . . . called appropriately 'The Sarstedt Brothers'.

Today, now a resident of California, he spends his time writing songs and occasionally sings in West Coast clubs and lounges.

KATHY KIRBY
British. Female. Singer.

Kathy Kirby always wanted to become a singer – a star singer. It started at the age of three when she won a talent contest in an Ilford, Essex, park. It progressed over the years until she achieved her ambition. And through her television appearances, hit records and club and concert engagements, she became one of Britain's best known singers.

. . . And then threw it all away!

She was born in Ilford in 1940 and educated at a local convent school where she was a member of the choir. She took singing lessons at the age of nine when her sights were firmly set on a career in opera.

At twelve, everything changed and she began to develop an interest in pop music.

Four years later . . . it all began to happen. Ambrose and his famous

KATHY KIRBY — from rags to riches and back again

radio Orchestra arrived for an engagement at the Ilford Palais de Danse and, after much persuasion, allowed the youthful Kathy to sing one number with his band. Bert Ambrose was so impressed with her powerful voice, that he offered her a job as a professional singer – a position she was to hold until Ambrose disbanded his Orchestra three years later. Then came two years of singing with the bands of Denny Boyce and Nat Allen, before Ambrose returned to the scene and became Kathy's manager. It was an association that lasted and flourished over a long period.

In May 1963, Kathy took one of the most important steps of her career. She successfully auditioned for the British television show 'Stars And Garters', and became a regular in the series. Within six weeks, she was receiving fan mail by the sackful.

A year earlier, however, Kathy Kirby had started making records. Her first – 'Big Man' – sold 50,000 copies. But it was a prelude to the hits singles that were to come: 'Dance On' and 'Secret Love' in 1963; 'Let Me Go Lover' and 'You're The One' in 1964. Then in 1965, she was signed for an eighteen-week television series for BBC TV. It proved so successful that she was immediately offered another.

The same year, she represented Britain in the Eurovision Song Contest and came second, singing 'I Belong', which went on to become another big hit.

Kathy consolidated all her success with concert and cabaret tours of Britain, and also played summer season. Indeed, she was virtually at the pinnacle of an outstanding career, nicknamed 'The Golden Girl Of Pop'.

Then it all began to go horribly wrong.

In 1971, Bert Ambrose died – and without her manager and mentor, Kathy's career went off the rails. She failed to honor existing contracts, crying off at the slightest irritation – a faulty sound system, an under-rehearsed band. And she soon got a reputation in showbusiness for being unreliable, and a temperamental prima donna! Very few people would employ her.

During the 1970s, however, she attempted several comebacks, playing at smaller and smaller venues, for smaller and smaller fees. A disastrous marriage in 1975 to journalist Fred Pye, which ended in divorce, didn't help her cause either. And her career went into suspended animation.

Three years later, she was declared a bankrupt by a London court, with debts in excess of £30,000 owed to the Inland Revenue. Then, at the start of 1979, she was arrested on a charge of

deceiving a London hotel of £304 and remanded on bail on the condition that she attended a mental hospital. The court order was dropped in April 1979 and later she was completely cleared of the charge. But it left a scar, and a huge question mark against her career.

Shortly after her first appearance in court, she hit the headlines once again when it was revealed that she was living in a London apartment with a woman – Laraine McKay – who had actually asked Kathy to *marry* her! They were having an affair, but the wedding ceremony never took place. Miss McKay was arrested on a deception charge and taken to Holloway Prison in London. The affair ended abruptly.

The same year, Kathy Kirby attempted yet another comeback playing a Kent bingo hall – singing in between each game.

She said at the time: "It may not be much of a start, but I had to begin somewhere again and it couldn't have been better. I know the mistakes I have made in the past, but I don't think it will ever happen again."

In the fall of 1980, she laid bare her soul and revealed intimate details of her life and career – her riches to rags story – in a leading British Sunday newspaper. And she ended the three week series by saying: "I am not going to write off my career. The stage is in my bloodstream. If I am no longer the glossy-lipped Golden Girl Of Pop, I have still got one asset left – that's my voice.

"Someone, somewhere will surely give me that one chance I need."

She's still waiting . . .

BILLY J. KRAMER
British. Male. Singer.

Billy J. Kramer actually picked his stage name from the Liverpool telephone directory in 1963, after he was discovered singing with the Mersey group The Coasters and signed up by Brian Epstein, on John Lennon's recommendation.

He was born William Howard Ashton in the Merseyside suburb of Bootle on August 19, 1943 – and after leaving school, he went to work for British Railways.

Billy started singing in his spare

time with various local bands, in clubs and ballrooms all over Liverpool, and it was here he was seen by Epstein who groomed him for stardom. Brian made him change his name, teamed him up with the crack Manchester instrumental group The Dakotas (Mike Maxfield – guitar; Tony Mansfield – drums; Ray Jones – bass; and Robin McDonald – guitar), and later pursuaded John Lennon and Paul McCartney to allow Billy J. to record their song 'Do You Want To Know A Secret'. It was his first record – and his first hit, reaching the Number 2 position in the British charts in June 1963.

Lennon and McCartney were responsible for writing several more of Kramer's hit singles including 'Bad To Me' (which topped the chart in Britain in August 1963) *and* made a sizeable dent in the U.S. Hit Parade; 'I'll Keep You Satisfied' (Number 4 in November 1963); and 'From A Window' (Number 10 in July 1964).

In 1964, however, Billy J. Kramer decided to break away from the Beatles' influence – for the time being at least – and, against great opposition from his management, he recorded a Mort Schuman composition – 'Little Children'. It proved to be his biggest-ever success, topping the British chart and clocking up massive sales in America where it registered strongly in the national Hit Parade. Further chart success came his way in May 1965 with Burt Bacharach's 'Trains And Boats And Planes'.

However, like so many of his Mersey contemporaries, Billy J. Kramer's recording career came to an abrupt halt in 1965 – and again, like so many of his former colleagues, he turned to the lucrative pastures of the British cabaret circuit to carve out a second career. He attempted a brief comeback in the mid-1970s, reverting back to his original name of William Howard Ashton, but without success.

Today, though, Billy J. Kramer – with a new group called appropriately The New Dakotas in tow – continues to perform in clubs all over Britain and occasionally ventures into the recording studios. Indeed, he has signed a new recording contract with JM Records and his first single for the label 'Silver Dream' was released in November 1980.

FRANKIE LAINE
American. Male. Singer.

Frankie Laine was born Frank Paul Lo Vecchio in the Italian section of Chicago, Illinois, on March 30, 1914. His parents were Sicilian.

The first time he ever sang in public was in the choir of Chicago's Immaculate Conception Church, but he was 15 before he sang professionally. While trying to make his way into showbusiness he worked at various jobs: office boy, book-keeper, dancing instructor and singing waiter, and also tried his hand at songwriting. But it was a hard struggle.

His first break came at the age of 24 when he was discovered singing 'That's My Desire' at Bill Berg's – a spa on Hollywood's Vine Street – by Hoagy Carmichael, who persuaded him to record the song for a fifty dollar advance. For the sake of the record sleeve his name was changed to . . . Frankie Laine. The record was a smash hit and he received his first royalty check for $36,000 within a few months.

It was the start of a magnificently successful career, which throughout the 1950s saw Frankie Laine as one of the world's major recording stars. And during this period, he achieved no less than *fourteen* Gold Discs for phenomenal sales of such recording classics as 'That's My Desire', 'Shine', 'Mule Train', 'Cry Of The Wild Goose', 'Lucky Ol' Sun', 'Jezebel', 'I Believe', 'Tell Me A Story', 'Moonlight Gambler', 'Black And Blue' and 'Sunny Side Of The Street', while five other Frankie Laine singles – 'Swamp Girl', 'Mam'selle', 'Music Maestro Please', 'Sunday Kind Of Love' and 'Rawhide' – went on to become million-sellers.

As early as 1952, he recorded the song that was to become his trademark all over the world . . . 'High Noon', from the outstandingly successful movie of the same name.

Thirty years later and Frankie is still receiving royalties for his record sales which today are in excess of 100 million!

Frankie's comeback to international prominence in the 1970s was due to Mel Brooks, who invited him to sing the title song from his film 'Blazing Saddles'. The song became a hit and Frankie's old fans emerged from holes in the woodwork.

Prior to that, however, he had starred in six motion pictures, with his voice enhancing the theme music for five – 'Blowing Wild', 'Man With A Star', 'Strange Lady In Town', 'Gunfight At The OK Corral', '3.10 To Yuma' and, of course, 'Blazing Saddles'.

Frankie Laine is one of America's most sought after singing entertainers and his charisma is unbeatable: he still retains that same charm and polish in his performance as he did in his earlier years. And at 66 he still plays to packed houses with every appearance.

In Britain, where he tours regularly – most recently in 1979 – he is accorded superstar status, and is very much in demand for concert and cabaret appearances.

Today, Frankie works 26 weeks of the year – he says one of the reasons is due to the way he sings: "I would strain my voice if I did any more!" The rest of the year is spent by bowling, fishing and relaxing with his wife Nan (the former actress Nan Grey) and his two daughters Pam and Jan. They live in San Diego in an ocean-front dwelling, less than 100 miles from where Frankie keeps his boat.

BRENDA LEE
American. Female. Singer.

The one thing that was never *small* about Brenda Lee was her talent. For after chalking up over thirty hit records in a spectacularly glittering career, there could be no disputing that!

She stood three inches under five feet tall, but packed so much energy and dynamism into her tiny frame, that throughout her phenomenally successful career, she was known as 'Little Miss Dynamite'.

Brenda Lee was born Brenda Mae Tarpley in Lithonia near Atlanta, Georgia on December 11, 1942, and educated in Nashville, Tennessee. She won a local talent contest at six, and cut her teeth as an entertainer with local and regional appearances in and around Atlanta. Following her father's death when she was eight, Brenda sang to help support the family income. Her first professional fee for performing came from an appearance in 1955 at a show in Swainboro, Georgia, to where her family had moved. For that one performance, she earned 35 dollars. At twelve, she was heard by the legendary country artiste Red Foley who signed her to appear on his Ozark Jubilee Show. Her appearance proved a great success and it led to further television slots *and* a recording contract with Decca Records. Her debut single for the label was 'Jambalaya'. Then followed a succession of chart singles, including five million-sellers and numerous Top Ten hits: 'Dynamite' (from which she took her name), 'Let's Jump The Broomstick', 'Sweet Nothins' (her first British success in 1960), 'Speak To Me Pretty', 'All Alone Am I', 'Here Comes That Feeling', 'Rockin' Around The

BRENDA LEE — Connie Francis' rival in the '60s

Christmas Tree', 'Losing You', 'As Usual', and 'Too Many Rivers'. At one time, she was acclaimed the world's leading female vocalist – and was the only girl singer in the 1960s to lead any kind of challenge to the supremacy of Connie Francis (see **Connie Francis**).

In 1963 she married Charles R. Shacklett; her daughter Julie was born a year later, and daughter Jolie arrived in 1969.

In 1967, Brenda stopped recording – "I felt the business changing, moving away from what I wanted to do", she said.

She returned in 1971 with a much more country flavor and approach to her act, and she had a big hit in 1974 with 'Nobody Wins'.

"Country music is increasingly being accepted by a wider range of people just for what it really is", she added.

Today, however, Brenda's career has taken second place in her life and affections to her family, and she could be said to be in temporary retirement.

She lives in Nashville with her husband and daughters and enjoys playing the housewife. She does occasionally venture into the recording studios, and in 1980 made a brand new album for the British based Warwick Records. Called 'Little Miss Dynamite', the album featured reworkings of many of her classic hits . . . and became a huge British hit in December of that year, reaching the Top Ten in the domestic album chart. Yet although her family certainly takes precedence in her lifestyle nowadays, she is often tempted back to live performances, singing her own kind of country music.

PEGGY LEE
American. Female. Singer.
Fifties star Peggy Lee was fighting to make a comeback in 1980, twenty-three years after enjoying her first British hit single with 'Mr. Wonderful' in 1957.

Born Norma Engstrom on May 20, 1920, she was raised by her father in the North Dakota farming town of Jamestown, after her mother died when she was very young. Peggy began singing in her teens and her early career was spent as a band singer with Will Osborne's Band.

In 1941, she joined the Benny Goodman Band and the same year, cut her first records. Two years later, however, she retired from showbusiness to marry composer David Balfour, settle down and raise a family. Their daughter Nikki was born in 1945 . . . but the marriage didn't last, ending in divorce in 1951. It was the first of four marriages for Miss Lee.

She returned to singing in 1948 and recorded her first million-selling single 'Manana', and for the next dozen years, she established herself as one of the world's leading nightclub singers. She enjoyed several more outstanding record successes, too, including another million-selling single with 'Lover' in 1952.

1957 saw her first British hit 'Mr. Wonderful', and the classic 'Fever' followed the next year. In 1961, 'Till There Was You' reached the lower reaches of the chart. Yet lack of substantial hit placings belies the fact that during her career, she recorded some 631 songs, and 59 albums! At the height of her

success, she was revered by the public, press and her fellow artists as one of the most dynamic entertainers in international showbusiness.

The early 1960s saw Peggy Lee already troubled by health problems . . . that still plague her today. In 1961, when she first performed in London, she caught pneumonia. Later she was forced to travel constantly with an iron lung! It was this ill health that eventually forced her to retire once more in 1976, after which she suffered a mystery illness that left her paralyzed. But she fought back, and re-entered showbusiness late in 1980, at the age of 60, with a North American tour, and engagements in Europe and Britain, which included appearances in the fall of '80 in The Royal Variety Show at The London Palladium, and a British tour.

She said: "I am grateful to be feeling well and to be truly enjoying my work again. I stand up stage, now, and say to myself – God, it's great to be here!"

JERRY LEE LEWIS
American. Male.
Singer/Instrumentalist.

Jerry Lee Lewis was born in Ferriday, Louisiana on September 29, 1935. And legend has it that when he was nine, his father heard him playing his Aunt Stella's piano and was so impressed that he decided to mortgage the family home for $900 in order to buy Jerry a keyboard of his own on which to practice. Today, nearly 40 years later, that piano is one of Jerry Lee Lewis's prize possessions.

He proved to be an accomplished pianist and even played in the school orchestra. Then, when he left school, he studied to become a preacher at the Ministry of God in Waxahatchie, Texas, where again legend has it, he was caught playing a boogie version of a hymn, and asked to leave. Another story credits his inability to finish the course to homesickness.

However, it was shortly after this unsuccessful attempt at entering the

JERRY LEE LEWIS — *The perfect snarl*

Church, that Jerry Lee turned to entertaining . . . and, singing the gospel (to a slightly rocking beat), he became a professional musician and entertained in nightclubs.

In 1956, he arrived at the influential Sun Records in Memphis, Tennessee, and auditioned for the studio. In actual fact, his audition tape of 'Crazy Arms' became Jerry Lee's first single release for Sun, and it was followed by some of the all-time rock 'n' roll classics: 'Whole Lotta Shakin' Going On' – which topped the American hit parade in 1957, 'Great Balls of Fire' (another chart-topper), 'What'd I Say', 'Green Green Grass Of Home' and 'Breathless', which all helped to establish the singer as a major star.

Jerry's career was shrouded in controversy, however, a few years later, when on tour in Britain. He was greeted with tremendous criticism and hostility by fans when it became known that he had married his cousin Myra Brown who *was only fourteen years old*! The tour was cancelled and the resulting bad publicity almost ruined him. Indeed, his career was never quite the same again!

He weathered the storm . . . and in 1963, he left Sun for Mercury Records and changed musical direction slightly, carving out a successful career in country music. It lasted for just six years and then Jerry Lee was back rocking 'n' rolling with the best of them. An appearance at the 1969 Toronto Rock 'n' Roll Festival put his name very firmly back in the frame.

Ten years later, after making several rock 'n' roll revival tours of Britain and America, he joined Elektra Records to begin yet another phase of his long career that *still* sees the name of Jerry Lee Lewis among the 'greats' of rock music and one of its most respected artists.

Despite enjoying great success professionally, Jerry Lee's personal life has been shattered on several occasions. Two of his children died prematurely; one was killed in a road crash and another died in a drowning accident. And throughout his life, Jerry has always had great difficulty shaking off a reputation as an alcoholic and womanizer!

JOHN LEYTON
British. Male. Singer.

John Leyton, pop star, was made, literally, by television! Indeed, up until 1961, he had enjoyed a fairly distinguished career as an actor, and had settled into the long-running British TV series 'Biggles', playing the part of 'Ginger', after serving his apprenticeship in repertory theater.

Then, in the summer of '61, he landed a part in the TV soap opera 'Harper's West One' which was to change his career, and establish him as a major force in British pop music.

Says John: "The series was built around a large London store, and the episode in which I appeared, featured the record department. I played pop singer Johnny St. Cyr, who was making a personal appearance at the store.

"During the action, the singer had to perform his latest record 'Johnny Remember Me' in front of the custom-

JOHN LEYTON — now returned to acting

ers. It was the producer's original intention for me to mime to someone else's recording . . . but I was adamant that I would sing the song myself, 'live'. I'd never actually sung in front of an audience in my life".

Within minutes of the show ending, the television station was inundated with requests for the song. So on the strength of massive public demand EMI Records, released it as a single. Within weeks 'Johnny Remember Me' was sitting at the top of the British hit parade . . . proving just how powerful a medium television had become. John Leyton – who was born in Essex on February 17, 1939 – was now a pop star, and the idol of millions.

For the next three years, Leyton's career spiralled. He followed up his debut record with several more chart singles which registered in hit parades throughout the world: 'Wild Wind', 'Son This Is She', 'Lonely City', 'Cupboard Love' were all monster-sellers . . . and as a result of his recording success, John undertook several major concert tours of Britain and Europe.

However, his acting career never entirely took a back seat. In 1962 he starred in the block-busting movie 'The Great Escape', followed by an appearance in 'Guns At Batasi'. Yet it was the film 'Von Ryan's Express', in which he played opposite Frank Sinatra, that proved to be a turning point in his career. The movie enjoyed

a phenomenal showing at the world's box-offices, and as a result, Leyton was offered a long contract for film and television appearances in Hollywood. He decided to quit Britain and settle in the States, where he was known only as an actor. His fame as a pop singer had yet to cross the Atlantic.

Over the next 10 years, Leyton starred in a succession of American TV series, including 'Convoy' and 'Twelve O'Clock High'. He also made several more excursions into the movies with appearances in 'Krakatoa East of Java' and 'The Idol'. Such was his success, that he landed his very own American television series called 'Jericho'.

Then in 1972, disillusioned with the American movie scene, he returned not only to Britain but to singing as well (for a short time at least) and signed a recording contract with York Records in London. He made a single and an album – though neither set the charts on fire.

Since then, John has turned more to writing, though he has continued to act. He has appeared regularly on British television, starring in the 1979 series 'The Square Leopard', and 'Dangerous Davies' in 1980.

LITTLE RICHARD
American. Male.
Singer/Instrumentalist.

Little Richard was born Richard Wayne Penniman, into a large family, on Christmas Day 1932 in Macon, Georgia – and by the age of fourteen, he was playing in his local church . . . and singing in the choir.

Shortly afterwards, his musical talents were put to the test when he joined Doctor Hudson's Medicine Show, with whom he sang, played piano and even tap danced! Then in rapid succession, he had a series of 'mundane' jobs which included working as a dishwasher at the Greyhound Bus Depot in Macon.

At the age of 19, after winning a talent competition in Atlanta, Georgia, he was signed, as a Gospel singer, to RCA and made several records for the label including 'Taxi Blues' and 'I Brought It All On Myself' before he moved to Peacock Records. Then in 1955, he sent demo tapes of his own composition 'Tutti Frutti' to Speciality Records in Hollywood who were immediately interested in signing him up. However, Richard was already signed to Peacock at the time . . . and it took a whole year before Speciality managed to buy out his contract. His first release for Speciality was a re-working of his demo-tape of 'Tutti Frutti' which he recorded in New Orleans, and it sold exactly *250* copies when it was first released. Yet, when the same song was re-released a few weeks later, it went on to sell a million. Next followed six more million selling records, all of which became rock 'n' roll standards: 'Long Tall Sally', 'Rip It Up' (his first hit in Britain in December 1956), 'Lucille', 'Jenny, Jenny', 'Keep A-Knockin' and 'Good Golly Miss Molly'.

. . . And Little Richard emerged as one of the most impressive Black rock 'n' rollers in America, with a devastating style of singing and playing piano. He was branded as 'the wild man of rock 'n' roll', 'the most exciting singer in the world' and he was even called 'the Bronze Liberace', for his outrageous and colorful showmanship on stage. He was also regularly seen on television and later starred in several major music movies of the day including 'The Girl Can't Help It' (the title song of which he recorded and it became a mammoth chart success in 1957, and gave Richard one of his biggest hits in Britain), 'Don't Knock The Rock', and 'Mr. Rock 'n' Roll'.

But in 1958, at the pinnacle of his success, his deep-set religious roots got the better of him, and he decided to dedicate himself to God. He left the music business and studied religion at Oakland Adventist College – and for the next five years worked as a minister, later adopting the name 'The Georgia Peach', a Seventh Day Adventist.

Richard returned to music and rock 'n' roll in 1963, first with End Records and later with Epic, Brunswick and Reprise. A year later, he was back in the chart with a classic song – 'Bama Lama Bama Loo'.

Since then, Little Richard has consolidated all his early success as one of the all-time greats of rock 'n' roll and he is recognized as a great influence on many of today's leading

LITTLE RICHARD — *in line with the Lord*

recording stars. He regularly tours the world in his own right as a headliner or with his contemporaries in rock 'n' roll revival shows, in between occasional bouts of returning to the Lord.

In 1977, he made a very welcome return to the British chart with a re-released single, comprising several of his former hits – 'Rip It Up', 'Good Golly Miss Molly' and 'By The Light Of The Silvery Moon'.

LOBO
American. Male. Singer.

Kent Lavoie took the name Lobo – which translated from the Spanish means 'Lone Wolf' – when he first recorded 'Me And You And A Dog Named Boo', because as he reasoned, if he failed to make the charts with the single, he could hide behind his anonymity and try his luck again, at another time. But he need not have worried. The record was a massive hit in America and Britain in 1971 and eventually went on to sell a million copies. His follow-up release, 'I'd Love You To Want Me' topped the American Hit Parade in 1972 . . . and the 'Lone Wolf' was one of the most popular singers in showbusiness.

He was born in Tallahassee, Florida in 1944 of French/Indian stock, and started playing guitar at college. Indeed, while working his way through school, he earned money singing and playing guitar in Florida clubs with various local beer bands. He later graduated to the more substantial night club circuit.

In 1968, Kent met the distinguished record producer Phil Gernhard, who signed him to a contract as a song-

LOBO — writing for TV

writer. Three years later, he recorded 'Me And You And A Dog Named Boo' for Big Tree Records. And with the acclaim he received when the record charted, Kent was established as a major new star in America, and set about touring the States, *and* appearing on television. His follow-up success consolidated his position . . . and for the next few years, his stock was high.

Today, he combines his performing activities with writing songs and recording. He has also carved out an enormously successful career for himself writing radio and television jingles, and recording demo-tapes in his home studio.

JOHN D. LOUDERMILK
**American. Male.
Singer/Songwriter.**

Still very much a country music favorite and one of the most prolific songwriters in the world today, John D. Loudermilk was born in Durham, North Carolina, on March 31, 1934.

A former Salvation Army bands-

man, he learned to play trumpet, saxophone, trombone and drums, he started his singing career on local radio, at the age of 11. At twelve he was appearing on television. Six years later he sang 'A Rose And A Baby Ruth' on local television when George Hamilton IV – then at University – saw the performance, decided he wanted to record the song, and met up with Loudermilk. The two hit it off immediately and formed a partnership with the result that 'A Rose And A Baby Ruth' sold over 4 million copies in 1956.

Two years later, he married Gwen Cooke and made his way to Nashville, Tennessee where he met Chet Atkins (see **Chet Atkins**), became his assistant, and started his own recording career with RCA. In 1961 he enjoyed a big hit with 'Language Of Love'. Next followed 'Callin' Doctor Casey' and his famous and amusing 'Road Hog'.

However, although John D has undertaken several major singing tours of the world including appearances at the Wembley International Country Music Festivals and has continued to record, it is as a songwriter that he is best known. He has penned some of the all-time pop, rock and country classics, including 'Abilene', 'Tobacco Road', 'Ebony Eyes', 'Indian Reservation', 'Talk Back Trembling Lips' and 'Sad Movies'.

These days, he prefers to stay at home in Nashville, with his wife and two sons and continues to write his special kind of songs – the royalties

from which have made him a millionaire.

He has an unusual hobby, too: he's a devoted hurricane freak and travels all over the Atlantic coast when news of an impending hurricane blows up, so that he can be on site immediately it reaches its peak!

LOVIN' SPOONFUL
American. Male.
Vocal/Instrumental Group.
Original line-up: John Sebastian (guitar); Zal Yanovsky (guitar); Joe Butler (drums); Steve Boone (guitar).

It was 1965, and the only answer America had to Beatlemania sweeping the world was The Bryds (see **The Byrds**), on the West Coast . . . and Lovin' Spoonful, on the East.

The Spoonful were given their name by founder member John Sebastian, taken from a line in a Mississippi John Hurt song. Born into a musical family – his father was a harmonica virtuoso – Sebastian closely studied traditional music and the blues in his teens, and teamed up, in the early '60s with Zal Yanovsky. Together they formed The Mugwumps with Denny Doherty and Mama Cass Elliott, who later became half of The Mamas and Papas (see **The Mamas and Papas**). The Mugwumps didn't last, and after the split, John Sebastian toured the U.S., but eventually returned to New York, and with Yanovsky, persuaded drummer Joe Butler and rhythm guitarist Steve Boone to form Lovin' Spoonful. And together they performed in the Night Owl Cafe in Greenwich Village, where they were discovered.

With their infectious humor, enthralling live performances that attracted The Bryds, Bob Dylan and Phil Spector – and their endless self-penned compositions – they became an instant hit. A record contract followed and 'Do You Believe In Magic?' was their first chart success, followed by 'Daydream', in the spring of '66, which gained them an international audience. 'Summer In The City' was their third release and second million-seller.

Hits cascaded from the group – mostly penned by the hugely talented Sebastian – 'Nashville Cats', 'Darling Be Home Soon', 'You Didn't Have To

Be So Nice' and 'Younger Girl'. He also turned his hand to film scores.

It had actually been the intention in 1965 to devise a zany TV series around the group's talents by producer Don Kirshner. Unfortunately, Lovin' Spoonful proved unsuitable. In the end the series was made with four unknowns forming the group known to millions as The Monkees (see **The Monkees**).

1967 saw change, however. Yanovsky was involved in a drugs' bust, and through the various problems this created, left the band. His place was taken by Jerry Yester, whose brother Jim was a member of The Association. The Lovin' Spoonful tried hard to recapture some of their earlier spirit, but couldn't quite make it, because of the strain of constant touring. The fun seemed to have gone out of the act, and they disbanded

LOVIN' SPOONFUL — (top l-r): John Sebastian, Joe Butler, (bottom, l-r), Steve Boone, Zal Yanovsky

gracefully. Though in the mid-'70s Sebastian did try briefly – and unsuccessfully – to reform the group.

Yanovsky, who had left amid problems, tried a solo career, but with only moderate success.

John Sebastian, too, went solo, and enjoyed a variety of successes, although never quite repeating his Spoonful days. By 1969 he had moved to Los Angeles, and appeared at Woodstock, playing accoustic guitar amid the notorious downpour. He had a U.S. Number 1 hit in 1976 with 'Welcome Back' the theme to John Travolta's American TV series, before turning to sessions with a variety of top acts, including Crosby, Stills, Nash And Young, Rita Coolidge and Keith Moon.

LULU
British. Female. Singer.

Lulu (real name Marie McDonald McLaughlin Lawrie) was a mere fifteen years old, and still at school in 1964, when she cut her first record – a version of the old Isley Brothers classic 'Shout' – with her group The Luvvers. But age has never been any drawback in showbusiness, and it proved the start of a glittering career for the diminutive Scots girl. The record jumped into the British hit parade and eventually reached the Number 3 slot . . . to become the cornerstone of her career, which has taken her across the full spectrum of entertainment; films, television, concert, cabaret and, of course, records.

She was born in Lennox Castle, Lennoxtown, near Glasgow, Scotland, on November 3, 1948, and started singing – "about as soon as I could talk". Lulu was five when she won a talent competition on holiday in Blackpool, and by the time she had reached the ripe old age of 9, she was appearing regularly with a local accordion band. She later graduated to local pop groups – and was soon working in clubs all over Glasgow. It was in one such club, in 1963, that she was discovered by Marion Massey . . . who today still manages her.

During the mid-1960s, Lulu emerged as Britain's 'Number 1 Female Singer' – an award she received from a leading British musical trade newspaper on several occasions. And she consolidated her claim to that title with her own top-rating TV series for the BBC, *and* several more best-selling singles including 'Here Comes The Night', 'Leave A Little Love', 'The Boat That I Row', 'Me The Peaceful Heart', 'I'm A Tiger', and (into the '70s) 'The Man Who Sold The World'.

In 1967, she made her movie debut in the film 'To Sir With Love' appearing alongside Sidney Poitier. She also recorded the title song. Within weeks of release of the film, the title track – 'To Sir With Love' – was sitting comfortably at the top of the American hit parade, where it stayed for five consecutive weeks. Ironically, the song didn't register at all in the British chart.

A year later, she represented Britain in the Eurovision Song Contest

LULU — in 1965

when she sang the winning entry 'Boom Bang A Bang', and later the same year, she hit the headlines once again with her marriage to Bee Gee Maurice Gibb. It lasted six years before ending in divorce in 1975.

Despite failing to register in the international hit parades since 1974, however, Lulu has retained her position as one of the brightest stars in British entertainment. She has completed no less than ten television series for BBC and undertaken series in North America. In 1980, she starred in the international TV series 'Let's Rock', for ITC, which was made in Britain and later screened throughout America.

Remarried, she lives with her hairdresser husband, John Frieda, and son, Jordan, in London.

M

THE McCOYS
American. Male.
Vocal/Instrumental Group.
Original line-up: Rick Zehringer (guitar); Randy Zehringer (drums); Randy Hobbs (bass); Bobby Peterson (keyboards).

The McCoys were formed in 1962 as a high school rock group in Union City, Indiana, by the Zehringer brothers, schoolfriend Bobby Peterson and their next-door neighbor Randy Hobbs. And they took their name from the Venture's hit single 'The McCoy'.

For the next few years, the group appeared extensively in Dayton, Ohio, where they supported the likes of The Beach Boys, The Drifters and Chuck Berry. Then, in 1965, they were discovered by r & b record producer Bert Berns who signed them up and recorded them for his own composition 'Hang On Sloopy'. It was their first release . . . and within a few weeks had become a million-selling single all over the world. They followed it up with 'Fever', but failed to consolidate their initial impact.

When Bobby Peterson left the group, The McCoys continued to perform as a trio, and they worked as resident band at Steve Paul's Scene Club in New York in 1968. A year later, Paul – who managed Johnny Winter – took over the group's management and they later became the backing group for the albino rock 'n' roller on his 'Johnny Winter And' album, which Rick Zehringer produced.

Randy Zehringer, however, left the group after the release of that album. Brother Rick, decided to change his stage name to Derringer, and together with Randy Hobbs, toured America with Winter. A year later, Rick joined Edgar Winter's group White Trash, and produced several of their albums in 1973. The following year, he produced his own solo album 'All American Boy'.

He left Winter in 1976 and formed his own group (Derringer) for touring and recording which he has continued to do ever since.

THE McCOYS — led by Rick Zehringer

VAN McCOY
American. Male. Instrumentalist.

Long before he enjoyed massive world-wide success in 1975 with the million-selling, American chart-topping single 'The Hustle', Van McCoy was well-established and respected in music circles as a record-producer and songwriter.

He was born in 1940 in Washington DC and joined his first group – The Starlighters – while just fifteen and still at high school. Shortly afterwards, he teamed-up with another group, The Heartbeats – who were signed to Gone End Records – with whom he made three singles.

In 1959, he recorded 'Hey Mr. DJ' and two years later, signed to Rock Records where he took a course in record production – and later worked in this capacity with The Shirelles. In 1962, now also developing as a songwriter, he worked with Leiber and Stoller, writing for the likes of Gladys Knight And The Pips and Bobby Vinton.

1964 saw him signed to Blackwood Music as a staff writer and he penned songs for Aretha Franklyn and Peter And Gordon.

Van McCoy formed his own companies, Van McCoy Productions and Vanda Records, in 1967, and by the early 1970s, he was producing and arranging for The Stylistics.

In 1975, he wrote and recorded 'The Hustle', which became an exciting new dance craze all over the world – and he followed it up with three more big hit singles, 'Change With The Times' (1975), 'Soul Cha Cha' (1977), and 'The Shuffle' (1977).

He died, tragically at the height of his recording success, in 1979.

COUNTRY JOE McDONALD
American. Male.
Singer/Songwriter.

There was a lot going on in Berkeley, California, in the mid-'60s; a spreading political awareness, and a growing interest in drugs. In the midst of it all appeared a 23-year-old former U.S. Naval Serviceman, Joe McDonald.

Country Joe had been born on New Year's Day, 1942, in El Monte, Los Angeles, and had been christened Joe by his leftist parents, after Joe Stalin.

His early performances were in the Berkeley folk clubs – his songs of a political nature. Then, as a member of the Instant Action Jug Band, he met the highly accomplished guitarist Barry Melton, and the two of them formed the core of Country Joe and the Fish.

Although the make-up of the band was prone to change, its best-known line-up was McDonald (guitar, vocals, harmonica); Melton (guitar); David Cohen (keyboard, vocals); Bruce

Barthol (bass); and 'Chicken' Hirsch (drums).

With this considerable mixture of talent, Country Joe and The Fish started out, soon establishing themselves with the classic 'I Feel Like I'm Fixin' To Die, Rag', a firmly anti-Vietnam War song. Then there was their anthem: 'Gimme an F, Gimme a U, Gimme a C . . .' and so forth, which found firm support among West Coast students and the 'doves', who saw in the group something of an anti-war spearhead.

COUNTRY JOE McDONALD — *over twenty albums in over two decades*

It was the later '60s, however, that were to see Country Joe and The Fish at their highpoint, with McDonald himself being hailed as the new Woody Guthrie. In 1969 came arguably, the band's finest hour, with their appearance at the famous Woodstock Festival, in upstate New York.

Soon after, McDonald — who had always been interested in cinema — tried his hand at film scores, most notably with a Dutch version of Henry Miller's classic novel, 'Quiet Days In Clichy', and he later became more deeply involved in the anti-Vietnam War Movement, linking himself with Jane Fonda and Donald Sutherland's 'Free The Army' revue.

After a spell of touring the major U.S. and European festivals, he disbanded his group and went to England, where he spent the next five years. And with the backing of English musicians recorded, 'Hold On It's Coming'.

However, prior to his excursions on the other side of the Atlantic, Joe had been fined $500 for shouting a four letter word at a concert in Worcester, Massachusetts during his famous 'Gimme An F . . .' routine. He was convicted under a law dating back to 1783.

He returned to America in 1975 and signed for Fantasy Records and recorded a number of acclaimed albums. Two years later, he was back in Britain for concert appearances.

Since then, he has continued to write and record his own kind of songs and continued, too, to play his own kind of music – he has made over 20 albums. And he regularly tours America: "I'm a member of the working class", he says about his current incessant workload. "I just go from one job to another" . . . with a guitar in hand and a song in the air.

BARRY McGUIRE
American. Male. Singer.

It was the classic protest song, 'Eve Of Destruction', that assured Barry McGuire a place in the history of popular music. Originally from Oklahoma, where he was born on October 15, 1937, Barry's gravel-toned voice was his trade-mark and made his name as lead singer of the New Christy Minstrels, on such hits as 'Green, Green', which he wrote and recorded at the age of 26, and the perennial children's favorite 'Three Wheels On My Wagon'. He also

BARRY McGUIRE — *one solo hit*

penned 'Green Back Dollar', a big hit for The Kingston Trio in 1963.

It was 1964, in Los Angeles, however, that he met Lou Adler and as a result, Barry left the Minstrels and recorded P. F. Sloan's 'Eve Of Destruction', on Adler's Dunhill record label. It was hastily followed up by an album, 'This Precious Time', in which he was backed by the embryonic Mamas and Papas.

'Eve Of Destruction' went on to top the American Hit Parade in 1965 and reach the Number 3 slot in Britain. He never followed up that success.

His commercial heyday, however, was over almost as quickly as it had come, and he became a devout Christian convert. The emphasis of his life had by then moved away from its earlier musical aspirations.

SCOTT McKENZIE
American. Male. Singer.

The peace and love hippy movement was in full swing in 1967, with American music company bosses, in full realization of the fact that the attention of the nation's youth was focused on San Francisco, and all that was going on musically and culturally there. And they did their best to exploit its commercial gain!

One result was the John Phillips song 'San Francisco (Be Sure To Wear Flowers In Your Hair)' recorded on Lou Adler's new Ode record label, by Scott McKenzie.

McKenzie, a former member of Phillips' folk group The Journeymen, was born on October 1, 1944, in Arlington, Virginia. After The Journeymen disbanded Phillips moved to California where he later formed The Mamas And Papas (see **The Mamas and Papas**) leaving McKenzie in New York, where by now he was recording for Capitol.

But he didn't stay long, having been summoned by Phillips, to the West Coast . . . to join in all that was going on out there!

McKenzie recorded 'No, No, No, No, No,' in 1967, and followed it up with the enormously successful 'San Francisco' which became an anthem to the 'love and peace' brigade. The record became a world-wide hit, topping the charts in Britain and selling over 7,000,000 copies internationally! *And*

SCOTT McKENZIE — author of the hippy anthem, 'San Francisco'

McKenzie appeared on the BBC's highly successful 'Top Of The Pops' . . . on film, complete with floral shirt, and headband, extolling the virtues of the love-and-peace city, in his song. He followed it up with the moderately successful 'Like An Old Time Movie'.

As a result, McKenzie became a true convert to the flower power movement. His record was not a cynical exploitation of the phenomena. That, in part, may explain why his only subsequent record was a country rock album, 'Summer of Love', recorded in 1970. Since then he has been completely absent from the recording scene. However, in 1977 the disc was re-released which revitalized his flagging – almost non existent – career.

THE MAMAS AND PAPAS
American. Male/Female. Vocal Group.
Original line-up: John Phillips; Michelle Phillips; Cass Elliott; Denny Doherty.

A classic set-piece of the '60s. The Mamas and Papas appeared, on the surface, to combine the traditional American folksy sounds with updated treatments. While that was true to a point, the real strength lay in the skillful marketing the band enjoyed, promoting their fashionable hippy image, and providing them with essentially easy-on-the-ear material.

The group was the brainchild of singer/songwriter John Phillips who, as a member of The Journeymen, had met Michelle Gilliam – an aspiring model – in New York, in 1962, and had married her.

An early Mamas' single, 'Creeque Alley', traces the formation of the foursome. Suffice to say that Michelle and John teamed up with 'Mama' Cass Elliott, a former actress, and Denny Doherty, who had both previously been with a group called The Mugwumps which included a future Lovin' Spoonful member (see **Lovin' Spoonful**), Zal Yanovsky.

Having pulled the band together after a session in the Virgin Islands, Phillips decided to take them all to Hollywood, and the West Coast, where they met Barry McGuire who in turn introduced them to producer Lou Adler, who signed them to Dunhill Records.

Between 1966 and '67 – capitalizing on their off-beat line-up and image, *and* their undoubted vocal abilities – The Mamas And Papas rose to become one of America's most popular musical acts.

Hit singles included 'California Dreamin'', 'Monday, Monday', 'I Saw Her Again' and the whispy 'Dedicated To The One I Love'.

In 1967, the foursome appeared at The Monterey Festival which Phillips had helped organize. Meanwhile, the ubiquitous artiste had already written the huge hit 'San Francisco (Be Sure To Wear Flowers In Your Hair)', sung by his friend, and one-time fellow Journeyman, Scott McKenzie (see **Scott McKenzie**) who was now a hippy convert.

And in addition, there was a string of highly successful LPs. By 1968, however, it was all over!

Phillips' marriage had run into problems, and the group felt it was time to dissolve and go their own separate ways. They did reform temporarily for a reunion concert in 1971.

John Phillips himself cut a solo album, but later became more and more involved in songwriting and production, basing himself at his Malibu home.

'Mama' Cass – she had been christened Cassandra – became a top cabaret artist, and returned to acting. With a highly promising solo career before her, the overweight star was found dead in London on July 29, 1974, just after completing a successful season at the London Palladium. She was 30.

Michelle went into acting and appeared in Ken Russell's 'Valentino' and several 'made for television' movies. Her name was also linked with 'Easy Rider' star Dennis Hopper's, after her divorce from Phil-

lips and she later lived with superstar Warren Beatty for three years. Doherty, too, went solo, but failed to recapture his early success, and drifted into obscurity.

Numerous re-releases of Mamas and Papas songs hit the market throughout the '70s, testimony to an appeal that lingered after the group were long gone.

In Spring 1981, John Phillips was jailed on a drugs charge and fined a reported $15,000.

MANFRED MANN
British. Male. Vocal/Instrumental Group.
Original line-up: Manfred Mann (organ); Paul Jones (vocals); Mike Vickers (guitar); Mike Hugg (drums); Dave Richmond (bass).

Manfred Mann – from whom the name of one of the most successful British groups in the 1960s was taken – was born Michael Lubowitz in Johannesburg, South Africa.

In 1961 he arrived in Britain with hopes of playing jazz piano and teaching musical theory. But by the summer of 1962, the need to earn a living and eat, forced him to abandon his original plans, and take a job in an English holiday camp. In the resident group he joined there, he met drummer Mike Hugg and, realizing they had the same musical tastes, became firm friends. When the summer season residency ended, they decided to form their own group – The Mann-Hugg Blues Brothers – playing essentially jazz.

Yet, by 1963, they had changed their name to Manfred Mann and abandoned the idea of playing jazz in favor of the more commercially acceptable r & b. And soon established themselves on the rapidly-expanding club circuit in Britain. The same year, they were signed to HMV Records and their first single release was the instrumental 'Why Should We Not?', followed by 'Cock-A-Hoop', both of which failed to register. However, it was their third single, '5-4-3-2-1', released in December 1963, which set the standard for an outstandingly successful career. The single charted in January 1964 and eventually reached the Number 5 slot in the British Hit Parade, after being adopted as the

theme tune for the country's leading television pop-rock show – 'Ready-Steady-Go! The release also coincided with the first change of line-up for the group, which saw Tom McGuinness replacing Dave Richmond on bass.

'5-4-3-2-1' was just the start of an avalanche of hit singles for Manfred Mann, which saw them chart many times over the following two years with such hits as 'Hubble Bubble Toil And Trouble', 'Do Wah Diddy Diddy' – their first British and American chart-topper, in 1964 – 'Sha La La', 'Come Tomorrow', 'Oh No Not My Baby', 'If You've Gotta Go, Go Now' and 'Pretty Flamingo' – another British chart-topper in 1966.

The year before, however, Mike Vickers left the group to branch out on an outstandingly successful solo career that later saw him penning many TV and movie soundtracks. He was replaced by Jack Bruce (see **Jack Bruce**), who played bass, while Tom McGuinness switched to guitar. Bruce stayed with Manfred Mann for a mere six months, before leaving to form his own group Cream (see **Cream**). His departure also coincided with Paul Jones' decision to leave the group for his own solo singing and acting career. And two new members replaced them – Klaus Voorman (on bass) and lead-singer Mike D'Abo, who was formerly with a Band Of Angels.

Still . . . although the group now contained only *two* original members – in Mann himself, and Hugg – Manfred Mann's assault on the music charts of the world was unabated. And they scored once more with singles 'Just Like A Woman', 'Semi-Detached Suburban Mr. James', 'Ha Ha Said The Clown', 'Mighty Quinn' (their third Number 1 hit in Britain, in 1968), 'My Name Is Jack', 'Fox On The Run', 'Ragamuffin Man' – and several top-selling albums. During this unbroken run of success, Mike Hugg penned the soundtrack music for the movie 'Up The Junction' which the group also recorded.

In 1969, they decided to call it a day – they had gone about as far as they could go – and disbanded, with Manfred Mann and Mike Hugg leaving to form the short-lived, jazz-orientated

Manfred Mann Chapter Three, with whom they recorded two albums – 'Manfred Mann Chapter Three' and 'Chapter Three, Volume Two'.

In 1971, Mann formed yet another new group – Manfred Mann's Earth Band – featuring Colin Pattenden (bass), Chris Slade (drums), Mick Rogers (guitar) and Chris Thompson (vocals) and in 1973, they enjoyed British singles chart success with 'Joybringer', followed in 1976 by 'Blinded By The Light', 'Davy's On The Road Again' (1978) and 'Don't Kill It Carol' (1979).

Since then, despite many changes of line-up – the present group comprises Manfred, Pat King (bass) and John Lingwood (drums), although Chris Thompson (guitar/vocals) and Steve Waller (guitar/vocals) often perform on record and tour with them – Manfred Mann's Earth Band have consolidated all that success with the release of *ten* best selling albums, the most recent of which 'Chance', was issued in the fall of 1980.

The group – with Thompson and Waller in tow – toured Britain and Europe again for the first time in two years, at the beginning of 1981.

After the original break up of Manfred Mann in 1969 Mike Hugg and Klaus Voorman branched out into session work and carved highly successful careers for themselves – with Hugg turning his hand to writing and producing. German-born Voorman later played 'live', and recorded with, Delaney and Bonnie, Eric Clapton, Ringo Starr, George Harrison and John Lennon's Plastic Ono Band. *And* at one stage it was rumored that he would be co-opted into a reformed Beatles' line-up to play bass in place of Paul McCartney, though the rumors proved groundless.

Mike D'Abo, too, branched out on a solo career and made several singles, though, recently he has concentrated on writing and producing.

Guitarist Tom McGuinness, like Manfred Mann, formed his own group, teaming up with former John Mayall's Bluesbreaker Hughie Flint on drums, to front *McGuinness Flint*, featuring Dennis Coulson, and hit songwriters/performers Benny Gallagher and Graham Lyle. And the group enjoyed two British hit singles

(in a short-lived career) with 'When I'm Dead And Gone' and 'Malt And Barley Blues', and three best-selling LP's. When Gallagher and Lyle went their own separate ways, Tom McGuinness formed the group *Coulson, Dean, McGuinness and Flint*.

However, towards the end of the '70s, McGuinness and Flint came back into the commercial limelight once more as part of the successful group The Blues Band, featuring another former Manfred – singer Paul Jones. And they have continued to tour and record together ever since, building up a large following all over Britain.

Prior to *his* joining The Blues Band, Paul Jones had enjoyed his own success as a solo singer, hitting the chart with best-selling singles 'High Time' (1966), 'I've Been A Bad, Bad Boy' (1967), 'Thinkin' Ain't For Me' (1967) and 'Aquarius' (1968). Yet, besides a successful singing career, Jones also turned his talents to writing *and* acting. He starred in the movie 'Privilege' in 1966, before heading more towards the legitimate stage and classical theater, appearing in drama productions on television, and in plays in London's West End.

WINK MARTINDALE
American. Male. Singer.

Wink Martindale's career as a pop singer was relatively short-lived. Indeed, his only success was one record, 'Deck Of Cards', but between 1959 and 1973, the record charted five times, and sold over a million copies.

Born Winston Conrad Martindale in 1933, he first became known as 'Wink' during school, in Jackson, Tennessee.

He started his professional career at 17 as a DJ in Jackson, before going to Memphis, only to return in 1954 to marry his childhood sweetheart, Madelyn Leech, by whom he was later to have four children.

A former choir singer, Wink later attended Memphis State University where he gained a BA degree in speech and drama.

Five years later he went to Hollywood, met DOT Records chief Randy Wood and cut 'Deck Of Cards' – a pseudo-religious monologue about a soldier who uses a pack of playing cards as a Bible – shortly afterwards. It gained no critical acclaim – in fact, just

WINK MARTINDALE — *found a new slot as host on an American quiz program*

the opposite. But its quirky originality caught on in Britain after it was played on the popular 'Family Favourites' radio show and it reached the Top Twenty in 1959. The record has subsequently been released on two more occasions in Britain, reaching Number 5 in 1963; and Number 22 in 1973.

Since then, Wink has concentrated his career on acting, using all the technique and training he acquired at Memphis State University. During 1980 he acted as host on an American TV quiz program 'Tic Tac Dough'.

THE MARVELETTES
American. Female. Vocal Group.
Original line-up: Gladys Horton; Katherine Anderson; Wanda Young; Georgeanna Tillman; Juanita Cowart.

The Marvelettes were discovered in 1961, singing in a talent contest at Inkester High School, on the outskirts of Detroit, by America's leading r and b group of the day The Miracles, who immediately arranged for them to be signed to their own record label, Tamla Motown. It was a shrewd move. Within a few weeks, the five girls had released their first single – 'Please Mr Postman', and it proved to be an outstanding hit, topping the American hit parade for several weeks. The record made history becoming Tamla Motown's first Number 1 and only the label's second million-seller!

The girls followed up their initial

success with several more hits – 'Playboy', 'Beachwood 4-5789' and 'Someday, Someday' – and by the end of 1962, they had established themselves as one of America's leading female vocal groups, with a formidable track record. And for the next five years the hits continued to flourish: 'Strange I Know', 'Locking Up My Heart', 'Don't Mess With Bill', 'When You're Young And In Love' (their only British hit) and 'The Hunter Gets Captured By The Game', were all sizeable chart entries in America.

Between 1961 and 1968, however, the line-up had reduced from a quintet to a trio. Georgeanna Tillman was forced to retire through ill-health; Juanita Cowart also left. And at the end of 1968, Gladys Horton quit to get married. She was replaced by Audrienne Ferguson-Smith, who leads the group today, ably supported by Sadi Bryant and Cathy Jones.

Since the early 1970s, The Marvelettes have appeared all over the world, undertaking major concert and cabaret tours. They are now based in Britain, where they have become an attraction on the provincial nightclub circuit.

CURTIS MAYFIELD AND THE IMPRESSIONS
American. Male.
Vocal/Instrumental Group.
Original line-up: Curtis Mayfield; Jerry Butler; Sam Gooden; Richard Brooks; Arthur Brooks.

One of the most influential Black groups to come out of America around the turn of the 1960s was The Impressions. And the creative force behind them was singer, guitarist, songwriter Curtis Mayfield.

But it wasn't just in the history of Soul that Mayfield earned his place. As a representative for racial matters and leading civil rights personality, Mayfield has made his mark.

The original Impressions were formed in Chicago in 1956 by Curtis Mayfield and Jerry Butler – a friend whom he had met through the church choir – and 'For Your Precious Love' was their first big hit in 1958. However, it was short-lived success because Butler left soon afterwards and for a time the group split up, with Curtis managing to earn a living as a song-

writer. By 1963, they were back together, although by this time without the Brooks brothers, leaving the group with its most famous line-up – Gooden, Cash and Mayfield. It was the Impressions most successful period during which time they established themselves as one of America's most outstanding vocal groups with a string of classic r 'n' b song hits: 'I'm So Proud', 'Talking About My Baby', 'You Must Believe Me', 'Keep On Pushing' and 'People Get Ready'.

Mayfield left the group in 1970 to go solo – his place to be taken by Leroy Hudson – although their next big single hit in Britain wasn't to come until 1975, with 'First Impressions'.

By then, however, Curtis Mayfield was recording solo, and had established his position as a serious composer for his 'Superfly' film score. He has since undertaken more film work, including acting in the American prison-life film 'Short Eyes'.

SERGIO MENDES
Brazilian. Male.
Instrumentalist/Composer.

Sergio Mendes has carved a unique position for himself in international music – and for 15 years has exerted a powerful influence over American popular music. His distinctive approach – a fusion of American and Brazilian music and rhythms – has maintained his place as an international star. Since the stunning impact of his first hit album '66', Sergio Mendes and his group may have changed personnel and names – through Brasils '77 and '88 – but they have consistently been in tune with public tastes the world over.

He was born in Rio De Janeiro, and started playing piano at the age of seven, and later had classical training at the Rio Conservatory. However, it was while studying at this celebrated academy, that he fell under the influence of jazz . . . and at the age of sixteen, decided to form his own jazz combo. It didn't take him too long to establish himself in his native country as a leading musician.

In 1962, he and several other leading Brazilian stylists appeared in concert at New York's Carnegie Hall. That performance saw Mendes emerge as a major force in North America, and shortly afterwards such was the demand for his music, that he started touring the U.S. regularly, and recording with the influential Cannonball Adderly.

Three years later, he decided to make his home on the West Coast, and settled in Los Angeles where he formed his first group in America – Brasil '66. Then followed a number of unique hit singles – 'Mas Que Nada', 'Scarborough Fair', 'Fool On The Hill' and 'The Look Of Love', all given that distinctive Mendes flavor and style, which certainly went a long way to consolidating his position as a musician with his very own 'sound' and technique.

Since then, Sergio Mendes has continued to enjoy success all over the world and to reap new harvests of international acclaim. In 1979, he completed an outstanding tour of the Far East, during which time, he won a major award at the Tokyo International Music Festival, in Japan. The same year, he scored Francois Reichenbach's 'Pele', the story of the

world-famous soccer player and a Brazilian national hero. And a year later, Sergio and Brasil '88 joined Frank Sinatra for a series of concerts in Britain.

THE MERSEYBEATS
British. Male. Vocal/Instrumental
Group.

Original line-up: Tony Crane (guitar); Billy Kinsley (bass); Aaron Williams (guitar); John Banks (drums).

The Merseybeats were formed at Newsham Secondary School in Liverpool in 1962 under the name of The Mavericks.

THE MERSEYBEATS — (l-r): Aaron Williams, Tony Crane, Billy Kinsley, John Banks

They changed their name a year later – when Merseymania swept the world – to mark the release of their first single on Fontana in August 1963, which was a re-working of the old Shirelles song 'It's Love That Really Counts'. It reached Number 24 in the British Hit Parade. Their follow-up release – 'I Think Of You', reached Number 5 in January 1964 . . . and for the next two years, they enjoyed great success in the British chart with 'Don't Turn Around', 'Wishin' And Hopin'', 'Last Night', 'I Love You, Yes I Do' and 'I Stand Accused'. They also undertook major concert tours and television appearances all over the world.

They disbanded initially in 1966, after undergoing several changes of line-up, with only Crane and Kinsley remaining from the original group.

However, the two of them resurfaced shortly afterwards as a vocal duo called, simply The Merseys, and in the summer of '66, they enjoyed tremendous chart success with their one and only hit record, 'Sorrow', which reached Number 4. Yet, with their backing group – the bizarre named Fruit Eating Bears – in tow, they toured the country for the next three years.

"Then Tony and I split up", says Billy Kinsley. "He wanted to go into cabaret, but I wasn't too keen. In actual fact,

Tony re-formed The Merseybeats and as Tony Crane (and The Merseybeats), carved out a new career for himself, playing major British nightclubs. I drifted into sessions and had a spell working with Jackie Lomax, before I played in Chuck Berry's backing group for a major European tour.

"Then, after returning to the session scene to work occasionally, I branched out on my own solo singing career with CBS Records in 1973. The same year, Tony asked me to re-join the old group for a tour of America. Some guy was trying to recreate the original Mersey Sounds of the 1960s – and he'd got together several top-line bands from that era, for that purpose."

Back in Britain, Tony Crane And The Merseybeats continued with their cabaret commitments, while Billy formed a new group, from local Liverpool musicians – Tony Coates (guitar), Roger Craig (keyboards) and Derek Cashin (drums) – who over the years had all performed on stage with The Merseybeats in various line-ups. And as Liverpool Express they hit the road. They were signed to WEA Records and in the summer of 1976, enjoyed their first chart success with their second single release 'You Are My Love' and followed it with three more major hits – 'Every Man Must Have A Dream', 'Hold Tight' and 'Dreamin''.

Today, now known as LEX (for short), they continue to tour Britain and Europe . . . *and* South America, where they have a particularly strong fan following.

The Merseybeats, meanwhile, are still going strong under the guidance of Tony Crane, and regularly appear in domestic cabaret seasons, as well as touring the Continent.

MILLIE
Jamaican. Female. Singer.

March, 1964, and the name Millie became almost a household word when her recording of 'My Boy Lollipop' crashed into the British and American hit parades, falling just short of the coveted Number 1 spot. The pint-sized Jamaican singer was just 16.

She followed up her initial chart success with a second single – 'Sweet William' – though it could never hope to repeat the tremendous impact of her debut song. But for eighteen months, Millie Small (she never used her surname professionally), enjoyed star status and even appeared on television in a Beatles 'special'. Then she disappeared from the pop scene almost as quickly as she had arrived.

Says Millie, born on October 6, 1948 in Clarendon, Jamaica, who was hailed as the 'First Lady of ska' all those years ago: " 'My Boy Lollipop' was such a big hit that I have been fortunate and I haven't needed to work since then,

MILLIE — true 'one-hit wonder' status

because I still get money from my old royalties.

"However, since that time, I've written extensively, and hopefully some of my songs will be recorded. Actually, I haven't sung since 1974. My time has been well spent though, in the service of Christ, speaking His word, and spreading His gospel."

THE MONKEES
American/British. Male.
Vocal/Instrumental Group.
Original line-up: Davy Jones
(vocals/keyboards); Mickey Dolenz
(drums/vocals); Peter Thorkelson
guitar/bass/vocals); Mike Nesmith
(guitar/vocals).

Following the success of Richard Lester's Beatles' movies 'A Hard Day's Night' in 1964 and 'Help' a year later, American television executive Don Kirshner decided to adopt and adapt Lester's zany approach to filming, and devise an American TV series based on the antics of a 'crazy' pop group.

His original intention was to build the series around the talents of the highly successful Lovin' Spoonful, but when major problems arose, Kirshner decided to 'manufacture' a group of his own, and advertised in the American showbusiness trade newspaper Daily Variety for four likely actors/musicians to play the roles. The advertisement read: "Madness Wanted: a quartet of hip, insane, folk-orientated rock 'n' rollers, seventeen to twenty-one, with courage to work". Not unnaturally Kirshner's ATV company was inundated with replies, from which, after much deliberation, he chose the talents of Mickey Dolenz, Mike Nesmith, Peter Thorkelson (Tork), and Davy Jones, who collectively became known as The Monkees.

The series was first screened on America's NBC Network in 1965, and for the next three years, The Monkees became an international hit – second only in popularity to The Beatles. Their music – written by many of the leading contemporary songwriters like Harry Nilsson, Neil Diamond, Neil Sedaka, Goffin and King, and Bobby Hart and Tommy Boyce – sold incredibly well. Their hit single 'Last Train To Clarksville' topped the American chart in the fall of 1966, followed in December by 'I'm A Believer' (written by Diamond) which topped the British and U.S. chart almost simultaneously and stayed there for two months. Their other singles all clocked up fantastic sales, too, 'A Little Bit Me, A

Little Bit You', 'Alternate Title', '-Pleasant Valley Sunday', and 'Daydream Believer'. In all, they went on to sell more than 20,000,000 records around the world.

In 1968, however, after their feature-length movie 'Head' flopped badly at the box-office, Peter Tork left to form his own group Release, and for a short time, The Monkees continued as a trio. Then, Mike Nesmith went his own separate way and formed the First and then the Second National Bands with whom he recorded several albums. Then during the mid-1970s, he formed his own recording company for whom he wrote and produced. In 1977, he clocked up a major hit single with 'Rio'.

Both Mickey Dolenz and Davy Jones branched out on individual careers as well. Mickey went into film production and direction; Davy returned to his 'vaudeville' roots, and appeared on television. Then in 1975, they reformed the group with writers Tommy Boyce and Bobby Hart, and toured America, Australia and the Far East.

Three years later Jones and Dolenz arrived in Britain and starred in Harry Nilsson's (see **Harry Nilsson**) musical 'The Point', which played a season at London's celebrated Mermaid Theatre, before they both pursued their former careers, with Davy Jones starring in a British TV series – 'A Horse In The House'.

THE MOVE
British. Male. Vocal/Instrumental Group.

Original line-up: Carl Wayne (vocals); Roy Wood (guitar); Chris 'Ace' Kefford (bass); Trevor Burton (guitar); Bev Bevan (drums).

One of Britain's leading pop-rock groups of the late '60s, The Move were formed in 1965 when members of several moderately successful Birmingham bands decided to join forces and form a mini-Midlands 'supergroup'.

Says former lead-singer Carl Wayne: "We signed a management contract with Tony Secunda – who at that time was looking after The Moody Blues, Joe Cocker (see **Joe Cocker**) and Procul Harum (see **Procul Harum**). And one of the first things he secured for the group was a residency at London's Marquee Club. Then we

launched into the whole publicity routine, in order to get our name known, including smashing up television sets on stage, burning life-size dummies of famous people during our act – and we even set fire to the Marquee at one time, causing a riot. Needless to say, our stage antics became notorious!"

However, in the fall of 1967 they capitalized on their reputation with the release of their first single 'Night Of Fear', which reached Number 2 in the British Hit Parade. They followed it up with an inspiring list of hit singles – all written by group member Roy Wood – which captured perfectly the rapidly emerging mood of psychedelia and Flower Power: 'I Can Hear The Grass Grow', and 'Flowers In The Rain' – which had the distinction of being the

very first record played on BBC Radio One, when the new station was launched in 1967. But the resulting publicity campaign surrounding that particular single, which satirized the then British Prime Minister Harold Wilson on a series of saucy postcards, landed the group in court. Wilson sued for damages, and won his case in the High Court, which resulted in all subsequent royalties from 'Flowers In The Rain' being donated to charity.

But then followed two more hits with 'Fire Brigade' and their first chart-topping single 'Blackberry Way' in 1968. Shortly after that success, bassman Ace Kefford left The Move to form his own group. A few months later Trevor Burton followed, and teamed up with Denny Laine and Alan White to form the ill-fated and short-

Electric Light Orchestra
Out of the Blue

lived trio Balls. He was replaced by Birmingham-born Rick Price. Since then Burton has become a vital member of The Steve Gibbons Band.

Another hit 'Curly' followed in 1969, before Carl Wayne decided to call it a day – and attempt a solo singing career – in 1970.

Says Carl: "I left the group for several reasons. Towards the end it became like a marriage gone wrong. We were no longer getting kicks out of recording hit records, or touring. By then, it was all down to living with each other's personality and we couldn't manage it."

He turned to the variety stage and television, a complete reversal of his 'bad boy' image with the group. In 1973, he starred in his own television series for ATV and later turned his attentions to cabaret, summer season and pantomime. In 1980, he appeared in summer season at the Winter Gardens Theatre, Margate, with another chart-singer from the '60s, Susan Maughan. However, it was at the Margate theatre, that Carl and Roy Wood made an impromptu return together,

to star in a special gala charity show in August 1980.

Wayne's place in The Move went to Jeff Lynne, formerly with the Birmingham group Idle Race, and with this line-up they charted four more times in the early '70s with 'Brontosaurus', 'Tonight', 'China Town' and 'California Man', the B-side of which 'Do Ya', gave them their only chart success in America in 1972.

A few months later, though, the group spawned The Electric Light Orchestra and, augmented with violins and cellos, they chalked up their first hit with '10588 Overture'. However, by the end of 1972, Jeff Lynne and Roy Wood were at creative loggerheads with each other – and they parted company. Lynne and Bevan remained with ELO and they have since gone on to enjoy magnificent success all over the world – while Wood and Price formed a new group, Roy Wood's Wizzard and hit the charts with seven massive singles between December 1972 and December 1974 which included British chart-toppers 'See My Baby Jive',

and 'Angel Fingers'. And during Wizzard's short-lived success, Roy Wood also established his own solo recording career with such hits as 'Dear Elaine', 'Forever' and 'Oh What A Shame'.

The group split up in 1975 and Rick Price quit performing to take over as personal assistant-cum-road-manager to the British singing duo Peters And Lee. Today, he works as personal assistant to top British comedian, Jim Davidson.

Roy Wood, meanwhile, has continued writing and producing and has worked with such established artists as Lynsey de Paul and Darts, and a number of unknowns.

In December 1980, he formed a new band called Helicopters for a short British tour – featuring John Camp (ex-Renaissance – bass); Mike Deacon (ex-Darts – keyboards); Paul Robbins (keyboards) and Ken Gorin (drums).

ANNE MURRAY
Canadian. Female. Singer.

Beyond the sparkle of platinum albums, Number 1 singles and SRO crowds of all ages and persuasions, there is a handful of recording artists able to maintain star qualities, such as those without succumbing to the trappings of pretension. Those are the artists who care about winning during the season as much as during the playoffs. Anne Murray, who had a year in 1978 successful enough to turn most stars' heads, is among that handful; she remains disarmingly honest and down-to-earth, just like her music.

After more than a year out of the spotlight (she suspended her career until her first-born son, named William Stewart Langstroth after his father, was a year old), she returned to her heavy schedule of concerts, television appearances and recording.

And between then and now, Ms. Murray took home an American gold single (her second) for the Number 1 pop and Number 1 country smash 'You Needed Me'. In her native Canada, 'You Needed Me' won Gold and Platinum honors.

Outside the musical realm, Anne's alma mater, the University of New Brunswick, presented her with an Honorary Doctorate of Letters degree in 1978, and in conjunction with the United Nations decree that 1979 be 'The Year Of The Child', the Canadian Save The Children Fund chose her to be its National Chairperson for 1979.

She was born and raised in the coal mining town of Springhill, Nova Scotia, with five brothers. "We all took piano lessons," she recalls. "I was singing for as long as I can remember, but at 15, I began taking singing lessons from Karen Mills, who had sung with symphonies."

She switched to the University of New Brunswick during the mid '60s. Her second year there she auditioned with 200 other performers for a Halifax television show called 'Sing A Long Jubilee', but she wasn't chosen to appear. Two years after her audition, representatives from the show contacted her and offered her a slot in their summer program. Through the show she met television producer William Langstroth (who Anne married in June 1975).

At the end of the summer Anne returned to school and graduated with a degree in physical education, which she then taught for a year in High School on Prince Edward Island. She returned to 'Sing Along Jubilee' for another summer and then performed regularly on another television show, 'Let's Go'. By then everyone was trying

to convince her to give up teaching and to pursue singing as a full-time career.

"I thought they were crazy," says Anne. "Singing was something you did in the bathtub and around bonfires. I felt there was no security in singing."

Anne began her recording career with a small Canadian label, Arc Records, which in 1968 released her debut LP, 'What About Me', The album greatly interested Capitol Records of Canada, which quickly signed her, and released her first LP, 'This Way Is My Way' in Canada.

After its significant Canadian showing, the album was retitled 'Snowbird' and released in the United States by Capitol Records in August 1970. Both the album and the title-track single achieved American Gold certification, qualifying Anne as the first female Canadian recording artist to win American Gold. 'Snowbird' was a huge international hit, winning Gold in many countries, and was also a smash on the American country charts (even though Anne claims she didn't listen to country music back then), beginning her highly successful career in that market. Soon after, she had a regular spot on Glen Campbell's acclaimed television show, which led to a duet LP ('Anne Murray/Glen Campbell' in November 1971) and a joint appearance in Las Vegas.

Since then she has become a favorite concert and television performer throughout North America, both for her easy-going singing style and her warm and personal stageside personna. She has hosted more than ten CBC 'Superspecials' and in America has appeared on a multitude of music, talk, and variety shows.

Anne Murray has also won countless awards and honors world-wide including a boxfull of Canadian Juno Awards (she won 'Best Female Vocalist' honors five years in a row). Adding to her American Grammy success, she holds similar awards from Great Britain. Most significantly: in 1975 Queen Elizabeth bestowed upon Anne Murray the highest honor possible for a Canadian citizen – Officer Of The Order Of Canada.

RICK NELSON
American. Male. Singer.

Fame came early for Ricky Nelson, helped in no small way by the fact that he was born into a showbusiness family. His father was band leader Ozzie Nelson; his mother was the singer Harriet Hillard and together they hosted their own radio show 'The Adventures Of Ozzie And Harriet', which transferred to television in the mid-1950s. By this time the shows began to feature the singing 9-year-old Ricky.

At the age of 16, he set out on his own solo career, and a year later chalked up his first disc success with the million-selling 'A Teenager's Romance' followed by 'Be-Bop Baby' and 'Stood Up'. Then came a series of hits, destined to keep him in the charts for a long, long time. Indeed, in Britain, he was to be in the Hit Parade for 132 weeks – although he never achieved a Number 1 hit. The late 1950s and early 1960s saw his recordings of 'Poor Little Fool', 'Someday', 'It's Late', 'Young World', the classic 'Fools Rush In', 'Teenage World' and another classic, 'Hello Mary Lou' established him as an enormous chart star. And in the words of one of his biggest hits – 'A Teenage Idol'.

ANNE MURRAY — still going strong with a new image

He also took his career a stage further by acting in films, including 'Rio Bravo' and 'The Wackiest Ship In The Army'.

By 1963 he had dropped the 'y' from his Christian name as part of his quest for maturity, but in so doing, it seemingly heralded the onset of decline in his fortunes.

However, before the end of the decade, he was back vying for top billing with his newly-formed Stone Canyon Band, which featured, among others, would-be Eagles member Randy Meisner, and Tom Brumley. The title track of his 'Garden Party' album charted in 1972, and regarding what amounted to a comeback, things looked good again for Nelson.

But, strictly, this was not to be the case!

He was born Eric Hilliard Nelson on May 8, 1940, in Teaneck, New Jersey, and during the latter days of the 1970s took part in numerous sessions – but failed to re-establish the magnitude of his former '50s success. However, his music now veers very much toward the country-rock field where as one writer recently said: "he currently meanders". Though, he can still muster a selective fan following.

THE NEW CHRISTY MINSTRELS
American. Male/Female. Vocal/Instrumental Group.

The story of the New Christy Minstrels spans nearly 150 years! It started in America as far back as 1842.

Edwin 'Pops' Christy, who gave the group its name, had a passionate belief that folk music would generate a new exciting culture in America if performed with the harmony and variety of a folk group. So with these aims in mind, he formed his own . . . and for the next 80 years, the Christy Minstrels entertained all over the States, becoming one of the most successful and popular acts of its kind in history. Indeed, as late as 1917, 'The New Christy Minstrel Show' was performing on Broadway as the longest-running show in the history of showbusiness! A record that still stands today! That show at one time featured two entertainers who were later to

THE NEW CHRISY MINSTRELS — led by the gravel-voiced Barry McGuire

find world-wide fame and fortune – Eddie Cantor and Al Jolson.

The Christy Minstrels disbanded in 1921 only to be re-formed – and Christy's original ideal revived – 40 years later in 1961. And The *New* Christy Minstrels made their debut at the famous Troubador Club in Los Angeles.

Since then, the group has gone on to become quite simply a major phenomenon in showbusiness, through a weekly, top-rated American TV series for NBC and hit records, including 'Green Green' (which sold three million-plus copies). The Minstrels have also passed virtually every milestone of professional achievement – and more important – continue to entertain audiences all over the world. Indeed, in 1980 they undertook a highly successful British and European concert tour which met with outstanding business at the box-office.

Over the years, The New Christy Minstrels have seen numerous changes of line-up. Yet the group goes on and on . . . Former Minstrels have included actress Karen Black, John Denver, Kenny Rogers, Barry McGuire see (**Barry McGuire**), Roger McGuinn and Gene Clark (creators of The Byrds see **The Byrds**), The Association (see **The Association**), comedians Skilles & Henderson, Larry Ramos, Tara Leigh and Bill Zorn. An amazing track record – but nothing new, for The Minstrels have a long tradition of discovering new talent and presenting it to the public.

Back in their early days in the mid-19th century, Edwin Christy virtually discovered poet Stephen Foster and did more than anyone to bring *his* own special talents to a wider audience.

NEW VAUDEVILLE BAND
British. Male. Vocal/Instrumental Group.

Original line-up: Henri Harrison; Mick Wilsher; Shuggy Watts; Chris Eady; Stan Haywood; Robert Kerr; Alan Klein.

Formed in 1966 as a 1930s revival band from members of the British rhythm and blues group Cops and Robbers, The New Vaudeville Band enjoyed tremendous success in the British chart during 1966 and 1967 with several hits including 'Winchester Cathedral', 'Peek-A-Boo' and 'Finchley Central'.

'Winchester Cathedral' later went to the top of the American Hit Parade and it was their Stateside success that prompted the group to move to Canada where they were based for

He was born in Brooklyn, New York, U.S.A. on June 15, 1941, though at the age of 15, he moved with his family across America to California.

When he left school, Harry landed a job as a computer programmer with a local West Coast bank, and in his spare time, he wrote songs and gradually broke into the music business as a part-time demo singer. After seven years with the bank, however, he was offered a recording contract with RCA Records, which proved to be the springboard to an exciting career.

But it was as a songwriter that Harry

Nilsson first made a name for himself in showbusiness when The Monkees (see **The Monkees**) recorded one of his songs – 'Cuddly Toy' – and featured it on their hit American TV show. However, it wasn't until he recorded his first album, 'The Early Years' in 1968, on which he featured a clever version of The Beatles' 'You Can't Do That', that he at last gained some kind of lasting recognition. It was the start, too, of a long association with the Fab Four – John Lennon spon-

HARRY NILSSON — made a comeback in 1980

the next three years. Then followed an extensive series of engagements in America, including a year-long season in cabaret at the Aladdin Hotel, Las Vegas.

Back in Britain at the start of the '70s, the New Vaudeville Band set about re-establishing themselves, only this time on the domestic cabaret circuit, with a change of line-up and a change of musical direction. Instead of concentrating on a pure '30s sound, the group turned towards contemporary material, and comedy, to become an entertaining showgroup.

Today – still led by Henri Harrison, with Robert Lewis Hay-Smith, Steve Ashton-Shaw, Paul Frederick Wright, and Ian Ffortescue-Carfrae – the New Vaudeville Band are still very much in demand for engagements in cabaret throughout Britain.

HARRY NILSSON
American. Male. Singer/Songwriter.

It's hard to believe, but Harry Nilsson has never actually appeared 'live' in concert in public, despite enjoying outstanding success with two monster-selling singles – 'Everybody's Talkin'' the theme from the movie 'Midnight Cowboy' in 1969, and 'Without You', which topped the British and American Hit Parades in 1972.

sored him (and later produced the album 'Pussy Cats'). A year later, he scored heavily in the chart with the single 'Everybody's Talkin'".

In 1970, Harry conceived an idea for a musical play which he called 'The Point'. After successfully selling the idea to ABC Television in America, he then teamed up with the Academy Award winning animator Fred Wolf to create and produce the first ever feature-length cartoon film for television, which was screened in 1972. Since then, it has been seen all over the world, winning awards at the coveted Montreaux Television Festival, and the Atlanta Film Festival. A stage version of the musical was performed in London's West End in 1978 featuring former Monkees Davy Jones and Mickey Dolenz.

After topping the U.S. and British Hit Parades in 1972 with 'Without You', from the hit album 'Nilsson Schmilsson', Harry Nilsson enjoyed even more success in America with a string of superb and witty LPs, including 'The Son Of Schmilsson' and 'A Little Touch Of Schmilsson In The Night', which spawned a highly entertaining international TV 'special'.

In 1973, he teamed up with Beatle Ringo Starr (see **Ringo Starr**) – he later appeared on his album 'Ringo' and sang on the hit single 'You're Sixteen' – to star in the movie 'Son Of Dracula'. A year later, he hit the headlines once again, but this time for all the *wrong* reasons, when he and John Lennon were forcibly ejected from the Los Angeles Troubador Club for causing a disturbance. Much the worse for drink, they sang 'I Can't Stand The Rain' to the annoyance of patrons, during the Smothers' Brothers cabaret act.

Harry Nilsson has remained one of the enigmas of the pop industry and has never quite established himself as a major force-to-be-reckoned-with. However, he continues to sing – he has recorded with virtually every top name in the music industry – *and* to write his witty, amusing, charming and often eccentric songs which have been recorded by artists as diverse as John Lennon and George Burns.

In 1980 he wrote the music and lyrics for the Walt Disney movie, 'Popeye'.

NINA AND FREDERICK
Danish. Male/Female. Vocal Duo.

During the late 1950s and early '60s, Danish singing duo Nina And Frederick established themselves as one of the most popular singing acts in Europe – and regularly toured the world, appearing in concert and cabaret engagements . . . and on television. They enjoyed many hit records, too, particularly on the Continent, though in Britain they scored with 'Mary's Boy Child', which reached Number 26 in the domestic chart in 1959; 'Listen To The Ocean' in 1960; 'Little Donkey' – their biggest-selling single, which reached Number 3 in 1960; 'Longtime Boy' (1961); and 'Sucu Sucu' (1961). And on stage, husband and wife, presented an idyllic act. They seemed to be the perfect partnership.

The partnership actually started in 1954 when Nordic beauty Nina married wealthy Danish aristocrat Baron Frederick Van Pallandt – and together they emerged as Europe's most popular folk duo. For the next fifteen years, their marriage went hand-in-hand with their musical careers. They even found time – in between engagements – to raise three children, ranging in age today from 16 to 21.

Then in 1969, they split up – "He didn't want to sing anymore", said a friend at the time. "She did!"

"We had a good time together for most of the time," says Nina. "But working *and* being private together puts a lot of strain on a relationship."

They were divorced in 1976 – "Somewhere along the way we thought we might get back together, but in the end *he* didn't want it," she added. "It's sad, I feel we had so much together."

The couple went their own separate ways. Frederick into almost hibernation to live the life of a recluse on the island of Ibiza where he bought a farm; Nina went into cabaret singing . . . and acting.

However, during the early 1970s, she hit the headlines in the most controversial way, when she became involved with Clifford Irving, who was later imprisoned for fraud following the famous Howard Hughes biography scandal. Nina had gone away on holiday with him to Mexico when news of the conspiracy broke. Irving claimed he had been commissioned by Hughes to write his 'official' biography, but in fact he had never even met the man. Nina, for her part was branded 'the other woman', and looked upon with suspicion and a certain contempt.

She told an English newspaper all about it: "That affair gave me a stigma that will stick with me for the rest of my life. It's ironic, isn't it? One weekend with a gentleman in Mexico, and I went straight from fame in Europe to infamy in America!"

However, it didn't affect her career too much – and she made her movie debut in the film 'The Long Goodbye' in 1973 which was acclaimed by one critic as "the most important film debut in the last ten years".

Since then, she has continued to work in films, starring in 'A Wedding' and 'American Gigolo' – playing a pimp – with Richard Gere in 1980. And she sees her career very firmly set on celluloid. However, she still finds time to involve herself in other activities and works regularly with a day clinic in Los Angeles.

"I've always been interested in this kind of work," she says.

Baron Frederick has rarely strayed from his hermit-like existence on Ibiza. Though in November 1979, he paid over $250,000 for the rights to publish Burke's Peerage, the distinguished British guide to aristocracy. Yet within eight months, he sold out – and as a friend later explained: "Van Pallandt is fascinated by genealogy. But he's more interested now in his farm on Ibiza."

PETER NOONE
British. Male. Singer.

HERMAN'S HERMITS
British. Male. Vocal/Instrumental Group.
Original line-up: Herman (Peter Noone) — vocals; Karl Green (bass); Derek Leckenby (guitar); Barry Whitman (drums); Keith Hopwood (guitar).

During those lazy, hazy, crazy days of the 1960s when Merseybeat and Merseymania virtually dominated the international music scene, one of the few groups to pose any sort of threat to its supremacy, came from 'down the road' in Manchester. They were called Herman's Hermits.

Led by Peter Noone, Herman's Hermits enjoyed amazing success, particularly in America and Britain – and in a career spanning eight years, they sold a phenomenal 50,000,000 records world-wide, with 20 hit singles.

Herman's Hermits first arrived on the scene in 1964, with the release of

HERMAN'S HERMITS — (l-r): Keith Hopwood, Barry Whitman, Peter Noone, Karl Green, Derek Leckenby

their debut single – 'I'm Into Something Good'. It topped the charts on both sides of the Atlantic. Next followed an incredible run of hits – 'Silhouettes', 'Wonderful World', 'A Must To Avoid', 'No Milk Today', 'There's A Kind Of Hush', 'Something's Happening', 'Sunshine Girl' and 'Mrs. Brown You've Gotta Lovely Daughter' (both American Number 1 hits in 1965) and 'Years May Come, Years May Go' – *and* (as Peter Noone and Herman's Hermits) 'Oh You Pretty Thing'.

Peter Noone was born in Davyhulme, Manchester, England, on November 5, 1947, and christened Peter Blair Denis Bernard Noone. At the age of 11, he went to the Manchester School of Music to study drama, music and singing and it was during his training that he began a short acting career, appearing in such British television series as 'Knight Errant' and 'Coronation Street' (in which he played Len Fairlough's son, Stanley).

He next tried his hand at singing and joined the Manchester group, The Heartbeats, which evolved into Herman's Hermits.

Peter left the group in 1972 to go solo, but he later moved to France (home of his wife Mirelle) and virtually retired from the music industry.

He says: "Basically I quit because I didn't want to become an end-of-the-pier performer."

Still, it was in France, that he started writing songs, several of which were recorded by Debby Boone, and Deniece Williams, and set about learning the techniques of record production. Next stop was America, where, besides the writing and production work, he still found time (and the money) to open a clothes shop in New York called The Zoo Boutique. However, he did eventually return from his self-imposed isolation to perform again, though this time with the unknown rock group The Tremblers, featuring Gregg Inhoffer, Robin Williams, Geo Connor and Randy Rice.

Meanwhile Herman's Hermits – with a Peter Noone sound-and-look-alike on vocals – have continued performing, playing the rounds of American concert halls and clubs as a 'nostalgia' group, reliving their halcyon days of the 1960s.

103

ROY ORBISON
American. Male Singer/Songwriter.

In the course of his last Las Vegas show, Elvis Presley took the time to introduce some fellow singers in the audience, including Engelbert Humperdinck. The last man he introduced he called "the greatest singer in the world". It was Roy Orbison.

Undeniably, Big 'O' *has* one of the finest voices of his generation.

He started his career on Sun Records with the likes of Elvis, Jerry Lee Lewis (see **Jerry Lee Lewis**), Carl Perkins (see **Carl Perkins**) and Johnny Cash. Then in 1963, he was acclaimed the number one vocalist in the world (in terms of chart records).

Roy Orbison was born in Vernon, Texas, on April 23, 1936, but grew up in the town of Wink, where he started playing guitar and singing on the local radio station's talent hour each Saturday. "By the time I was thirteen, I had my own group The Wink Westerners," says Roy. "And we toured around West Texas, playing at jamborees and the like."

After high school, he attended North Texas State University and spurred on by the example of a fellow student – Pat Boone (see **Pat Boone**) – and the success of Elvis Presley, formed another group which won several local talent contests. He recorded a demo of his own song 'Ooby Dooby' and on the recommendation of Johnny Cash, he was signed to Sun. The actual demo of 'Ooby Dooby' was released as his debut single. It was his first hit and sold nearly 500,000 copies.

Orbison toured with many of his Sun stable companions – Perkins, Cash and Lewis, then left the label in 1957 to concentrate his career on songwriting. He penned 'Down The Line' for Jerry Lee; the Number 1 success – 'Claudette' (named after his wife) for The Everly Brothers; and songs for Buddy Holly.

In 1959, he joined Fred Foster at Mercury Records and started singing and recording once again. He wrote 'Only The Lonely' not long afterwards and was hoping to persuade either

Elvis or The Everly Brothers to record it. In the end, he recorded it himself. It became a smash hit, topped the British charts in 1960, and ended up selling more than two million copies!

That was the beginning of an unbroken stream of chart records and Top Ten hits on the Monument label, among them 'Running Scared' (his first American Number 1 in 1961), 'Cryin'' (1961), 'Dream Baby' (1963), 'Blue Bayou' (1963), 'It's Over' (1964) and 'Oh, Pretty Woman' (1964) . . . which topped the charts on both sides of the Atlantic). To date, he has sold nearly 40,000,000 records world-wide.

In 1963, Roy decided to step into the global musical arena in a big way and was contracted to tour Britain with the up-and-coming Beatles. It was the beginning of the international fame that has become the mainstay of his career. Indeed, he regularly toured Britain, Europe and Australia throughout the 1960s and 1970s – making his last excursion to Britain in 1980. It also marked the establishment of his

ROY ORBISON — Big O, still lurking behind the shades

characteristic image, through a minor, and almost accidental, change of his physical aspect. On the way over to Britain, Orbie left his glasses on a plane and was obliged to wear his prescription sunglasses for the entire tour. He has retained the dark-glasses look ever since.

Three years later, tragedy struck, when his wife Claudette was killed in a motorcycle accident. Then in 1968, two of his three sons were killed in a fire at his Nashville ranch home.

Orbison was shattered, but threw himself into his career and worked harder than ever, touring almost ceaselessly, throughout America, Britain and Europe – where, in Germany, in 1969, he met his second wife, Barbara.

Since then, Roy Orbison has retained his position as one of the giants of pop music . . . and an inspiration to many of today's leading performers including The Eagles and

Bruce Springsteen. He still undertakes concert tours of America and Britain – where he has a strong affiliation and big fan following.

In recent years, although not having any chart singles of his own, Roy has certainly enjoyed great success as a songwriter. Both Linda Ronstadt with her Platinum-selling 'Blue Bayou' and Don McLean with 'Cryin'' have topped international Hit Parades singing Roy Orbison numbers.

PAPER LACE
British. Male.
Vocal/Instrumental Group.
Original Line-up: Cliff Fish (bass); Michael Vaughan (guitar); Phil Wright (drums); Chris Morris (guitar); Carlo Santana (guitar).

Paper Lace made history in 1974 when their single 'The Night Chicago Died' went to the very top of the American Hit Parade – and later sold over a million copies – to become one of an elite band of British groups to achieve this distinction. On the homefront, however, the single fared less well, reaching Number 3 in the British chart.

The group was formed in 1969 in Rochdale where they landed a residency at Tiffany's Club in the Lancashire town. They later undertook club and concert engagements up and down the country and in 1974 made their TV debut on the talent series 'Opportunity Knocks', winning one of the shows in the process. Earlier in the year, the group had been signed by songwriter Mitch Murray to his own record company – Bus Stop – and with Peter Callander, he wrote their debut single 'Billy Don't Be A Hero'. They featured the song on their very first television show and it proved an instant success. Within weeks it was at the top of the British chart. Their follow-up release 'The Night Chicago Died' consolidated their potential . . . and they scored for a third time with 'The Back Eyed Boys'.

At the height of their success, Paper Lace toured Britain and America, and appeared at major venues, including the London Palladium, in June 1974. A year later, they were chosen to appear in the Royal Variety Show.

In 1978 Carlo Santana left the group to go solo – though as yet he has failed to make any major impact in Britain.

Paper Lace, on the other hand, have continued to entertain – appearing in clubs in Holland, Germany, France and Scandinavia, where they have retained a large fan following. And four of the original members are still very active within the group.

In 1978, after being out of the commercial eye for two years, they teamed up with Nottingham Forest Football Club to record the single 'We've Got The Whole World In Our Hands', which reached 24 in the British chart.

PAPER LACE — (l-r): Cliff Fish, Mike Vaughan, Phil Wright, Chris Morris

CARL PERKINS — rocking at a London show, backed by Dave Edmunds

CARL PERKINS
American. Male. Singer.

It was Carl Perkins who wrote and recorded 'Blue Suede Shoes' long before Elvis Presley got his hands on the song which was to establish him as a world beater!

" 'Blue Suede Shoes' was the easiest song I ever wrote," he says. "I got up at 3.00 a.m. one morning when me and my wife Valda were living in a government project in Jackson, Tennessee. I had the idea in my head, seeing my kids by the bandstands so proud of their new city shoes – you gotta be real poor to care about new shoes like I did. And we were *real poor*! That morning I went downstairs and wrote out the words on a potato sack. We didn't have any reason to have writing paper around!"

'Blue Suede Shoes' went on to top pop, country and r & b charts in America, all at the same time/and to register a Top Ten success in Britain, as well. And, almost overnight, Carl Perkins became a star. It was 1955.

His success was to last a mere twelve months for in March 1956, while travelling to a television show, he was involved in a serious car accident which killed his brother Jay, and his manager . . . and put Carl in hospital for a whole year with a broken neck and fractured skull. His spectacular career was in ruins!

Carl Perkins was born on April 9, 1932 in Tipton County, Tennessee, in extreme poverty. From an early age, he was fascinated by the blues he heard sung all around him. He bought his first guitar at the age of ten for three dollars and taught himself to play. At fourteen, he bought a homemade bass, which he taught his brother Clayton to play. His other brother, Jay, played rhythm guitar – and The Perkins Brothers Band was formed. It wasn't long before they were entering *and* winning local talent contests and building up something of a reputation for themselves in and around their hometown. Then in 1955, adding drummer W. S. Holland to their ranks, the family group auditioned for Sam Phillips at Sun Records in Memphis, Tennessee, and were signed to a recording contract to join the rapidly emerging Sun stable of stars – Elvis, Jerry Lee Lewis (see **Jerry Lee Lewis**), Charlie Rich, Johnny Cash and Roy Orbison (see **Roy Orbison**). Carl's first record – 'Blue Suede Shoes' – was an instant success . . . and he became one of the leading lights in rock 'n' roll, until that fatal car smash.

When he recovered, Carl Perkins' career was never quite the same again – time had passed him by. Elvis, meanwhile had recorded 'Blue Suede

Shoes' and enjoyed outstanding success with the song that everyone thought was his own. Perkins did resurface in the American chart with 'Matchbox' (later recorded by The Beatles), but somehow the sparkle had gone, and he turned more and more towards country music for his living.

In 1967, he joined Johnny Cash to work on his top-rated television series . . . and he has worked regularly with the star ever since, adding his own, distinctive style of guitar playing to Johnny's music.

Still recognized as one of the rock 'n' roll legends, the world over, Carl Perkins is still touring in his own right . . . and played extensive concert engagements all over Europe in 1978 (with Bo Diddley – see **Bo Diddley**) and 1979. During both visits, he appeared at the famous International Festival of Country Music in Wembley.

He returned to Britain in the spring of 1981 for a further Country Festival appearance . . . and projected tour.

PETER, PAUL AND MARY
American. Male/Female.
Vocal/Instrumental trio.

Peter, Paul and Mary emerged from Greenwich Village in the early '60s, and during the next 10 years made the voice of protest – as evidenced in their polished, but still sing-along music – acceptable.

At the same time, during the early years, they were the first group to put Bob Dylan's songs before a mass audience. Manager Albert Grossman brought vocalist Mary Travers (born on November 7, 1937, in Louisville, Kentucky) and vocalist/guitarists Peter Yarrow (born in New York on May 31, 1938) and Paul Stookey (born in Baltimore, Maryland on November 30, 1937) together in 1961.

Peter Yarrow had studied psychology at Cornell University where he was also an instructor in a folk ballad course. He sang in folk clubs in his spare time and was discovered at the Newport Folk Festival in 1960. Paul Stookey started *his* career in various rock groups at school and worked on local TV. He later met a young folk

singer, Mary Travers, and helped her to make a singing comeback after a disastrous excursion into Broadway in the musical 'The Next President'.

They started playing as a trio in folk clubs in Greenwich Village, and essentially, their material was topical/protest, with a few odd numbers, such as 'Puff The Magic Dragon' – a children's favorite – thrown in for good measure. Their first hit, however, was 'If I Had A Hammer', by Pete Seeger. Other hits included, 'This Land Is Your Land', and 'Go Tell It To The Mountain', before they broke through with Dylan's 'Blowin' In The Wind', towards the end of '63. A year later they had another Dylan hit with 'The Times They Are A-Changin' '. By then the threesome had built up a huge following and regularly toured the world. They could play concerts, or for that matter, protest rallies, as they did on many occasions later in the Vietnam era. But wherever they appeared they assured themselves a massive audience.

In 1969, they paved the way for another new performer's career when they recorded John Denver's 'Leaving On A Jet Plane', which went to Number 1 in America and sold a million. However, the following year they decided that they had had enough, and split to go their own, solo, ways.

It was a fortunate decision, because

on March 26, 1970, Peter Yarrow was jailed for 3 months after being found guilty of a sex offence, "taking immoral liberties with a 14-year old girl", of which he was vindicated ten years later. The group had just received a coveted Grammy Award for producing the 'Best Children's Record Of The Year'.

They reformed a year later for a one-off concert at a George McGovern rally . . . and shortly afterwards all three made solo albums.

Yarrow came back with a vengeance as a session musician and later worked with Jim Capaldi. In 1976, he wrote Mary MacGregor's huge hit 'Torn Between Two Lovers'.

Mary Travers went into radio and television work as an interviewer and had her own chat show, while Paul Stookey has returned to his folk roots, working in his self-built studio in Maine and performing in American folk clubs.

WILSON PICKETT
American. Male. Singer.

Wilson Pickett established himself in no uncertain terms as one of the most revered soul artists in the world during the 1960s. He was one of the guiding lights of soul . . . and helped to introduce the music all over the world. His reputation as a 'King Of Soul' was never in any doubt.

PETER, PAUL & MARY — (l-r): Paul, Mary, Peter

Born on March 18, 1941 in Prattville, Alabama, Pickett moved with his family to Detroit when still in his teens. And it was in the Motor City that he soon fell under the inviting spell of all the varied forms of music on display throughout Michigan – from rock 'n' roll to soul and r. & b. He plumped for Gospel music . . . and for two years sang with various local groups.

In 1959, he joined the Detroit band The Falcons – who earlier that year had a million-selling single with 'You're So Fine' – at the invitation of group member Willie Schofield as a replacement for lead-singer Joe Stubbs (brother of Four Tops singer Levi Stubbs). Wilson became a vital member of the five-piece outfit and wrote many of their subsequent hits,

including 'I Found Love'.

He stayed with the group until 1963, when he joined Double L Records and branched out on a solo career. 'If You Need Me' was his first hit single for the label, followed by 'It's Too Late', both self-penned songs.

A year later, he signed to Atlantic Records and the hits continued from the Pickett production line. He wrote most of them himself including: 'I'm Gonna Cry' and 'For Better Or Worse'. In 1965, he wrote and recorded the million-seller 'In The Midnight Hour', which gave him his first British hit, followed by 'Don't Fight It', '634 – 5789', 'Land Of A Thousand Dances', 'Mustang Sally' and 'Funky Broadway'.

With such a track record behind him, Wilson Pickett emerged as one

of the biggest soul singers in the business, in demand for tours and television appearances all over the world. He could do no wrong. Indeed, during the latter days of the '60s, he amassed a string of hits with cover versions of several former million-selling songs – given his own inimitable treatment – including Hendrix's 'Hey Joe' and The Beatles' 'Hey Jude', which were outstanding chart successes in Britain and America in 1969.

However, as the '60s moved into the '70s, recording success started to drift away from him as the music industry turned every which way, without very much direction.

He moved to Philadelphia in search of a new sound and even more hit records. He found both in 1971 with two more million-selling singles – 'Don't Let The Green Grass Fool You' and 'Don't Knock My Love'. Two years later, he left Atlantic for RCA, and yet another change of style and sound.

These days, Wilson Pickett is still searching. He still performs regularly *and* is very active on the recording scene. He has been hailed as one of the most dynamic 'live' entertainers in the business and described by one British rock writer as "a superlative performer able to win over even the most restrained audience with his extrovert dynamism!"

During 1980, he did just that with regular appearances on the Manhattan rock club circuit, and often frequented the stage of New York's Lone Star club.

GENE PITNEY
American. Male.
Singer/Songwriter.

In 1961, Gene Pitney recorded a demo-disc of a song he had written himself – 'I Want To Love My Life Away' – and without much hope of ever finding a market for himself as a singer, hawked the song around from publisher to publisher with the intention of putting it out for grabs. Yet, no-one was interested in recording the song! However, Musicor Records decided to take a chance on the singer and the song, and actually released the demo, featuring Pitney's over-dubbed voice (seven times), with the twenty-one-year-old also playing drums, piano and guitar. The gamble paid off in no uncertain terms. 'I Want To Love My Life Away' became an immediate hit ... Gene's first chart success in America. It was the first of many.

Following that initial breakthrough, came an unbroken sequence: 'Town Without Pity', 'Liberty Valance', 'Mecca', 'Twenty-Four Hours From Tulsa', 'It Hurts To Be In Love', 'I'm Gonna Be Strong', 'Lookin' Through The Eyes Of Love', 'Something's Gotten Hold Of My Heart' ... and many more.

Gene's songwriting activities, too, flourished, with singers like Roy Orbison, Steve Lawrence and Tommy Edwards recording much of his material. But four of his self-penned songs have gone on to become pop classics

in their own right – 'Today's Teardrops' by Orbison, 'Hello Mary Lou' (Ricky Nelson), 'Rubber Ball' (Bobby Vee) and 'He's A Rebel' (The Crystals). The royalties alone from these have made Pitney a millionaire.

It was 'Twenty-Four Hours From Tulsa' which introduced Gene Pitney to British audiences in 1963. The single was an enormous hit and since then, he has regularly toured the country undertaking concert and cabaret engagements, most recently in 1981.

Pitney's interest in music took over a previous passion for electronics, while he was studying at the University of Connecticut. Born in Rockville, Connecticut on February 17, 1941, he spent many hours as a ham radio operator, regularly chatting to other enthusiasts all over the world. This interest led him to study electronics at the State University, but a simultaneous role as leader and vocalist of a college band determined him to follow a musical career.

Although his work schedule keeps him moving around the world at an

amazing pace for several months a year – he undertakes two tours of Britain each year, and a bi-annual tour of Australia. Pitney has also become a shrewd businessman, and can boast ownership of a beach and yacht club in Connecticut, where in poorer days he worked as a chef. He also takes an active role in his publishing operation which includes three separate music and production companies. Today he lives in Connecticut with his wife Lynne and three sons.

BRIAN POOLE AND THE TREMELOES
British. Male. Vocal/Instrumental Group.

Original line-up: Brian Poole (Vocals); Alan Blakely (guitar); Dave Munden (drums); Ricky West (guitar); Alan Howard (bass).

Brian Poole was born in London on November 3, 1941, and formed his backing group The Tremeloes in Dagenham, Essex, in 1959. For the next two years, the group worked semi-professionally in clubs and dance

halls all over the south of England . . . and in 1961 decided to turn professional.

Regular guest-star appearances on BBC Radio's 'Saturday Club' show followed. But in those early days, the group made a name for themselves by covering other people's hit records on a small budget-priced record label. In this capacity, they made several albums including 'Big Hits Of '62' for Ace Of Clubs.

However, in 1963 they hit the chart jackpot in their own right when they recorded 'Twist And Shout', the old Isley Brothers classic which The Beatles featured on *their* debut album 'Please Please Me'. The record went to Number 4 in the British chart in July of that year, and helped to establish their name in the first division of pop music. By September, they were sitting at the top of the Hit Parade with 'Do You Love Me' – and next found even greater success with 'I Can Dance', and further hits 'Candy Man', 'Someone Someone', 'Three Bells' and 'I Want Candy'.

Bassman Alan Howard left the group at the height of their success to be replaced by Micky Clark, who in turn later joined The Rubettes.

In 1966, Brian Poole decided to branch out on his own solo singing career but with little success. And he later returned to his original career as a master butcher with his own family firm in Barking, Essex . . . where today he is running a thriving business.

Meanwhile, The Tremeloes branched out on their own. They reformed shortly afterwards with Len 'Chip' Hawkes on bass, and in February, 1967 enjoyed chart success with the Cat Stevens' song 'Here Comes My Baby'. Their next release 'Silence Is Golden' went on to top the British Hit Parade.

For the next four years, the group headlined major concert tours all over the world . . . and they made the British chart again with several best-selling singles: 'Even The Bad Times

BRIAN POOLE AND THE TREMELOES — *Ricky West, Brian Poole, Dave Munden, Alan Blakely, Alan Howard*

Are Good', 'Suddenly You Love Me', 'My Little Girl', 'Hello World', 'Call Me Number One', 'Me And My Life' and 'Call Me Buddy'.

However, a series of tragedies marred their success in the early 1970s. In 1972, Ricky West was injured in a car crash and left the group, returning in 1974 to replace Chip Hawkes when he, too, was severely injured in a similar smash.

In 1975 Alan Blakely decided to leave, which at that time left just two original members — West and Munden, who were joined by Bob Benham and Aaron Woolley . . . and they continued to record and play selective concert engagements. Chip Hawkes meanwhile returned to the music scene in Nashville, Tennessee, where he performed and recorded with Crystal Gayle, The Crickets and Barefoot Jerry. In 1978, though, he returned to

Britain and re-joined his former group.

Today, The 'new' Tremeloes — West, Hawkes, Munden and new member Vic Elms (formerly with Christie of 'Yellow River' fame) — have continued to tour and spend most of their time combining engagements in Holland, Germany, and Scandinavia with seasons of British cabaret.

P. J. PROBY
American. Male. Singer.

P. J. Proby was born James Marcus Smith in Houston, Texas, on November 6, 1938.

As a teenager, he became great friends with Elvis Presley, who dated his sister. During his early twenties, Jim went to Hollywood, where he spent most of his time working in the movies as an extra and bit-part actor. However, under the name of Jet Powers, he started singing and recording,

and not long afterwards he was employed to make demo tapes for his old buddy Elvis.

In 1964, now working as P. J. Proby (and sporting flamboyant clothes and his hair tied in a pony tail) he was brought to England by producer Jack Good to appear in a Beatles television special. His performance on the show was dynamic, and almost overnight, P.J. was a star. He followed up his television success by making the British Top Ten with three singles in 1964 — 'Hold Me', 'Together' and 'Somewhere' (from West Side Story) and it really did seem that he had the British public eating out of his hand!

Then it went sour. At the beginning of 1965, while headlining an extensive British concert tour with Cilla Black, Proby's skin-tight velvet trousers split in mid song at the Ritz Theatre, Luton . . . and he was pulled off the stage by the theater management. They stated later that his lewd and highly suggestive stage act was inciting the audience! A few days later, he was banned from appearing in theaters owned by the massive ABC Cinema circuit, and shortly afterwards he was prohibited from appearing on British television. Public outrage had won the day. Yet, in one defiant gesture, Proby smashed back into the British chart with the aptly titled single — 'I Apologise'. In actual fact, he enjoyed several more hit singles after the trouser-splitting incident, including 'Let The Water Run Down' (1965), 'That Means A Lot' (1965), 'Maria' (1965 — his second hit from 'West Side Story'), 'To Make A Big Man Cry' (1966), 'I Can't Make It Alone' (1966) and 'It's Your Day Today' (1968).

However by 1968, his flamboyant life style — the free-loaders, the manic drinking sessions, the women — caught up with him, and he was declared a bankrupt. The same year, he returned to America in the hope of re-kindling his career.

Three years later, he was back in Britain and again it was through Jack Good, who cast him as 'Iago' in his rock musical-version of 'Othello' . . . 'Catch My Soul'. And for the next few years, Jim knuckled down to find a fair modicum of success on the British domestic cabaret circuit.

In 1977, he made a spectacular come-back, starring as 'Elvis Presley', in the rock musical 'Elvis' in London's West End. Proby was acclaimed by the press for his performance, yet a short while after the show opened, he left the company in a blaze of publicity after an argument with the management. Proby's old habits died hard . . . and he went back into his own self-imposed showbusiness exile.

PROCUL HARUM
British. Male. Vocal/Instrumental Group.

Original line-up: Gary Brooker (piano); Matthew Fisher (organ); Dave Knights (bass); Bobby Harrison (drums); Ray Royer (guitar).

Formed by Gary Brooker, an ex-member of the British r & b group The Paramounts – who featured Brooker, Barry Wilson, Robin Trower and Chris Copping and enjoyed chart success in 1964 with 'Poison Ivy'. Procul Harum came together in 1966 to record the Gary Brooker/Keith Reid composition 'A Whiter Shade Of Pale'. The band had been assembled from would-be applicants answering a musical trade newspaper advertisement, and the record was independently produced for a few hundred dollars. However, when it was released by Deram in May '67, it became one of the fastest selling singles in history – topping the British chart for six weeks and clocking up Gold Disc sales in America.

It proved the start of an interesting, if not spectacular career for the group, named after a breed of Burmese Cats. But they never really consolidated their early promise, due in the main to a fluctuating line-up. Indeed, Harrison and Knights only played on the one hit record, before being replaced by former Paramount members Barry Wilson and Robin Trower.

The group followed up their single success with 'Homburg' in October 1967, reaching the British Top Ten, and later made two outstanding albums – 'Procul Harum' and 'Shine On Brightly'. But they rarely appeared 'live' together in the early days, apart from a series of lengthy American tours. And indeed, it was in the States that they amassed a large fan following –

which necessitated regular visits for concerts. But these tours were interspersed with long periods of inactivity.

After producing their third album 'A Salty Dog' in 1969, Matthew Fisher left the group to go solo, and he was followed by Dave Knights. The fourth Paramount Chris Copping (bass) replaced them both, and Procul Harum continued to work as a four-piece. In this capacity, they made two more best-selling albums – 'Home' (1970) and 'Broken Barricades' a year later.

The line-up changed yet again in 1971 when Robin Trower quit and with Frankie Miller formed the short-lived group Jude, before breaking out on his own once more with the outstanding Robin Trower Group. He was replaced by Dave Ball on guitar, and bassman Alan Cartwright – with Copping changing to organ. And together,

PROCUL HARUM — The 1967 line up including Barny Wilson and Robin Trower

they recorded their successful 'Procul Harum In Concert With The Edmonton Symphony Orchestra' – and toured America once more. From the 'Edmonton' album, the single 'Conquistador' was taken which gained moderate sales and a chart position in Britain of 22 in 1972. For their 'Grand Hotel' album in 1973, Mick Grabham came in on guitar.

Alan Cartwright left the group in 1976 to be replaced by Pete Sollie which allowed Chris Copping to double on bass once more. The revised line-up recorded several more albums including 'Exotic Birds And Fruit' and 'Procul Harum's Ninth' and enjoyed a final hit single with 'Pandora's Box' (16 in the British chart) before splitting up completely in 1977, never quite having realized their full potential. It was a sad fact of life that the group were acclaimed in America throughout their career, but couldn't repeat that success at home in Britain.

Gary Brooker – the mainstay of the band who with Keith Reid penned much of their outstandingly original material – went solo, and (with Reid) continued to write and produce songs.

GARY PUCKETT AND THE UNION GAP
American. Male.
Vocal/Instrumental Group.
Original line-up: Gary Puckett (guitar/vocals); Dwight Bement (sax); Kerry Chator (bass); Gary Withem (keyboards); Paul Whitbread (drums).

Essentially a singles' band, Gary Puckett and the Union Gap emerged – dressed in American Civil War uniforms – in 1967, from San Diego, California, where the band was formed the same year. Puckett ('The General') – was very much the front man. He was born in Hibbing, Minnesota, on October 17, 1942, and grew up in Washington, near a small town

called Union Gap, hence the group's name.

They hit the headlines (and the international charts) in '67 when their single 'Woman Woman' made the American Top Five and sold over a million copies. Up until then, the group had attracted a large fan following on club and college engagements. Then came an avalanche of hits, the next year – 'Young Girl', which topped both the British and American charts; 'Lady Willpower' (another U.S. Number 1) and 'Over You'.

Yet the Union Gap boom faded as quickly as it had arrived, and in 1971 they disbanded.

Puckett, already an accomplished songwriter, turned to acting, and created a second lucrative career in films, television and theater.

'Young Girl' was re-released and made the Top Ten once more in Britain in 1974.

G.P. AND THE UNION GAP — (l-r): Kerry Chater, Gary Whitlem, Paul Whitbread, Dwight Bement, Gary Puckett

MARVIN RAINWATER
American. Male. Singer.
Although *not* a member of that exclusive 'one hit wonder' club, Marvin Rainwater is best-remembered for just one hit single – 'Whole Lot Of Woman' which topped the British chart in 1958 and sold over a million records in America alone.

An American Cherokee Red-Indian, Marvin Percy was born in Wichita, Kansas on July 2, 1925 (he took his mother's maiden name for recording) and studied to be a veterinary surgeon at Washington State University. After serving with the U.S. Navy during World War II, he set out on a singing career and was discovered almost overnight when he appeared on the celebrated Arthur Godfry Talent Scouts program. Singing one of his own compositions, 'Gonna Find Me A Bluebird', Marvin's prize for winning the talent contest was a recording contract with MGM and a week-long engagement on Godfry's early morning radio show.

Not un-naturally, 'Gonna Find Me A Bluebird' was Marvin Rainwater's first single release in 1957 and it became a monster hit all over the States – selling over a million and reaching Number 3 on the national Hit Parade. It stayed in the Country chart for twenty-six weeks. Later that year he teamed up with Connie Francis (see **Connie Francis**) and together they recorded the million-selling 'Majesty of Love'. The next year, he enjoyed world-wide success with 'Whole Lot Of Woman' followed by three more million-sellers, 'My Love Is Real', 'My Brand Of Blues' and 'Half Breed'. He later joined the cast of the successful radio show 'Jamboree' in West Virginia, and regularly appeared on Red Foley's TV shows.

However, during the 1960s, after refusing to change his somewhat dated image and style, Marvin Rainwater fell from chart grace and although he continued to record, he never consolidated his early promise.

Incidentally, his cause wasn't helped in the mid-'60s by a serious

throat operation, which halted his recording for nearly five years.

A great favorite in Britain, Marvin Rainwater's career has enjoyed a renascence on this side of the Atlantic during the last decade, playing to enthusiastic audiences on several concert tours. (In America, his main market has been the supper clubs of New York). But . . . how the mighty have fallen. In the winter of 1980 he was booked to appear in concert at the Hastings Town Football Club in a quiet backwater of Southern England.

Still, as 'the singing Cherokee' says: – "I keep singing – that's all I ever really wanted to do". In Spring 1981 his fortunes took an upturn with an appearance at the International Festival of Country Music in Wembley, London

JOHNNIE RAY
American. Male. Singer.

They called him 'The Prince of Wails' and 'The Cry Guy' for the emotional and expressive way he sang. They also called Johnnie Ray 'one of the most exciting singers in the world'. And despite having the physical handicap – for a singer – of being deaf, he established himself, during the 1950s, as one of the world's most popular entertainers, with an incredible female following long before Beatlemania swept the world.

He was born John Alvin Ray on January 10, 1927 in Dallas, Oregon – and raised on the family farm in nearby Salem. John loved the outdoor life, but at the age of eleven suddenly became withdrawn and silent. It wasn't until he was fifteen that it was discovered he was deaf. The same year, he was fitted with his first hearing aid, and as soon as he could hear again, he determined to become an entertainer, throwing himself into everything musical he could find: church and choir clubs; high school bands; and songwriting. At seventeen he wrote 'Little White Cloud', which was later to become a million-seller.

When he was sixteen, Johnnie sang on an amateur radio show in Portland, Oregon . . . and became a regular contributor. His first professional singing job came as a production singer in a Portland burlesque show.

By now a competent piano player as

well as a developing singing star, he left home in 1949 for Hollywood, intent on making a name for himself. For the next twelve months, he scraped together a living singing and playing piano in Los Angeles bistros and seedy burlesque clubs, before he decided to try his luck in New York. However, he had little money for the journey, and set about *singing* his way across the States in small supper clubs for equally small wages.

"They were all the same," says Johnnie. "They always told me: 'Don't sing – just play nice piano!'"

However, it was good experience, and he found plenty of time to write new songs and feature them in his act. Then, while working in Detroit, he was lucky enough to record two of his own songs 'Tell The Lady I Said Goodbye'

and 'Whiskey And Gin'. Local radio disc jockeys liked them and started to play them on air . . . and Johnnie Ray was on his way to one of the most phenomenal careers in showbusiness.

In 1952, he sky-rocketed to success when he was discovered singing in the Motor City by a major record executive who signed him up and flew him to New York for a recording session. It was here that he recorded the legendary 'Little White Cloud That Cried', and 'Cry', and both songs sold in excess of four million copies to bring Johnnie Ray instant international acclaim. He toured the world, enjoying outstanding success wherever he appeared *and* chalked up many more worldwide million-selling hits (many of which he composed himself): 'Such

WHATEVER HAPPENED TO . . .?

A Night' (1954); 'Just Walkin' In The Rain' (1956); and 'Yes Tonight Josephine' (1957) – his three British Number 1 successes; 'Please Mr. Sun', 'Walkin' My Baby Back Home', 'Broken Hearted', 'Glad Rag Doll', 'With These Hands', 'Look Homeward Angel', 'If You Believe', 'Somebody's Stole My Gal', 'Hey There' and 'I'll Never Fall In Love Again'. He also notched up a hit in 1957 with Frankie Laine ('Good Evening Friends') . . . and three hits with Doris Day in 1953 with 'Ma Says, Pa Says', 'Full Time Job' and 'Let's Walk That-a-way'.

At the height of his career, Johnnie starred in the motion picture musical 'There's No Business Like Showbusiness' with Ethel Merman – and later turned to acting in major U.S. theater productions of 'Guys And Dolls' and 'Bus Stop'.

The Johnnie Ray recording story ended abruptly in 1960 – but the singer continued to work extensively for the next ten years, appearing in cabaret in Las Vegas; on television – and touring the world in concert. He had lost none of the excitement and none of his pulling power. In 1969, he toured Europe with Judy Garland and appeared with her in concert at Copenhagen's Falconer Centre in March of that year. It proved to be Judy's final performance.

When Johnnie Ray made it to stardom in 1952, he established the Johnnie Ray Foundation For The Deaf with the express purpose to supply underprivileged children and adults with hearing aids.

His work reached even further than he anticipated. Through Johnnie's personal donations and the generosity of others, training devices for the hard-of-hearing children were purchased and given to deaf schools. Scholarship grants were obtained for the training of teachers for the deaf.

In 1969, he discovered Pasadena's H.E.A.R. Foundation and their amazing work in aiding deaf children, through specially trained teachers and sophisticated auditory equipment.

Realizing that such equipment and personnel cost money, Johnnie launched countless benefit performances, TV talk shows and other tactics to help mount donations for the foundation. He is affectionately

tagged 'our singing disciple' by his fellow H.E.A.R. board of trustees members.

It has been his lifetime work, and today takes up most of his professional life. He still has a massive fan following – and regularly makes time to tour Europe and America. In the late 1970s, he played a season in Britain at the London Palladium.

In most every city where Johnnie Ray is appearing these days, he finds a deaf school or college, makes a visit, sings, talks, communicates and cheers up the children.

But these are things Johnnie Ray doesn't talk about much. He just does them.

OTIS REDDING
American. Male. Singer.

Otis Redding, one of the giants of rock 'n' roll 'n' soul music during the 1960s, was born on September 9, 1941 in Dawson, Georgia . . . the son of a Baptist minister. He was brought up in nearby Macon City, already influenced by Gospel music. At High School though, he was inspired to go into the music industry by the reaction local-boy-made-good Little Richard (see **Little Richard**) was getting all over America. He longed to emulate him.

He joined his first group as back-up-singer-cum-road-manager for Johnny Jenkins And The Pinetoppers, a local r & b outfit with whom he toured the college circuit in the Southern states. At the age of 19, he made his first record on the Bethlehem label – 'Shout Bamalama'.

In 1962, Johnny Jenkins was due to cut a record for the Atlanta label and Otis duly drove the band to the studio in Memphis, Tennessee. At the end of the session, there was still over half-an-hour of recording time left, so Redding pursuaded the group and technicians to let him record one of his own songs – 'These Arms Of Mine'. He turned in such an impressive performance in the studio, that he was immediately signed up by the record company in his own right, and 'These Arms Of Mine' became his first single release on Volt Records, a subsidiary of Stax. It proved his first American hit. And for the next two years, Otis Redding's output of singles was prolific –

and all of them, 'Pain In My Heart', 'That's How Strong My Love Is', 'I've Been Lovin' You Too Long' and 'Lover's Prayer' were big hits on the r & b charts. However, they didn't actually register strongly on the national chart.

In 1964, he changed his gentle style of singing altogether with the release of the gutsy 'Mr. Pitiful'. A year later, he blasted his way into the international arena and world Hit Parades with 'Respect', followed by a highly original version of The Rolling Stones' 'Satisfaction'. He also scored well with a tender version of The Temptations' 'My Girl', which gave him his first hit in Britain.

Besides emerging as one of the most dynamic soul singers in the business with his vast array of hit singles and several best-selling albums, Otis Redding also displayed a brilliance at song-writing, penning his own successes 'Ole Man Trouble' and the haunting 'Sittin' On The Dock Of The Bay', which was to become his biggest-ever international hit. Yet, he found time to write for other stars and picked up a hit with his 'Sweet Soul Music', which his protegee Arthur Conley took into the charts – it was a record, incidentally, that Redding produced himself. He also recorded an album – 'King And Queen' – with Carla Thomas in 1967 from which the hit single 'Tramp' was taken.

Otis Redding was one of the most charismatic 'live' performers in contemporary music – and regularly toured the world with backing groups Booker T And The MGs, or The Mar-Keys, or indeed his own band The Bar Kays. In 1967, he was voted the World's Number One vocalist by a British musical trade newspaper and he consolidated his claim to the title shortly afterwards with a devastating performance at the Monterey Pop Festival. Not long after, he recorded 'Dock Of The Bay'.

On December 10, 1967, he was killed when his plane crashed in heavy fog, into the frozen Lake Monana, near Madison, Wisconsin, to where he and his group were travelling for an engagement. He was a mere 26. Four members of The Bar Kays died with him.

At his funeral in Macon City, 4,500 people turned up for the memorial

service including many of the world's top soul artistes. Joe Tex (see **Joe Tex**), Joe Simon, Johnnie Taylor, Solomon Burke (see **Solomon Burke**), Percy Sledge (see **Percy Sledge**), Don Covay and Sam Moore (see **Sam And Dave**) were pall-bearers. Not long afterwards, 'Sitting On The Dock Of The Bay' topped the American chart and went on to sell over a million copies.

THE RIGHTEOUS BROTHERS
American. Male. Vocal Duo.

Acclaimed by aficionados to be the ultimate pop record, 'You've Lost That Lovin' Feeling' was a huge million-selling success for The Righteous Brothers in 1964. It also marked the highspot in production techniques for Phil Spector, who masterminded it.

In actual fact, though, The Righteous Brothers *were not* brothers. They weren't even related.

Bill Medley was born on September 19, 1940 in Los Angeles and, like his partner Bobby Hatfield (born in Beaver Dam, Wisconsin, on April 10, 1940), was a successful solo singer in Southern California. They met on the West Coast in 1962 and decided to team up together.

Minor success followed. Their first hit together was 'Little Latin Lupe Lu', which Medley had written – and they also appeared on Jack Good's TV show 'Shindig'. But it wasn't until 1964 when Phil Spector took an interest, that they hit the jackpot recording-wise with 'You've Lost That Lovin' Feeling', and their powerful follow-up 'Unchained Melody'. In 1966, they

enjoyed three more substantial hits with '(You're My) Soul And Inspiration', another American chart-topper; 'White Cliffs Of Dover' and 'Island In The Sun', though by now they had quit Spector's Philles label for Verve.

But in 1968, with Medley saying he felt restricted – and fearing his musical development might be stunted – they parted company to pursue solo careers. Hatfield took on a new partner, Jimmy Walker, while Bill Medley worked alone. He later admitted he didn't enjoy his solo career. A year later 'Lovin' Feeling' was re-released and back in the chart in Britain.

They re-formed in 1974 and enjoyed two more hits – 'Rock 'n' Roll Heaven' and 'Give It To The People', before splitting again in 1975. Two years later the second re-release of 'Lovin' Feeling', once more made the British charts.

Since then, both Bill and Bobby have carved interesting solo careers for themselves – and regularly appear in the American nightclub circuit.

JEANNIE C. RILEY
American. Female. Singer.

It was almost a rags to riches story! Jeannie C. Riley arrived in Nashville, from Anson, Texas, to work as a secretary, with ambitions of becoming a singer. And, just like all the best stories, her dreams really *did* come true when she recorded Tom T. Hall's 'Harper Valley PTA', on Shelby Singleton's new Plantation label.

The song contained the strong message of a liberated mother being confronted by small-town prejudice. It was an enormous hit, selling 1,750,000 copies in just two weeks and reaching Number 1 for 3 weeks in the American charts. In Britain the record stayed for 15 weeks in the charts during 1968. But if the song was the key to Jeannie's fortune, it was also her undoing in the sense that she became too strongly linked to it, and despite subsequent quality country records, Jeannie could not repeat her chart success in the late 1970s.

She was born on October 19, 1945, and had no showbusiness experience whatsoever before arriving in

JEANNIE C. RILEY — tied to strongly to one song

Nashville as a raw, starry-eyed twenty-two year-old typist, who made demo tapes in her spare time.

'Harper Valley PTA' went on to sell over four million copies and she followed it up with such singles as 'The Girl Most Likely', 'There Was A Time', 'Country Girl' and 'Good Enough To Be Your Wife', all American Top Ten hits.

When the hit singles deserted her, Jeannie turned to singing in night clubs, but later abandoned this lucrative showbusiness medium to concentrate on concerts. Today she lives in Brentwood, Tennessee, with her daughter Kim, and averages fifteen to twenty concert appearances each month.

She told an American magazine: "Of course, I owe a lot to 'Harper Valley', but I only wish it hadn't all happened so quickly. I realize now, it would have been much better for my career if I'd had a few hits before that came out."

MINNIE RIPERTON
American. Female. Singer.

Minnie Riperton's voice was a rare gift. Unique . . . crystal clear and very distinctive. Her major chart success 'Loving You' – a million-selling single in the spring of 1975, which topped the American Hit Parade – displayed her magnificent 5-octave range and powerful potential to the full. It was, in short, perfection.

Minnie Riperton was born into a musical family in Chicago on November 8, 1947, one of eight children. She started singing in the local church choir at the age of nine, and two years later she was trained formally in singing, and studied opera in particular.

At the age of fourteen, whilst still at school, she was signed up by Chess Records – and shortly afterwards, she formed her own all-girl vocal group

MINNIE RIPERTON — *a tragic victim of cancer*

called The Gems. And for the next four years, she and the group performed back-up vocals on numerous Chess recording sessions and appeared on radio commercials. In 1967, she left the group and became lead-singer with Rotary Connection. Three years later, she went solo and recorded her first album for Chess – on their Janus label – 'Come To My Garden'.

She left Chess in 1971 and moved to Gainesville, Florida, with her husband Richard Rudolph, where she went into semi-retirement, writing songs and raising a family. However, she was tempted out of hibernation and signed to Epic Records. Her first album for the label, 'Perfect Angel' – which featured songs written by Minnie and her husband – was produced by Stevie Wonder who also played numerous instruments on the sessions. 'Loving You' was taken off the LP and issued as a single.

She followed it up with more single success – 'Adventures In Paradise', from the album of the same name, and 'Stay In Love', before signing to Capitol Records in 1978 . . . and recording the album 'Minnie'.

In 1977 she was honored by President Carter at the White House when she was presented with the American Cancer Society Courage Award for her "continuing activity and openness about her ordeal", after discovering she had the disease in 1976.

She died on July 12, 1979 after undergoing three years of cancer

therapy. In the fall of 1980, however, Capitol Records released the posthumous Minnie Riperton album 'Love Lives Forever', from which the single 'Island In The Sun' was taken. The album featured a glittering array of sidemen, including Stevie Wonder, George Benson, Michael Jackson, and Roberta Flack.

JIMMIE RODGERS
American. Male. Singer.

Jimmie Rodgers was born in Camas, Washington (a small town thirty miles from Portland) on September 18, 1933. The son of country star Hank Snow, he was christened *Jimmie Rodgers Snow*, as a mark of respect to the legendary country star of the 1920s – Jimmie Rodgers – whom his father admired greatly.

As a youngster, Jimmie was taught to play piano by his mother, the former Minnie Blanche, herself a country singer of some renown . . . and he later taught himself to play guitar.

A spell in the U.S. Air Force followed and Jimmie served in Korea for four years. While stationed in Seoul, he purchased a beat-up guitar from a fellow airman for ten dollars, and set about entertaining. Within a few weeks, he had formed a musical group called The Rhythm Kings, who became tremendously popular with military personnel, and soon began performing at numerous bases throughout Korea, Japan and America.

After his discharge, he returned home to Washington and set about establishing a career for himself as a singer, but the going was tough and he was often forced to take a series of jobs away from showbusiness to earn a living, and occasionally worked on logging camps and farms.

But an appearance on Arthur Godfry's 'Talent Scout' television show changed all that. He won the show outright and was asked to audition for Roulette Records, which resulted in his being offered a recording contract. His first single release 'Honeycomb' sold over a million copies in 1957, and topped the American Hit Parade. For the next five years, he released several more singles which all met with outstanding chart success: 'Kisses Sweeter Than Wine', 'Oh Oh

I'm Falling In Love Again', 'Secretly', and 'Are You Really Mine'.

In 1959, at the height of his success, he was given his own television series 'The Jimmie Rodgers Show' – which became a top-rating program. And he combined his TV and recording commitments with top-line appearances in American nightclubs where he enjoyed a huge following . . . and great success.

In 1962, he switched to Dot Records for whom he worked not only as a performer, but as Chief of Artists and Repertoire for the folk music department. During this time he chalked up several more hit singles with 'No One Will Ever Know', 'The World I Used To Know', 'It's Over', 'Strangers' and 'Morning Means Tomorrow'. In Britain, he is best known for his Top Five success 'English Country Garden', released in 1962.

For the next few years, Jimmie toured the world, undertaking top nightclub appearances in Britain, Australia and America, consolidating his position as one of the most successful international singers of all time. Then in 1967, he was involved in a mysterious car accident in Los Angeles, where he was found in his *own* car with a fractured skull. He was unable to explain what happened! He knew nothing about it. However, during the following year, he underwent major brain surgery and it was unknown whether he would ever recover.

Happily, he did . . . and made a major comeback in 1969 with his own television series for CBS TV. A year later, he resumed his concert and cabaret tours.

Since then, Jimmie Rodgers' career has continued to thrive. He has embarked on major international concert tours, and starred in several television projects including many of his own 'specials'. He is still recording, too, although without the same success he enjoyed over twenty years ago.

Still a remarkably active entertainer – writing and producing many of his own singles and albums – Jimmie is an active evangelist and lives with his wife Trudy in Los Angeles.

TOMMY ROE
American. Male. Singer.

As the '60s drew to a close, a Number 1 success – 'Dizzy' – looked like launching singer-songwriter Tommy Roe into a hugely successful international career.

But the truth was, that Roe had been around a good ten years before that. Indeed during a 1963 British tour, The Beatles were actually among his support acts!

Born in Atlanta, Georgia, on May 9, 1942, Thomas David Roe started his musical career at school. His first group, which played local dances, was called The Satins. He was heading their line-up at 16, and composed their first record release on the Judd label in 1960 – 'Sheila' – which failed to

TOMMY ROE — climbing upwards in 1969

make any impact. But when he signed as a solo singer with ABC Paramount in 1961, he revamped the song and 'Sheila' became his first hit single, topping the U.S. chart – and later sold a million copies. He was 19.

Oddly enough at that time, his subsequent work was *not* acclaimed in America, but in Britain alone. So, he moved to England, and had hits in 1962 and 1963 with 'Susie Darlin', 'The Folk Singer', and 'Everybody'. In 1966 he sold a million copies of 'Sweet Pea'.

1968 saw him returning to the States for TV and concert work. He made 'Dizzy', his most successful song, and a year later hit the album chart with the wittily titled 'Twelve In A Roe' and the singles Hit Parade with another million-seller 'Jam Up Jelly Tight'.

The 1970s saw him as a major night-club attraction, a position he has retained ever since.

Twice-married Tommy Roe still has two homes – one in his native Atlanta, the other in Los Angeles.

THE RONETTES
American. Female. Vocal Group.
Original line-up: Veronica Bennett; Estelle Bennett; Nedra Talley.

Formed in 1959 by three New York Puerto Rican girls – two sisters and their cousin Nedra – The Ronettes started life out as a dancing act called The Dolly Sisters. However, after studying at New York's Camilucci Studio, they started to put singing into their act – and were later signed up as backing singers with Joey Dee And The Starliters (see **Joey Dee**) at the famous Peppermint Lounge, where they supported such artistes as Del Shannon (see **Del Shannon**) and Bobby Rydell. But attempts to establish themselves as a solo act failed.

In 1961, they toured with disc jockey Clay Coles and his Twist-A-Rama as a singing-dancing act and even appeared in the pop movie 'Twist Around The Clock'. They also worked on television with DJ Murray The K as a dance act. The same year, they signed with Colpix Records and over the next two years had five singles released all of which flopped badly. After failing to make the breakthrough to recording success, they were used more and more by the label as session singers and they sang on several hits by Jackie de Shannon and James Darren. And in 1963, Phil Spector signed them to his Philles label for the sole purpose of using them as back-up singers on sessions.

But not long after joining Philles, they recorded the Spector/Barry/Greenwich song 'Be My Baby' (featuring the famous Phil Spector sound developed earlier with The Crystals). It sold a million copies and set them on their way to a place in the record books. Their follow up single 'Baby I

THE RONETTES — groomed by Phil Spector

Love You', repeated its predecessor's success, selling another million, and their subsequent releases – 'Walkin' In The Rain', 'The Best Part Of Breakin' Up' and 'Born To Be Together', all sold well.

The group, now riding on the crest of amazing success, toured America with several of the chart-topping groups of the day, including The Beatles and The Rolling Stones, but by 1966 – and the demise of the Philles label – they slipped into obscurity.

In 1968, Veronica (Ronnie) Bennett married the group's mentor Phil Spector – and as a wedding present, he bought her a 23-roomed mansion in Beverly Hills. A year later, the group (minus their newly-married lead singer) made a brief comeback on the A & M label, but with little success. They had a final attempt at a revival in fortunes in 1973 on Buddah Records, but with a changed line-up.

Meanwhile, Ronnie was finding married life difficult. She told an English musical trade newspaper in 1980: "Phil kept me in seclusion. He wouldn't let me return to my career, to tour – or even *listen* to rock records. I wasn't even a housewife. I didn't cook, *I didn't even empty ashtrays.* After four years, I was going stir-crazy. It was like being royalty. I was locked in, literally. I sat around all day with nothing to do.

"There were all those people he'd been recording before our marriage: The Checkmates, The Righteous

Brothers, Ike And Tina Turner, but I wasn't anything except married to my husband. I assumed that I didn't have a voice any longer because if I did, my own husband – my writer and producer – would be doing something! Phil was always telling me that I was nothing, that it was *his* production and *his* writing that made me and that without him, I wouldn't make it again."

The couple – not unnaturally – were divorced in 1974 and Ronnie returned to singing shortly afterwards with Southside Johnny, but without success. However, she has continued performing ever since, trying to re-establish her career.

In the fall of 1980, she released her first-ever solo album – 'Siren'.

TIM ROSE
American. Male.
Singer/Songwriter.

Hailed as one of the most exciting musical finds to emerge from New York in the mid-'60s, Tim Rose a former student priest and airline pilot (an unlikely combination) based his reputation more on live performances than recordings. But he found himself in the limelight in 1967, when his first LP, 'Tim Rose' was released. It contained his best-known composition, 'Morning Dew', written with Bonny Dobson, which has subsequently been released under numerous cover versions and chalked up many hits. The album also contained a slow-working of 'Hey Joe', which was later picked up by Jimi Hendrix, and proved the springboard for *his* emerging career.

Further success of that high order was not to follow, and by 1974, when Tim – who was born in 1940 – had developed a drinks problem and become totally disillusioned with the American music scene, particularly in Los Angeles, he moved to London to sort himself out and find new inspiration.

Since then he has continued to write songs *and* regularly appear on the British club circuit. During the mid-'70s he occasionally teamed up for club dates with fellow expatriate American, Tim Hardin (see **Tim Hardin**). But great acclaim in the latter '70s eluded him.

PAUL AND BARRY RYAN
British. Male. Vocal/Duo.

Twin sons of Fifties singing star Marion Ryan and tour promoter Harold Davidson, Paul and Barry Ryan followed their illustrious parents into showbusiness in a blaze of publicity in 1965. Three months after turning professional, the duo had their first hit with 'Don't Bring Me No Heartaches'. It was their biggest Hit Parade success. Even though they made the British chart with a further seven singles, including 'I Love You' and 'Have You Ever Loved Somebody', they failed to live up to their early potential.

Born Paul and Barry Sapherson in Leeds, England, on October 24, 1948 (Paul being the elder brother by three minutes), the duo split up in 1968. Paul decided to take a backseat in the performing stakes and concentrate entirely on songwriting and record production. Over the next few years, he enjoyed tremendous success with his songs, several of which were recorded by an old family friend – Frank Sinatra. Indeed, Old Blue Eyes had a major international hit with the

PAUL AND BARRY RYAN — the twins pictured with showbusiness mother, Marion

Paul Ryan song 'I Will Drink The Wine' in 1971.

Barry Ryan, however, continued to sing and record. He branched out on his own solo career which got off to exactly the right start in October 1968, when his debut single on MGM 'Eloise' (writen by brother Paul), went to the very top of the British Hit Parade. For the next few years, he enjoyed great success in the charts with a further five singles, including the million seller 'Love Is Love'.

In 1976, he made the headlines once again when he married Princess Meriam of Johore, daughter of the late Sultan of Johore, who was one of the richest men in the world. The marriage lasted for four years before ending in divorce in 1980.

Two years previously, though, Paul and Barry had decided to pick up the threads of their former career and resume their partnership – and today, they undertake concert and cabaret appearances all over Britain and Europe.

BUFFY SAINTE-MARIE
American. Female.
Singer/Songwriter.

A highly-original voice, and the good fortune to have the composition credits for 'Universal Soldier' (a minor hit for Donovan in 1965) and 'Soldier Blue' – theme of the 1971 movie of the same name – have ensured a place in the history of popular music for Buffy Sainte-Marie.

Born in Sabagolake, Maine, on February 20, 1941, much of her early fame in the '60s Folk Revivalist boom stemmed from her Cree Indian descent, and much of her work both at that time and subsequently saw her devoting her talents to the American Indian cause. And for this, she gained a massive cult following.

She was adopted when still very young – never knew her real parents – and was raised in Massachussetts. Singing was always her first love and

in her teens, she regularly appeared in the New York Gas Light Café where she often worked with fellow Cree Indian, Patrick Sky. Appearances at the Newport Folk Festivals followed and by 1964 she was recording. Her first album release was 'It's My Way' for Vanguard Records.

She headed more in the direction of country music during the 1970s particularly with the release of the 'I'm Gonna Be A Country Girl Again' single and later dabbled with rock, as exemplified by her 1972 'Moonshot' LP. The same year 'Until It's Time For You To Go' – a song she had written in 1965 – became a massive hit for Elvis Presley.

In 1973, she left the label for MCA and three years later moved to ABC and recorded her 'Sweet America' album. Then came a period of inactivity in the commercial sense.

BUFFY SAINTE MARIE — still fighting for cause of American Indians

Still Buffy has continued to write and record, and carry out her one woman crusade for the cause of American Red Indians, and for this reason her concert tours of the U.S.A. are well patronized. Yet, beside her 'live' appearances, Buffy has also carved out a secondary career as a television star.

KYU SAKAMOTO
Japanese. Male. Singer.

Japanese singing star Kyu Sakamoto had American disc jockey Rich Osborne to thank for the suc cess of his 1963 best-selling single 'Sukiyaki' . . . which went on to top the U.S. national chart. For it was Osborne who brought the record to the attention of listeners to his show on station KORD in Pasco, Washington, after discovering the song on an obscure imported Japanese album. Soon afterwards, the radio station became so inundated with requests for the record to be played under its original title of 'Ueo Muite Aruko' (which translated means "walk with your head up") that Capitol Records decided to release it as a single.

In actual fact, at the start of 1963, an instrumental version of the same song – by Britain's Kenny Ball And His Jazzmen – had reached Number 10 in the British charts, under the title of 'Sukiyaki' (which is a Japanese meat dish). And when the American version by Kyu was issued in the States, it, too, carried 'Sukiyaki' as its name. With increased radio coverage – now on a national scale – the record really took off and within a handful of weeks it went to the very top of the chart, where it stayed for three weeks. In Britain, it reached the Number 6 slot . . . and sold a million copies.

Kyu Sakamoto was born in the Japanese city of Kawasaki and started his singing career in the Tokyo Tea Houses, before joining the group Paradise Kings. He soon emerged as one of his country's leading singers,

with a string of best-selling singles and albums to his credit, and regularly appeared on television. He also established himself as a competent actor and appeared in several major Japanese movies.

In 1960, he signed to Toshiba Records and a year later recorded the song that was to cause a sensation as 'Sukiyaka' – which in 1963 became the first-ever million-selling Japanese record in America. Needless to say, the song first topped the local charts and in doing so, sold 500,000 copies.

Sakamoto followed up his big hit with a further chart success in 1963 with 'China Nights', but it was to be his last international recording hit.

He returned to Japan . . . where today, he is still going strong as one of his country's leading television stars.

SAM AND DAVE
American. Male. Vocal/Duo.

It was their particular brand of tough, gutsy soul music which put Sam And Dave at the forefront of the Memphis Sound artists in the latter half of the '60s.

The duo – Sam Moore, who was born in Miami, Florida, on October 12, 1935, and Dave Prater (born in Ocilla, Georgia on May 9, 1937) – met as solo artists in Miami's King OF Hearts Club,

SAM AND DAVE — (l-r): Sam and Dave; the brotherly bond remains

in Sam's hometown in 1958. They teamed up professionally two years later, and signed for Roulette, later switching to Atlantic in 1965.

The following year they began recording on Stax, backed by writer/producers Isaac Hayes and David Porter. 'You Don't Know Like I Know' and 'Hold On I'm Coming', strong up-temp ballads, were released. But their first British chart hit came in 1967 with 'Soothe Me' followed by their enormously successful million-seller 'Soul Man'. The same year, they toured Britain and America and in 1968, an American college tour grossed nearly $2,000,000!

Their last big hit on Stax was 'I Thank You' and they later returned to Atlantic – when their former label was bought out – to make the classic 'Soul Sister Brown Sugar' in 1969 . . . which marked another year of outstanding world-wide success.

The duo split in 1970, to go their own separate ways, but reformed in 1971. Yet, their time was up – their brand of Soul was no longer so much in demand, and by the mid-'70s they had disappeared from the commercial limelight.

However, they have continued to perform together ever since, playing rock and soul clubs all over the States, and during 1980 they became a regular attraction on the Manhattan rock club circuit playing at such New York clubs as Tramps.

SAM THE SHAM AND THE PHAROAHS
American. Male. Vocal/Instrumental Group.
Original line-up: Sam The Sham (vocals); David Martin (bass); Ray Stinnet (guitar); Jerry Patterson (drums).

His real name was Domingo Samudio and he was born of Texan-Mexican stock in Dallas, Texas, in 1940.

But he's much better known as Sam The Sham, who fronted the legendary Pharoahs – an essentially fun group, which enjoyed considerable popularity in the mid-'60s.

Sam was a keen singer at school and sang with various local groups. But on graduation he joined the U.S. Navy, where he spent the next four

M.G.M. and released Sam's composition 'Wooly Bully', supposedly written about his cat! The song was a giant success, selling three million copies. Meanwhile, the group were working on their image, which by then consisted of their wearing brightly-colored arab clothes. They were riding the crest of the wave and their next single hit was another million seller, 'Li'l Red Riding Hood'.

1968, however, saw a change in their fortunes, when the 'fun' element went out of the group's music and their gimicky appeal faded . . . and they disbanded.

In the early '70s Sam tried to carve out a solo career as Sam Samudio without too much success, and today works in record production.

THE SANDPIPERS
American. Male. Vocal/Group.
Original line-up: Jim Brady; Richard Shoff; Michael Piano.

The last time The Sandpipers had a British chart hit was in 1976, with 'Hang On Sloopy', by which time the group had been together for over 16 years – although the three members had known each other since their boyhood when they were members of the acclaimed Mitchell Boys Choir, in Los Angeles.

However, all three had to leave the choir when their voices broke, but

years. After his discharge, he went to Arlington State College in Texas where he taught himself to play organ. He left to join a friend who had recently formed a band in Louisiana, and they played regularly in Memphis, enjoying outstanding local success. When eventually they disbanded, Sam and bassman David Martin were left to pick up the pieces. Out of the remnants emerged the idea for The Pharoahs, and co-oping guitarist Ray Stinnet and drummer Jerry Patterson (and later saxophonist Butch Gibson) they hit the road.

Sam, or rather Domingo as he was still called, hit on the 'Sham' idea from the r & b word 'shamming', which meant shuffling or hiving around to music.

In 1964 they were signed to Penn Records and released 'Haunted House'. A year later, they switched to

SAM THE SHAM AND THE PHAROAHS — led by Sam (seated) who has now swapped the turban for the PR man's hat

THE SANDPIPERS — still singing in eleven languages

they later formed a vocal trio, and initially called themselves The Grads.

For the next six years they worked hard, touring America, appearing on radio and television, and making singles, though without any marked success. Then in 1965, they joined the new A & M label and cut 'Everything In The Garden' while still calling themselves The Grads. Next followed the big break-through to success with 'Guantanamera'. And a brand new name.

Legend has it, that twenty minutes before the trio made the disc, a secretary at A & M suggested, speculatively, that they should call themselves The Sandpipers. The name stuck!

The catchily haunting song was an enormous success world-wide, and the threesome followed up with a string of top-selling singles including 'Quando M'Innamoro' (A Man Without Love) and the hugely popular religious song 'Kumbaya', which made the British charts in the Spring of 1969.

The trio who sing in eleven languages, are still very much in demand for live appearances all over the world – and are kept busy with concert and cabaret tours (which include sessions in Las Vegas, Lake Tahoe and Reno) . . . and major appearances on television. In 1978, they starred at The Talk Of The Town in London.

THE SEARCHERS
British. Male.
Vocal/Instrumental Group.
Original line-up: Tony Jackson (bass/vocals); Chris Curtis (drums/vocals); Mike Pender (guitar/vocals); John McNally (guitar/vocals).

One of the few remaining groups left over from the early 1960s, The Searchers are still going strong!

Formed in 1960 by John McNally originally as backing group to Johnny Sandon, they became the only other Liverpool group to present any serious challenge to the supremacy of The Beatles during those early days of Merseybeat. Indeed, like their Mersey rivals, they had their very own distinctive 'sound', which prompted the late Brian Epstein to openly state that he wished he had signed them to his rapidly increasing Nems stable. It was one of his only regrets in the business, because he admired and respected them so much.

The Searchers who took their name from the John Wayne movie of the same name, enjoyed their first hit single in the summer of 1963 with 'Sweets For My Sweet' which went to top the British Hit Parade, a feat their second single 'Sugar And Spice' just failed to emulate. However, it wasn't long before they returned to the pinnacle of the British charts with their third single release 'Needles And Pins', in 1964.

However, the success of the record brought a split in the ranks. Tony Jackson left the group after a disagreement over policy and was replaced by Frank Allen. But no matter . . . it certainly didn't affect The Searchers' popularity, for in June 1964 their fourth single – 'Don't Throw Your Love Away' – landed them with yet another Number 1. And the story continued for a further two years, during which time they sold more than 30,000,000 records!

Then, when the hits finally started to fall away, the group decided to concentrate on 'live' appearances and carried out a hectic schedule of engagements all over the world, embracing Britain, America, Europe and Australia. And the story has continued in similar vein ever since.

Indeed, the only change in line-up came at about the end of the '60s when Billy Adamson replaced Chris Curtis on drums.

The group signed a recording contract with the American label Sire at the end of 1979.

NEIL SEDAKA
American. Male.
Singer/Songwriter.

No one has to see the gold records and industry awards that line the walls of Neil Sedaka's home to know what his name means in the world of entertainment. Two decades of hitmaking, both as a performer and a composer, have made him an institution – one that guarantees sell-out concerts around the world, where audiences are just as wild for his spirited pop tunes as for his warm moving ballads. Whether it's by jogging an audience's memory with his hits of the 1960s or by bringing them up to date with his brand new compositions, Neil Sedaka is constantly reaffirming his enormous appeal.

Born in Brooklyn, on March 13, 1939, the son of a taxi driver Sedaka first began pleasing the public in New

NEIL SEDAKA — continuous touring has kept him in the public eye

York City at the age of eight as a piano prodigy, and a serious student of classical music, attending the prestigious Juilliard School. His songwriting career began at the age of thirteen with neighbor Howard Greenfield, who has remained a song-writing partner for more than 25 years. At first they wrote pop songs in the style of artistes like Johnnie Ray and Patti Page, but soon turned to rock 'n' roll and found their songs being recorded by many Atlantic Records recording artistes, produced by Jerry Wexler. At eighteen he became a full-fledged songwriter with his first major hit 'Stupid Cupid', for Connie Francis.

Sedaka's first years of singing stardom stretched from 1959 to 1963, when he sold more than 25 million copies of such records as 'Calender Girl', 'Carol', 'Stairway To Heaven', 'The Dairy', 'Breaking Up Is Hard To Do' and 'Happy Birthday Sweet Sixteen'. Then, with what Neil refers to as the "Beatle Invasion", he retired back to the piano and wrote hit songs for other performers such as Tom Jones, The Fifth Dimension and Andy Williams.

By the end of the '60s, at the suggestion of a friend, Neil took himself and his family to England. He performed a concert at London's Royal Albert Hall that combined his "oldies" with a crop of new material he had recently composed. The audience proved overwhelmingly receptive to the "new" Sedaka, and Neil's career once again took off with the speed of a skyrocket. He has consistently enjoyed succes in Britain ever since with such album releases as 'Solitaire', 'The Tra La Days Are Over', and 'Laughter And Tears', which achieved *platinum* status.

Neil returned to America in triumph, and re-established himself as an international sensation with the gold-rated 'Sedaka's Back', 'The Hungry Years', and 'Steppin' Out' as well as the Number 1 singles 'Laughter In The Rain' and 'Bad Blood'. One of Neil's songs, 'Love Will Keep Us Together' was the vehicle that propelled The Captain and Tennille into stardom. It was followed by 'Lonely Nights (Angel Face)', to which Neil wrote the music *and* lyrics, and another Captain and Tennille hit 'You Never Done It Like That'.

1976 was a particularly big year for

THE SEEKERS — (l-r): Athol Guy, Judy Durham, Keith Potger, Bruce Woodley

Sedaka. His strength as a composer was graphically documented when he was awarded no less than six awards from B.M.I. (a B.M.I. Award is granted when a song has been played over 400,000 times in one year on radio and television). Three of Neil's songs actually received over a million performances: 'Breaking Up Is Hard To Do', 'Love Will Keep Us Together' and 'Laughter In The Rain'. This was also the year of Sedaka's first television special for NBC, which not only had excellent ratings, but also earned praise from both music and television reviewers. He was acclaimed as an artiste representing every facet of the entertainment community.

Not a man to rest on his laurels, Neil continues to tour concert halls around the country an the rest of the world, where he is always introducing new material to the delight of all who see him perform. His performances in Vegas, Tahoe and Reno to SRO crowds only confirm that this stellar attraction remains an indefatigable performer on the road.

He toured Britain once more in the spring of 1981.

THE SEEKERS
Australian. Male.
Vocal/Instrumental Group.
Original line-up: Keith Potger (guitar); Bruce Woodley (guitar); Athol Guy (bass); Ken Ray (vocals).

The Seekers were formed in Melbourne, Australia, in 1962 as a *four-boy* group, singing in coffee bars and clubs in the evening, while holding down ordinary daytime jobs. They spent a year appearing in local engagements, before Ken Ray decided to call it a day and leave. And for a while, the boys continued as trio and later worked on a Pacific cruise liner, where besides performing in cabaret, they ran all the entertainment on board ship. However, on their return to Australia, they decided to augment their folk-influenced sound with the inclusion of a girl singer.

They chose Judith Durham, who had been making a name for herself, singing with various Melbourne jazz bands. And . . . for the following eighteen months, The Seekers continued to work all over Victoria as a semi-pro outfit. Hoever, by 1964, they were inunundated with work and regularly appeared on local radio and television. So, they decided to turn professional and set off in search of success in Britain. Yet prior to leaving Australia – working their passage to Britain on board a cruise liner – they had sent a demo tape and film clip of their act, to a top London theatrical agency. And on arrival in England, they found that the agency was *more* than interested in booking them. Their first major appearance in the country was on the top-rating television show 'Sunday Night At The London Palladium', on which they made so much impact, that they were signed immediately to a recording contract with EMI Records.

Their first single – 'I'll Never Find Another You' – topped the British Hit Parade at the beginning of 1965 and sold a million copies. It was hastily followed by a string of smash hits, which for the next three years, helped to establish The Seekers as one of the most successful attractions in show-business – *and* the first Australian group to succeed internationally. 'A World Of Our Own', 'The Carnival Is Over' – which topped the charts in the fall of 1965 – 'Someday One Day', 'Walk With Me', 'Morningtown Ride', 'Georgy Girl' (from the film of the same name, which reached Number 1 in America in 1966), 'When Will The Good Apples Fall' and 'Emerald City'. And they consolidated all their recording success with lengthy, sell-out tours all over the world. In 1967, they established a new Australian record for attracting crowds, when 2200,000 people turned up to see them appear at the Myer Music Bowl in Melbourne.

However, in the summer of 1968, riding an enormous wave of international success, The Seekers disbanded in a blaze of pulicity.

Said Keith Potger: "We had a pact that if anyone wanted to leave, they were to give six months notice, and Judith did just that. Any problems that might have been in the group were problems that had been there for six years."

After the split Athol Guy returned to Australia and made numerous appearances on radio and television, before forming his own marketing and promotions company. At the request of the Australian Government, he formed 'The Young Australians' for Expo '70 in Canada and later turned to politics. In December 1973, he stood for Parliament when the local member resigned, and was re-elected when he stood again in the election of 1974.

Bruce Woodley, too, returned home. "I found it difficult to resume a normal life," he said. "The fact that I'd been a Seeker was a hindrance rather than an asset. I started writing music for TV and radio commercials after a very hard battle to binto the market." However, once inside, he carved out a highly successful career for himself in this direction.

Keith Potger remained in Britain and formed The New Seekers and for a while appeared on stage with the group. He later took a backseat to handle the group's management and publishing activities, and also established himself as a successful record producer and songwriter.

Like Keith, Judith Durham, stayed in Britain . . . but returned to her jazz roots. She met, and married, pianist Ron Edgeworth and together they decided in 1972 to combine their immense talents to form the Hot Jazz Duo, which for a while was backed by their own mainstream jazz band, The Hottest Band In the Land. They have worked together ever since, appearing extensively in clubs and at festivals in Britain and America – including the celebrated St. Louis Jazz Festival and at Monterey. In 1980, they undertook lengthy seasons in Florida, New York, San Francisco and London.

The Seekers re-formed briefly in 1974 for concert and cabaret appearances in Australia and Britain, with original members Potger, Guy and Woodley, augmenting their sound with the delightful singing talents of Dutch-born Louisa Wisselling.

HELEN SHAPIRO
British. Female. Singer.

Helen Shapiro was a mere fourteen years-old and still attending Clapton Girls School in London, when she topped the British Hit Parade in the summer of 1961 with 'You Don't Know Me'. It was her second record release and the follow-up single to 'Don't Treat Me Like A Child', which reached Number 3, three months earlier.

She was born in London's East End on September 28, 1946, and was discovered singing at the Maurice Berman School of Singing at the beginning of 1961. She had been taking lessons for just a handful of weeks when record-producer John Schroeder – always on the look out for new talent – made a routine visit to the school, and heard Helen in the middle of a lesson. He was so impressed with her ability, and distinctive voice, that he arranged for a recording audition – and as a result, signed her to a contract. He also wrote her first single 'Don't Treat Me Like A Child'.

It was the start of a spectacular year of success. And at the end of 1961, having enjoyed her second Number 1 hit with 'Walking Back To Happiness', Helen Shapiro was voted Britain's Number One Female Singer of the Year. She retained the award in 1962, during which time she also enjoyed four more big hit singles – 'Tell Me What He Said', 'Let's Talk About Love', 'Little Miss Lonely' and 'Keep Away From Other Girls'. And for the next two years, she more than lived up to her reputation, touring the world and headlining concert and theater engagements. (On one such tour, she had The Beatles as her support group!) She also appeared extensively on television.

Helen had her last British hit in 1964 with 'Fever' which came at the height of Beatlemania . . . and then, for a while, she faded from public view. However, she continued to work extensively for the next fifteen years,

HELEN SHAPIRO — at the height of her success

126

and toured the world appearing in exclusive cabaret clubs and major hotels, entertaining international audiences with her unique and unmistakable voice.

Then, towards the end of the 1970s, Helen made a major career decision and veered much more towards stage musicals and productions. And in 1979 starred in London's West End at the Piccadilly Theatre in the musical 'The French Have A Song For It'. A year later, she starred as 'Nancy' at the Alberry Theatre in a revival of the hit musical 'Oliver'.

THE SHANGRI-LAS
American. Female. Vocal Group.
Original line-up: Betty Weiss; Mary Weiss; Mary-Ann Ganser; Margie Ganser.

Formed in the early 1960s at New York's Andrew Jackson High School in Queens, by two pairs of white sisters (the Ganser sisters were twins), The Shangri-Las were protegees of producer George 'Shadow' Morton, who guided their career to stardom. Indeed, it was Morton who produced all of their major hit singles, including the legendary 'Leader Of The Pack!'

However, when the group was first formed, they found great difficulty in achieving any kind of lasting success. Until 1964, they had recorded and released several singles, all of which failed miserably. It stayed that way until New York disc jockey Bob Lewis recognized their potential and recommended the group to Morton.

'Shadow' transformed them into one of the most dynamic groups of all time (their records still stand up today, a lasting tribute to Morton's skill as a producer. Indeed, in 1976 the group's 'Leader Of The Pack' was re-released in Britain and became another major hit). He used contrived recording gimmicks, over-dubbing sea gulls and breaking waves on their first single success 'Remember (Walking In The Sand)' and the sound of reverberating motor cycles on 'Leaer', and highlighted perfectly the emotional, shrill voice of Betty Weiss on lead vocals.

'Remember (Walking In The Sand)' issued on Leiber and Stoller's Red Bird label in the fall of 1966, reached

Number 5 in America and 14 in Britain. Their follow-up release 'Leader Of The Pack' topped the U.S. charts (reaching 11 in Britain) and sold over a million copies. And subsequent singles – 'I Can Never Go Home Anymore', 'Give Him A Great Big Kiss', 'Long Live Our Love' and 'Past, Present And Future' retained the chart momentum.

Yet by the end of 1966, the Red Bird label *and* the Shangri-Las folded, with the group going into total retirement. They did, however, re-form momentarily at the turn of the '70s for revival concerts – and in 1972 when 'Leader Of The Pack' hit the international charts again, rumors were rife about a relaunch, though nothing ever materialized. Four years later, when the same song reached the British Top Ten, more rumors abounded about a rapid return of the legendary quartet. But again, they proved groundless.

RAVI SHANKAR
Indian. Male. Instrumentalist.

Ravi Shankar hit the world's headlines in 1964 when he was virtually adopted by Beatle George Harrison as his spiritual mentor . . . and the man who taught him to play that traditional Indian instrument, the sitar.

"Even before I met George," he says, "I was playing in London folk clubs and people were listening to my

THE SHANGRILAS — *(above)*

RAVI SHANKAR — *(below)*

music and what I had to offer. Then suddenly, with the drug culture and hippies running rife, I was discovered".

Overnight he became a star.

Because of the Beatles' influence – they featured the sitar on many of their album tracks and singles, and introduced Indian music to the mass audience – Ravi Shankar gained fame and prestige. His music was taken up by Yehudi Menuhin and Andre Previn, and used on the sound track of the controversial tele-movie 'Alice In Wonderland'.

Born in Benares, India, in 1920, Shankar started his career as a classical musician and gained immense renown and respect among his contemporaries for his traditional approach to music. However, during the mid-1960s all that changed, and Ravi found himself regarded by the world almost as the 'Fifth' Beatle, when the foursome threw themselves into their very own mystical mystery tour of gurus, maharishis, flower power, and

transcendental meditation. And for several years afterwards, the Indian master musician thrived and gained a tremendous reputation. In 1967 he founded his Kinnera School of Music in Los Angeles. Then, after spending ten years in Britain and America preaching his own kind of gospel of Eastern culture, Ravi returned home, in 1973, to continue with his former career in classical music. His lifestyle changed greatly: his daily routine was now spent in meditation and music. Very little has changed.

However, he still ventures to the West on occasions to play concerts, though this time, playing purely traditional Indian classical music. In September 1980, he played a series of engagements in London to celebrate his sixtieth birthday.

DEL SHANNON
American. Male. Singer.

Del Shannon has been an innovator in the field of pop music since 1961 and his massive international chart-topper 'Runaway'. Far from being a mere "oldies act", his early records were solidly ahead of their time – and at any given time and at any given point his music has been thoroughly contemporary.

Del was born Charles Westover in Grand Rapids, Michigan on December 30, 1939 and raised in Coopersville. He became interested in music early. "In high school I used to get up in assemblies and sing Inkspots'

DEL SHANNON — *still recording with Island Records*

songs," he recalls. He served his musical apprenticeship in a small club in Battle Creek, Michigan, and began entertaining seriously in 7th Army's 'Get Up And Go Show', while serving in Germany. On demob, he set about playing local engagements. One day, improvising on the bandstand, he and his resident keyboard wizard, Max Crook, came up with 'Runaway'. A local DJ was enthused, and ultimately Big Top Records in New York allotted him an hour-and-a-half to record the tune.

Propelled by Del's dramatic delivery and the unusual musitron break in the middle of the song, 'Runaway' became a legendary Number 1 smash in early 1961. Hit after hit followed: 'Hats Off To Larry', 'So Long Baby', 'Hey Little Girl', 'Swiss Maid' – which was the first big writing break for an obscure Nashville composer named Roger Miller – and 'Cry Myself To Sleep', though not a huge hit, was probably the one single song that most greatly influenced Elton John's 'Crocodile Rock'. 'Little Town Flirt' and 'Two Kinds of Teardrops' continued the hit streak into 1963.

Del's records were equally big in England, and he toured overseas frequently. On one excursion he played with The Beatles, and decided to record their 'From Me To You', which he made a hit fully six months before America had even heard of the Fab

Four. In late '63 he formed his own label, Ber-Lee, making a couple of singles, and then in '64 he joined Amy Records.

During the full force of the 'British Invasion', when very few American artists were scoring hits consistently, Del proceeded to run up a highly impressive string. Jimmy Jones' 'Handy Man', transformed into a driving rocker, kicked off the winning run and was followed by 'Do You Wanna Dance' (months before the Beach Boys revived it), the monumental 'Keep Searchin'' and 'Stranger In Town' – brilliant, exciting, powerful records. He saw his composition 'I Go To Pieces' become a global hit for Peter and Gordon.

In early 1966 he switched labels to Liberty, working with Snuff Garrett, Leon Russell, the Stones' producer Andrew Loog Oldham, and other contemporary luminaries. He suffered a commercial decline, but made some excellent and rather underrated records, such as 'Show Me' and 'She'. He also recut 'Runaway' in late 1967, hitting the top of the charts in Australia; and had a sizeable regional hit in the States with a version of the Stones' 'Under My Thumb'.

In 1968 he released an ambitious self-composed album titled 'The Further Adventures of Charles Westover' (Del's real name); it sounded very contemporary and contained several striking cuts. Shortly afterwards, having enjoyed seven years of recording success and all conceivable honors, Del decided to try something fresh – producing. He saw a group in a local San Fernando Valley nightclub, rehearsed them and selected their material. Eventually they had a Top Ten smash in 1969, 'Baby It's You', as Smith on Dunhill.

Del himself made a couple of singles for Dunhill in '69, but his main interest was producing. His next project was with an old friend – another '60s hitmaker – Brian Hyland, who'd just signed with Uni Records. Del cut him on the old Impressions hit, 'Gypsy Woman', in 1970; and it became Hyland's biggest hit in the eight years, since 'Sealed With A Kiss'. In the producing line, Del has another longstanding desire – "I'd love to produce Waylon Jennings. He's something

else". Waylon has also recorded one of Del's songs, 'I've Got Eyes For You'.

Del Shannon has also emerged as a shrewd business man, investing his money well, particularly in California real estate In 1972 in one deal alone, he made more money from the transaction than he did in his ten most prolific years of singing.

Recently Del has been touring extensively "just for fun" all over the world, primarily in England where his audience is one of the most fiercely loyal anywhere. When he performs these days, he sings almost all of his hit records, explaining his philosophy this way: "When somebody hires me, they hire my name, my hits. Why not do the hits? It makes 'em happy".

But Del is also working on a variety

SANDIE SHAW — pictured soon after her Eurovision Song Contest victory

of contemporary projects as well, new material which arouses high hopes for the future in anyone who's heard any of it. Recently he got together with Jeff Lynne of the Electric Light Orchestra, who (in common with many musicians) had idolized Shannon for years, and attractive possibilities could arise from that projected alliance . . .

During 1980 and '81, he worked extensively in the Studio with Tom Petty, who produced a brand new Del Shannon LP.

SANDIE SHAW
British. Female. Singer.

Sandie Shaw is remembered as the slim, leggy, barefoot Cinderella. The Princess of Pop of London's 'Swinging' '60s.

She was born on February 26, 1947, the only child of Raymond and Rosina Goodrich and raised at their family home in Dagenham, Essex.

At school she was a bright though rebellious student, with a lively intellectual ability which her dreamy 'head in the clouds' nature stopped her from realizing in the usual academic qualifications of the day. Instead, she dreamed of the bright lights of London, and the rhythm and fashion of the pop music cult which had just started to grip the imagination of her teenage contemporaries.

Deciding to turn her dreams into reality she started singing at 15 with amateur groups around the local youth clubs and teenage dances. The word soon went round and after winning a local talent competition Sandie was asked to appear in a show in London with Adam Faith. In the capacity filled theater the audience enthusiastically responded to the first of her three songs. She was an instant success! It was such a shock to Sandie that she fled the stage, forgetting to sing her two other songs.

However, Adam Faith was so impressed with her singing, that he arranged for her to be represented by his manager Eve Taylor and she later auditioned for a recording contract wih Pye.

Her first single 'As Long As You're Happy Baby' released in 1964 did absolutely nothing. Her second release – 'There's Always Something There To Remind Me' (a cover version of the Dionne Warwick American hit) – topped the British Hit Parade followed by a further fifteen more chart singles including 'Girl Don't Come'; 'I'll Stop At Nothing'; 'Long Live Love' (her second Number 1, in 1965); 'Message Understod'; 'Tomorrow'; 'Nothing Comes Easy' and 'Monsieur Dupont'. And with such success, she was quite rightly acclaimed as Britain's leading female vocalist. She had a unique style and approach to singing.

Says Sandie: "In those days I felt I was the only person that really knew what was going on, so I interpreted my feelings of the times through my songs."

In 1967 she was chosen by BBC Television to represent her country in The Eurovision Song Contest – and singing 'Puppet On A String' – she landed the coveted first prize. The first time Britain had ever won the competition. 'Puppet On A String' went on to give her another chart-topping single and a million-selling song.

During this time Sandie made a huge impact on both television viewers and the TV industry with her innovating series called 'The Sandie Shaw Supplement', the style of which has become extensively imitated and absorbed by most TV musical presentations ever since.

In 1968, she married the celebrated fashion designer Jeff Banks and her career began to take a back seat to her family life. But in the Seventies, Sandie widened her extensive experience in recording, TV and stage performances, by taking on two major acting roles. She appeared in repertory theater in London playing the parts of Joan of Arc in Bernard Shaw's

THE SHIRELLES' — **Shirley Alston**

'St. Joan' and Ophelia in Shakespeare's 'Hamlet'.

In 1971 she had a daughter, Grace, an event which encouraged her to make fewer and fewer public appearances as the years drew into the eighties.

For the past few years Sandie has concentrated on developing her many and diverse interests, which she roughly names under the subject of 'Life', including philosophy, astrology, psychology, and fairy stories! She reads extensively and spends a lot of time in the countryside of Scotland and Ireland.

THE SHIRELLES
American. Female. Vocal Group.
Original line-up: Addie Harris; Shirley Alston; Doris Kenner; Beverley Lee.

Like the majority of Black r & b vocal groups of the 1950s, The Shirelles were formed at high school – in Passaic, New Jersey – where in 1957 they were discovered singing in a local talent contest and signed to a recording contract with Decca Records.

Taking their name from lead singer *Shirley* Alston, the group made their debut shortly afterwards with 'I Met Him On A Sunday', an later switched recording labels to the newly-formed Scepter Records (owned by the girls' manager Florence Greenberg). In 1959, they notched up their first million-selling single with 'Dedicated To The One I Love' which reached Number 3 in the U.S. chart. They followed it with two more million-sellers the next year – 'Tonight's The Night' and 'Will You Still Love Me Tomorrow', which gave them their first American chart-topper. Two years later, they topped the charts again with their fourth million-selling single 'Soldier Boy'.

During the height of their popularity – at the turn of the 1960s – the group influenced many of the young, up-and-coming groups of the day including The Beatles who admired their material so much, that they recorded two of their songs – 'Boys' and 'Baby It's You'.

The group continued to record until 1967 and enjoyed several minor successes before splitting up. Lead-singer Shirley Alston made a belated comeback to showbusiness in the latter days of 1970, though she didn't particularly set the charts on fire as a solo artist.

NINA SIMONE
American. Female.
Singer/Songwriter.

Nina Simone was born Eunice Waymon on February 21, 1933 in Tryon, North Carolina – one of eight children. At the age of five, she started playing piano and organ, and also sang in the church choir.

During her teens, Nina showed a tremendous potential for music, and on leaving High School, she had formal training at New York's celebrated Julliard School of Music. On graduation, however, she started to earn her living, playing and singing jazz in New Jersey and Philadelphia clubs.

In 1959, she was signed to Bethlehem Records and later released the million-selling single 'I Love You Porgy'. A year later, she changed record companies and joined Philips Records for whom she notched up her most famous singles 'Don't Let Me Be Misunderstood' and 'I Put A Spell On You'. Both songs were later covered, in turn by The Animals (see **The Animals**) and Alan Price.

Towards the end of'the 1960s, she

NINA SIMONE — increasing political commitment

became a leading member of the American Black Movement, and recorded several songs which became anthems of the Civil Rights Movement, though her music tended to be over indulgent and very bitter, including such songs as 'Backlash Blues' and 'Go To Hell'.

However, in 1968, she was back in the British and American charts with a classic from the hit rock musical 'Hair' – 'Ain't Got No – I Got Life'. She followed it up with a cover version of the Bee Gees' hit 'To Love Somebody'.

Nina Simone's career went into decline in the 1970s, her increasingly political involvement losing her many thousands of fans, and for a while, she even went into retirement. In 1979, she made a comeback with a European and British tour, which was fraught with problems.

THE SINGING NUN
(Soeur Sourire)
Belgian. Female. Singer.

Sister Luc-Gabrielle, better known as The Singing Nun, astounded the entire music world in 1963 when her recording (sung entirely in French) of a self-written song, 'Dominique', topped the American Hit Parade *and* sold over a million copies. Royalties from the single and accompanying album – 'The Singing Nun' – reached a massive $100,000 which was spent entirely on foreign missions by Sister Luc-Gabrielle's convent at Fichermont, near Brussels, Belgium.

The song was released on record almost by accident.

Sister Luc-Gabrille had been writing and singing songs to her own guitar accompaniment for many years, when in 1961 she started to entertain the young girls who studied at the convent. They were so impressed with the songs she wrote, that they asked her if there was any way she could record them for the girls to keep. So, spurred on by the girls' interest and enthusiasm, the Sister sought the advice of Philips Records in Brussels, who later agreed to a short non-commercial recording session. Sister Luc-Gabrielle and a chorus of nuns, then went into the studio and recorded over a dozen of the most popular compositions. The record company executives, were captivated

with their charm and simplicity, and decided to take a chance. They packaged the numbers into an album which was released under the title of 'Sister Smile' (Soeur Sourire). Their gamble paid off, handsomely. The album proved extremely popular in Europe, and as a result, was released in America shortly afterwards, where 'Dominique' was taken as a single. It enjoyed outstanding success!

Sadly – for the music world – however, the song proved to be the Sister's only record success.

Born Jeannie Deckers in Belgium in 1928, Sister Luc-Gabrielle left the convent in Fichermont in 1966 . . . and faded into obscurity.

SLADE
British. Male. Vocal/Instrumental Group.
Original line-up: Noddy Holder (guitar/vocals); Jim Lea (bass/violin); Dave Hill (guitar); Don Powell (drums).

Slade formed at the turn of the 1970s in the West Midlands city of Wolverhampton, as The 'N Betweens, before changing their name to Ambrose Slade and subsequently Slade shortly afterwards. However, it wasn't until they were discovered by former Animal Chas Chandler (see **The Animals**), that the group first hit the pop and rock headlines.

They were originally hailed as Britain's first skin-head group – a publicity campaign dreamed up to promote their single 'The Shape Of Things To Come'. Unfortunately, the idea misfired badly, the group's appearance horrified promoters who refused to book them because they feared the group would incite trouble and violence.

In 1971, though, they hit the British chart for the first time with a re-working of the Little Richard classic 'Get Down And Get With It'. Slade were on their way . . . to success. Next followed a stream of hits – which all set a precedent in recording circles for their excitement and vibrance . . . and the appalling grammar and spelling of the titles. Still, it was a nice touch and unique to the band – 'Coz I

SLADE — (l-r): Noddy Holder, Jim Lea, Dave Hill, Don Powell

Luv You' (a British chart-topper in 1971); 'Look Wot You Dun', 'Take Me Bak 'Ome' and 'Mama Weer All Crazee Now' (which both topped the charts in 1972); 'Gudbuy T'Jane' (1972), 'Cum On Feel The Noize', 'Skweeze Me Pleeze Me' (which both reached the Number 1 position in 1973); 'My Frend Stan', 'Merry Xmas Everybody' (their final Number 1 success in 1973); 'Everyday', 'Bangin' Man', 'Far Far Away' and 'Thanks For The Memory'.

Slade were a 'live' group in every sense of the word, and caused unrivalled scenes of 'support' at their sell-out concerts, working their audiences up into a frenzy.

In 1973, drummer Don Powell was seriously injured in a car crash – which killed his fiancee – and spent several months recovering. The group was never quite the same again.

During the halcyon days of their hit singles, Slade toured regularly and established themselves in no uncertain terms in America. But a disastrous (at the box-office) movie debut in 'Flame' left their career floundering. And by 1975, all their early American success had waned.

They left Britain shortly afterwards and made their home in New York, from where they hoped to re-establish themselves in America. The move proved to be unsuccessful, and the group returned to Britain in 1979 to find some success touring the domestic cabaret circuit.

They made a remarkable comeback to the British Charts in 1981 with a Top Ten single, 'We'll Bring The House Down'.

PERCY SLEDGE
American. Male. Singer.

Audiences can be fickle, and perhaps no one knows more so than Percy Sledge.

Born in Muscle Shoals, Alabama, in 1941, he recorded some of the classiest soul songs of the 1960s and built an enormous reputation. But, during the following decade, he found himself out in the cold!

He started singing at fifteen at school, and on leaving high school became a male nurse at Colbert County Hospital. He spent much of his spare time singing in The Gallilee

PERCY SLEDGE — fortune revived in a 1980 New York show

Baptist Church choir. At about the same time, he joined The Esquires Combo, and not long afterwards auditioned for Quin Ivy, the former disc jockey, who decided to record him in a small session studio in Sheffield. The resulting demo tape was heard by executives of Atlantic Records who signed him up.

His soulful tenor voice was just the right medium for such songs as 'It Tears Me Up', 'Dark End Of The Street', 'I Had A Talk With My Woman' and 'Take Time To Know Her', all substantial American hits. But his biggest success on both sides of the Atlantic was the million selling – 'When A Man Loves A Woman', in 1966, which elevated him to international stardom.

The end of the '60s saw the curtailment of his fortunes, but he didn't retire, re-emerging four years later with 'I'll Be Your Everything'. He disappeared promptly from the charts thereafter, but has continued to find a ready market in cabaret and the American supper club circuit.

In December 1980, he starred in a successful soul package show – with Carla Thomas and Clarence Carter – which appeared at New York's Ritz Theater.

HURRICANE SMITH
British. Male. Singer.

Greeted at the time as "the oldest singer in the business", Norman 'Hurricane' Smith first hit the British charts on June 12, 1971, with 'Don't Let It Die'

. . . at the tender age of 49.

And his gritty voice produced two subsequent hits with 'Oh Babe, What Would You Say?' the following April, and 'Who Was It?' in September, 1972.

He hit on the 'Hurricane' idea as a result of seeing the 1952 Yvonne de Carlo film, 'Hurricane Smith'. The idea was nurtured for twenty years.

Before his own recorded hits, Hurricane – who was married with two grown up children – had been working in the record industry, for EMI, producing for numerous artistes including Pink Floyd and The Pretty Things. And during the early 1960s, he worked with George Martin on many of The Beatles' tracks. However, prior to his days at EMI, he had earned a steady living as a jazz trumpeter.

But then, having made a substantial

amount of money from his three hit singles – and one successful LP – the moustached, gravel-voiced crooner decided to retire.

He now breeds racehorses in Surrey, England.

SONNY AND CHER
American. Male/Female. Vocal Duo.

Husband and wife teams haven't been that successful in popular music, though there have been many. Things tend to start well, with a hit single or album, but inevitably they disintegrate when that initial success cannot be followed. It has been the same old story, time and time again.

However, there is always one

SONNY AND CHER — *have finally split after many tribulations*

exception, and in this case it was Sonny and Cher. Yet, even *their* partnership was doomed ... because there is always an inevitability that one partner will gain more acclaim than the other. It was to be the half-Cherokee Indian, half-Armenian, Cher who would outshine Sonny!

Still, for a time, the partnership did work ... and it worked extremely well.

Sonny – born Salvatore Bono on February 16, 1935 in Detroit – started his career in showbusiness in 1951 as a part-time, would-be songwriter. However, his writing certainly *didn't* pay the rent to support his wife and young daughter, so he spent much of his time working at whatever jobs came along, which included truck-driving and working as a waiter and masseur. In his spare time, though, he hawked his songs around the Hollywood record companies, and also touted his talents as a singer. His marriage could never hope to survive on such an unstable base – and by the time he landed a job as a trainee record producer at Speciality Records, it had ended in divorce.

In 1963, Sonny – and Jack Nitzsche – co-wrote a song that was destined to enjoy magnificent international success for The Searchers (see **The Searchers**) – 'Needles And Pins'. The same year, he started working as Phil Spector's (see **Phil Spector**) assistant at Philles Records, where he met his future wife – Cher (born Cherilyn Sakisian La Pier on May 20, 1946 in El Centro, California) who was employed at the studios as a session singer.

The following year, the couple married in Tijuana, Mexico, and Sonny hoped that Spector would eventually produce Cher as a solo artist. But at first, she was only used as a back-up singer. However, she *was* featured on The Crystals' (see **The Crystals**) big hit 'Da Doo Ron Ron'. When Darlene Love failed to turn up for the session – Cher stepped in.

By now, the couple had developed their own double act and were working extensively in nightclubs, under the name of Cleo and Caesar. Then in

1965, they reverted back to their real names to record the song 'I Got You Babe' for Atco Records. It topped the charts on both sides of the Atlantic within weeks of its release, and sold over a million copies. It was the first of a battery of best-sellers between 1965 and 1971 which boosted their fame – *and* their joint annual income to over $2,000,000.

Sonny and Cher were a revelation to the pop industry. Their music was fresh and original – their dress and appearance, often bizarre: long flowing hair, exotic and flamboyant clothes often made out of shaggy sheepskins.

They followed up their first hit with several more – 'Baby Don't Go', 'But You're Mine', 'What Now My Love', 'Little Man', 'The Beat Goes On', and 'All I Ever Need Is You'. And at the same time, both Sonny and his wife clocked up hits in their own right as solo artistes with 'Laugh At Me' (Sonny); 'All I Really Need Is You', 'Bang Bang', 'I Feel Something In The Air', 'Sunny' and 'Gypsies Tramps And Thieves' (Cher). In 1966 they made their film debut together in 'Good Times', followed three years later by their second movie 'Chastity' (named after their daughter).

A year later, Sonny and Cher turned to the bright lights of Las Vegas and cabaret – and they also started what was to become a long-running and highly successful TV career, headlining their own top rating series 'The Sonny And Cher Show'.

Then in 1974, as Cher began to take the limelight away from her husband, following further million-selling solo hits 'Half Breed' and 'Dark Lady', the partnership, that nearly ten years earlier had seemed idyllic, fell apart, culminating in a bitter divorce.

Sonny returned to a successful career in record production, while Cher went from strength to strength, emerging as one of Hollywood's many personalities. She later married Greg Allman (of The Allman Brothers) and within 9 days filed for divorce! However, they eventually got their marriage together sufficiently to produce their son Elijah Blue in 1976. Cher later toured America and Britain with her husband but their concerts were received with moderate acclaim. In

135

1979 she released her first single – 'Take Me Home' – on the Casablanca label.

Since splitting from Sonny, Cher has modelled for Vogue and starred in her own TV shows.

Today, though, she is a member of America's personality set, on "the celebrity circuit" as Greg Allman called it. *And* the gossip columnists delight . . .

Cher's stormy marriage to Greg Allman ended in divorce in 1979, and the same year, the rock star married Julie Bindas.

PHIL SPECTOR
American. Male. Producer.

It was to become known as "Wall of sound technique", as blanket, full production, crammed with clever over dubbing and mixing . . . and containing a fullness and broad range of effects. It was *the Phil Spector Sound*!

Phil Harvey Spector was born in New York on Boxing Day, 1940, but moved to Los Angeles in 1953, after the death of his father. At 18 he wrote

PHIL SPECTOR — *still the classic entrepreneur*

'To Know Him Is To Love Him', which, so the story goes, was the inscription on his father's headstone. The song was a million-seller and a huge hit on both sides of the Atlantic for The Teddy Bears, a group that actually included Spector, with Marshall Lieb and Annette Bard. He lost out badly on the whole thing, however, and decided to finish his education. Lack of cash forced him to earn a living. So he became a court reporter, before heading back to New York to become an interpreter. He had, however, already met producers Lester Sills and Lee Hazelwood, and back in New York he soon found himself very much involved in the music business again, working with Leiber and Stoller, and penning – with Stoller – 'Spanish Harlem', a big '60s hit.

After a spell with Atlantic records, Spector, became an independent producer, and his first hit in that capacity was with Roy Peterson's

'Corinna, Corinna', at the end of 1960.

Phil, however, was tiring of the pressures of New York, and returned to the West Coast, where a year later, he had a Top Five hit on Sills' Gregmark label with 'I Love How You Love Me', recorded by The Paris Sisters. Two more big hits followed – Curtis Lee's 'Pretty Little Angel Eyes' and Gene Pitney's 'Every Breath I take' – before Spector and Sills formed their own label, Philles (an amalgam of their names) which was distributed from Philadelphia.

The label's first success was with a group Spector had encountered in New York – The Crystals (see **The Crystals**). The record was 'There's No Other', which demonstrated the rapidly developing Spector sound.

The following year Spector bought his partner out of the record label, and took total control. Still only 21, he was by now a millionaire.

The Crystals then recorded the classic 'He's A Rebel', followed by million-sellers 'Da Doo Ron Ron' and 'Then He Kissed Me'.

Meanwhile, Spector had also signed up another new all-girl act, The Ronettes (see **The Ronettes**), who's first release, 'Be My Baby', sold a million. More successes followed with 'Baby I Love You', 'The Best Part Of Breakin' Up' and 'Do I Love You'. The signing was made yet more significant because Spector was later to marry one of the group – Veronica 'Ronnie' Bennett.

The hits followed on with few problems. One, notably The Righteous Brothers' (see **The Righteous Brothers**) 'You've Lost That Loving Feeling' in 1964, has on more than one occasion been called the ultimate pop record.

There were few hitches with the exception of the 1963 'Phil Spector Christmas Album' – a massive project employing all the Philles artists performing traditional festive songs against the accompanying Spector production job. It was a gigantic labor of love, but was released on the day President John Kennedy was assassinated. The result was that the American public were in no mood for the Spector Christmas Sound, and it was initially a flop. It has since been re-released, and enjoyed the success it deserves.

But even then there was an indication that the American music industry was tiring of the Spector talent. Not because he was *not* innovative enough. In fact, just the opposite. His records showed polish and sophistication few other labels or producers could match. The fall had to come though, and it did so spectacularly with Ike and Tina Turner's 'River Deep, Mountain High'. The song was a success only in Britain. In America it managed to be blackballed by the music industry, and as a result Spector, 'the wizz-kid', opted for virtual retirement. For the rest of the '60s, apart from an appearance in the movie 'Easy Rider,' Spector remained out of the limelight.

In the '70s, however, he re-emerged, refreshed and raring to go . . . to work with John Lennon, Cher (see **Sonny And Cher**), George Harrison (see **George Harrison**), and Dion (see **Dion**), on several spectacular record projects. He also financed Bruce Lee's last movie, 'Enter The Dragon'.

Yet despite his numerous achievements, Spector remains an enigmatic figure.

In 1975, he survived two near-fatal car crashes – and became very much a recluse, loathing to talk about his work or appear publicly.

By the '80s he had become something of a figure of the past, albeit a cult figure. Nonetheless, his contribution to popular music had been immeasurable.

Although, *genius* is a word overused, in the case of Phil Spector, it genuinely applies. He did emerge from almost total seclusion in 1981 to record a new LP with Bette Midler at Hollywood's Gold Star Studios.

SPENCER DAVIS GROUP
British. Male. Vocal/Instrumental Group.

Original line-up: Spencer Davis (guitar); Muff Winwood (bass); Steve Winwood (guitar/keyboards); Pete York (drums).

The Spencer Davis Group was formed in Birmingham in 1963 as The Spencer Davis Quartet, and they spent much of their early life together playing r & b in Midlands pub. Indeed, they landed a residency at the Golden

SPENCER DAVIS GROUP — (l-r): Steve Winwood, Pete York, Muff Winwood, Spencer Davis

Eagle in Birmingham.

The group had come together from local jazz groups. Davis, a former lecturer at Birmingham University, played Leadbelly blues with various jazz bands, while the Winwood Brothers had been former members of a mainstream jazz band, which Muff fronted. Pete York's pedigree was in big band jazz.

In 1964, they were discovered by producer Chris Blackwell who signed them to Fontana Records, for whom they had a series of non-successful singles and albums released over the following eighteen months, although 'I Can't Stand It', 'Strong Love' and 'Every Little Bit Hurts' were minor British hits. Then in 1965, they recorded the Jackie Wilson song 'Keep On Running' and helped by Stevie Winwood's distinctive voice, the record went to the top of the British Hit Parade, hastily followed by 'Somebody Help Me' (their second Number 1, in 1966); 'Gimme Some Loving' (their first American Top Ten hit); and 'I'm A Man'.

In 1967 however, Steve Winwood (see **Steve Winwood**) left the group to form Traffic – and later launched the ill-fated supergroup Blind Faith, (before returning to again re-form Traffic). His brother Muff followed suit and joined Chris Blackwell at Island

Records, for whom he later became an executive. Today Muff is head of A & R (UK) for Epic Records.

The group, meanwhile, was unsuccessfully reshaped with Eddie Hardin on keyboards and augmented with Phil Sawyer on guitar and Charlie McCracken on bass. It was the first of many re-formed line-ups. Eddie Hardin and Pete York later launched out on their own career as the duo Hardin – York, and The Spencer Davis Group disintegrated, for the time being at least, when Phil Sawyer decided to leave. But undeterred Davis continued, bringing Nigel Olsson and Dee Murray. But the new line-up's lifetime was limited.

In 1969, Spencer Davis disbanded the group and moved to California where he teamed up with Alun Davies and Peter Jameson, and worked as an acoustic trio. They later worked with Fred McDowell. Then in 1973, he met Eddie Hardin in Los Angeles and together they re-formed The Spencer Davis Group (Mark Four) for just a handful of months which included tours of Britain and America.

. . . But that was it.

Today, Spencer Davis is a record executive, working on America's West Coast.

DUSTY SPRINGFIELD
British. Female. Singer.

Hailed by many as the "best female singer Britain has ever produced", Dusty Springfield was born Mary

DUSTY SPRINGFIELD — *unsuccessful comback in 1980*

O'Brien in Hampstead, London, on April 16, 1939. Convent educated, she left school to work in a record store.

In her spare time, Dusty appeared with her brother Tom in a Latin American music combo, and later joined a trio of girl singers called the Lana Sisters. However, it wasn't long before she teamed up with her brother once more and, with Tim Field, they formed the folk-orientated Springfields. Their first single, 'Dear John', was released in 1961. Tim Field was later replaced by Mike Hurst, and for the next two years, the trio regularly appeared in the British best-seller charts with such hits as 'Breakaway', 'Island Of Dreams', 'Say I Won't Be There' and 'Come On Home'. They also achieved success in America with their single 'Silver Threads And Golden Needles', which was recorded in Nashville, and later made the U.S. Top Twenty.

In 1963, Dusty left the group to go solo – her brother Tom went into composing, arranging and record production and Mike Hurst, too, went into production and later produced for Cat Stevens – and she scored with her first single 'I Only Want To Be With You'. It was followed by numerous hits, including 'I Just Don't Know What To Do With Myself' (1964), 'In The Middle Of Nowhere' (1965), 'Some Of Your Lovin'' (1965), 'You Don't Have To Say You Love Me' (her only British Number 1, in 1966), 'Going Back' (1966) and 'Son Of A Preacher

Man' (1968). By now she was acclaimed one of the world's leading (white) soul singers.

During the latter days of 1968, her stranglehold on the international Hit Parades relaxed somewhat, as her career became dominated more and more by problems in her personal life. Sadly, Dusty went into a decline. Yet she was still able to record the classic album 'Dusty In Memphis', generally regarded as her finest LP.

The 1970s saw Dusty Springfield living in almost semi-retirement in America, though she would sometimes resurface to add her own distinctive vocal backings on songs that were to become American hits. She toured Britain in 1972 without much success. There was even talk of Elton John revitalizing her career, though nothing ever materialized. Dusty then returned to her own self-imposed exile.

1979 saw her back in Britain for a series of engagements which were fraught with problems and difficulties . . . and the comeback tour, which was heralded in a blaze of publicity, whimpered into oblivion.

ALVIN STARDUST
British. Male. Singer.

Alvin Stardust was born Bernard Jewry in Muswell Hill, London, on September 27, 1944, and at the age of two, moved with his family to Mansfield, where his mother bought a boarding house.

"Mum used to take in the acts appearing at the local Mansfield Palace Theatre," he says. "Music Hall was still thriving in Britain at that time, and we were never short of guests." And because of these showbusiness connections, Alvin made his professional stage debut at the age of four . . . at the Mansfield Palace Theatre in the pantomime 'Babes In The Wood.'

When he was twelve he fronted his first rhythm group singing and playing guitar. And during his teens, he became road manager for a local Nottingham group called Johnny Theakston and The Tremeloes who were building their reputation in the Midlands. A tape of the group had been sent to the BBC and the 'Beeb' in turn had decided to audition the group for possible inclusion on their weekly

series 'Saturday Club'. For the purpose of the tape, the group had changed the name to the more rock orientated . . . Shane Fenton and The Fentones.

Then tragedy struck. Johnny, who had been seriously ill as a child, was suddenly taken ill again and rushed to hospital where he died two days later.

"That was the end as far as we were concerned," adds Alvin. "We cancelled all our engagements, and virtually decided to split the group up. There seemed no point in continuing. But it was Johnny's mother who finally persuaded us to stay together and go through with the BBC audition. She told us that Johnny would have wanted us to continue . . . with *me* on lead vocals."

Shane Fenton and The Fentones were on their way to a rapid rise to stardom. After becoming one of the regular guest groups on 'Saturday Club', they landed a recording contract with EMI and their first single 'I'm A Moody Guy', written specially for the group by Jerry Lorden, and coupled with 'Five Foot Two, Eyes Of Blue', stormed into the British charts to land a double-sided hit in 1961. Next followed several more hits including 'Walk Away', 'It's All Over Now' and 'Cindy's Birthday'.

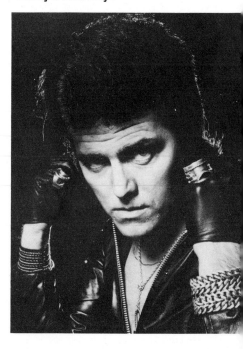

ALVIN STARDUST — *concentrating nowadays on the theatre*

In 1965 at the height of his success, Alvin quit the group and went into management/agency work, handling such artistes as The Hollies and Lulu.

"Then I gave it all up – and went off round the world," he adds. "But when the money ran out, I came back home, re-formed The Fentones and set out playing authentic rock 'n' roll in the British cabaret clubs."

He worked steadily, and after gaining a fair amount of success met record producer/songwriter Peter Shelley in London.

"Peter was in the process of forming a new recording company," adds Alvin. "And he asked me how *I* was fixed recording wise. When I told him I had no contract whatsoever, he invited me into the studios to lay down a few tracks ... and suggested I signed a contract with Magnet Records. I was the first artist to sign with the company.

"Anyway, we went into the studios hoping to record something for possible release as a single, and put down several tracks. Actually, things worked out so well, that we were going to release more than one single at the same time. Naturally, we couldn't issue them all from Shane Fenton, so we decided to make up a few appropriate names to carry on the record labels. One of the names we hit upon was *Alvin Stardust*.

"However, none of the records was released, for two weeks later, Peter came up with a song called 'My Coo Ca Choo' which subsequently went out on the market as Alvin Stardust's debut disc."

The song was an immediate hit, crashing into the British Top Ten from nowhere with very little pre-publicity to help it on its way. And almost overnight, Alvin Stardust had emerged as one of Britain's brightest stars ... and the career of Shane Fenton had turned almost full circle.

His success was consolidated a few months later when his second release 'Jealous Mind' went to the very top of the British Hit Parade ... followed by 'You You You', 'Red Dress', 'Tell Me Why', 'Sweet Cheatin' Rita' and 'Move It' which were all substantial hits in Britain and abroad.

However, when the hits finally came to an end, Alvin returned to domestic cabaret to trade his wares – though for four years from 1975, he built up a massive following on the British University-campus-circuit.

At the beginning of 1979, Alvin starred in a series of concerts called 'Oh Boy!', devised and produced by Jack Good, at London's Astoria Theatre, and he later starred in two television versions of the show. And a further series – 'Let's Rock' – made entirely for the American TV market, and screened during late 1980, early 1981.

Yet, for the 1979/80 Christmas season, Alvin starred as 'Robinson Crusoe' in the pantomime of the same name at The Palace Theatre, Plymouth and in the fall of 1980, he made his straight acting debut, playing 'Walter' in the Trevor Baxter play 'His Life And Times' in London's fringe theater.

EDWIN STARR
American. Male. Singer.

Edwin Starr was born Charles Hatcher on January 21, 1942 in Nashville, Tennessee. He was educated in Cleveland where at fourteen, he formed his first band – and on the nationally syndicated television prog-

ram 'The Uncle Jake Show', he won a week-long engagement as co-star with the legendary Billie Holliday.

On graduation from High School, he enlisted in the Army and was posted overseas to Europe where he formed another group and – in his spare time – set about entertaining in clubs.

Back home in America, he joined the Bill Doggett Combo, and later formed another group. And shortly afterwards, he was signed to the Ric Tic Records label in Detroit. His first single 'Agent Double O Soul' in 1965 established him immediately, when it crashed into the American Top Thirty, followed by 'Headline News' and 'S.O.S. – Stop Her On Sight' which became his first hit in Britain.

During the latter days of the 1960s, Starr's career went into decline in America and he turned to the lucrative pastures of the European and British markets, where he emerged as a headline star. Today, he readily admits that these markets sustained him during the lean years.

Edwin crashed back to success, however, in 1969 with '25 Miles' on the Tamla Motown label, followed in 1970 by the million-selling U.S. chart topper 'War (What Is It Good For)?'

Edwin Starr's strength has always been his ability to sit back and take stock of his career, to listen to advice and diversify his talents to take in new avenues of showbusiness. And during the 1970s when the hits had deserted him, he turned his hand at producing and writing – and he penned several movie scores.

Today, he spends most of his time writing and recording, but he still continues to perform as a soul and r & b artist of immense talent, turning his hand to a more disco-orientated market.

In the spring of 1980, he toured Britain and Europe with Marvin Gaye.

KAY STARR
American. Female. Singer.

Kay Starr was born Katherine Starks on July 21, 1922 on an Indian reservation in Dougherty, Oklahoma, and at the age of fourteen, moved with her family to Dallas, Texas.

At the age of thirteen, however, she sang on the local WRR radio station for 15 dollars a week – and later, when the family moved again – this time to Memphis, Tennessee – fifteen-year-old Katherine changed her name to Kay Starr and sang with the famous violinist Joe Venuti And His Band, as well as singing on Radio WREC with the studio orchestra.

When she left high school – now a seasoned showbiz trouper, she turned professional with Venuti's band and toured America. On one such engagement, she was heard by Glen Miller who arranged a recording audition for her with Victor Records.

Next step . . . and Kay joined Bob Crosby's Orchestra and went to New York to appear on his famous Camel Caravan Show.

At the age of twenty-one, she joined Charlie Barnet's Band with whom she appeared for the following two years, touring and even making movies. She soon established herself as a major attraction with the band. But then, on the verge of stardom, she was stricken by throat trouble and ordered *not* to sing for at least a year. It was a shattering blow to her budding career and many thought she would never recover.

She returned to showbusiness in 1945, however, after seriously thinking about a permanent retirement from performing, and set about re-establishing her name as a solo performer, signing a recording contract with Capitol Records. Her first hit was 'The Loneliest Girl In The World' which enabled her to headline numerous major American concert tours. She also appeared extensively on radio with Bing Crosby.

In 1952, now well entrenched as a major recording star and one of America's leading female vocalists, Kay enjoyed a million-selling single success with 'Wheel Of Fortune', which topped the U.S. chart for nine weeks. She followed up with an outstanding line-up of hit singles including 'Comes A-Long A-Love' – a British chart-topper in 1952; 'Side By Side' (1953); 'Changing Partners', 'Am I A Toy Or A Treasure?' (1954); 'Frankie And Johnny' and 'Stormy Weather' (1955).

She also turned her attentions towards cabaret and was a regular bill-topper in Las Vegas, Nevada.

In 1956, she recorded the classic song 'Rock 'N' Roll Waltz', which topped charts on both sides of the Atlantic, selling over a million copies.

From such a springboard, Kay turned to television and starred in her own American TV series – *and* often deserted her singing to appear in dramatic roles, during the latter days of the 1950s.

Then in 1960, she took a major career decision and decided to limit her live appearances and to go into semi-retirement. And since then her performances have been very few and far between.

Today, Kay Starr has been good to her word. She lives with her husband – she's been married six times – in Hollywood, California and only sings "when I want to."

RINGO STARR
British. Male. Singer.

By comparison with the careers of John Lennon, George Harrison (see **George Harrison**) and Paul McCartney since The Beatles split in 1969, Ringo Starr's career looks positively light-weight. There has been much emphasis on good ole rock 'n' roll, most notably in the 1971 smash hit 'It Don't Come Easy', followed by 'Back Off Boogaloo', 'Photograph' and 'You're Sixteen'. In addition, there have been several LP's that have all enjoyed success, particularly 'Ringo' (Apple), in 1973.

But the ex-Beatle drummer – born Richard Starkey in Dingle, Liverpool, on July 7, 1940 – felt that one particular direction he wanted to explore was movies, having had a cameo part in the 1968 movie, 'Candy', and a more substantial part in Peter Sellers' 'The Magic Christian' in 1970, apart that is from the three Beatles films.

With 'That'll Be The Day', in 1973, starring opposite David Essex, he gained particular success, although critics later accused him of over-reaching himself with his direction of 'Born To Boogie', a film documentary about rock star Marc Bolan (see **Marc Bolan**).

But through his movies – or more precisely – his latest film, 'Caveman', he met the new love in his life, beautiful 33-year-old actress Barbara Bach. The couple plan to wed when her divorce is finalized from her Italian industrialist husband. Ringo, whose beard is now flecked with grey, is divorced from his first wife – his childhood sweetheart, Maureen. Since the break-up of their marriage, his life has become of no mean interest to gossip columnists all over the

RINGO STARR — finding ways to spend his money

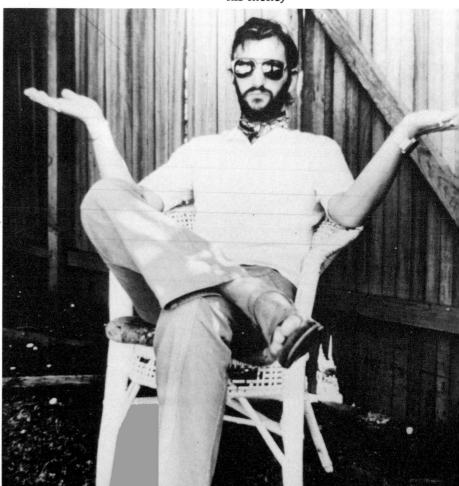

world, who have linked his name with a succession of attractive women, including petite blonde singer Lynsey de Paul, and actress Nancy Andrews.

The former Beatles' funnyman – his taciturn humor was an essential element of the group – continues to divide his time between homes on both sides of the Atlantic, since the emphasis of his popularity has long been embedded in the States. He also continues to co-own a furniture design business.

But as he says: "I've got to make it on my own talent now, not the memory of who I used to be."

STEPPENWOLF
American. Male.
Vocal/Instrumental Group.

Original line-up: John Kay (guitar/vocals); Jerry Edmonton (drums); Goldy McJohn (keyboards); Michael Monarch (guitar); Rushton Moreue (bass).

Steppenwolf came to prominence in 1969 when their recording of 'Born To Be Wild' was featured extensively in the smash box-office movie 'Easy Rider'. The song went on to become an anthem for the rapidly emerging heavy metal rock brigade. Needless to say, with the outstanding exposure from 'Easy Rider', it was a big hit both in Britain and America.

The group had been formed in 1967 by John Kay, from members of the Canadian blues band Sparrow, and although they performed heavy rock, Steppenwolf (who took their name from a novel by Hermann Hesse) still managed to retain elements of their blues roots. After 'Born To Be Wild', they enjoyed several more American hit singles: 'The Pusher', 'Magic Carpet Ride' and 'Rock Me'. They also clocked up eight U.S. Gold albums!

They split in 1972 after a series of line-up changes, with Kay going solo (he later made two successful solo albums). Edmonton and McJohn formed their own group Manbeast. Yet two years later, they re-formed for a series of concerts, before going their own separate ways once again.

In the fall of 1980, John Kay decided to re-form the group for the second time, after massive publicity in America exposed several bogus groups who had been exploiting the

STEPPENWOLF — inspired by novelist Hermann Hesse

name Steppenwolf.

He explained the situation to a London journalist: "Various people who had been fired from the band over the years and were unable to make ends meet on their own talents, thought it was a good idea to use the name Steppenwolf – at one time there were *three* Steppenwolfs touring the States at once – all cashing in on our success. So, I decided to re-form the original band to put them out of business once and for all."

CAT STEVENS
British. Male. Singer/Songwriter.

Cat Stevens was born Steven Georgiou, the son of a Greek restauranteur, in London, on July 21, 1947, and initially achieved fame as a clean-cut teen-idol when his debut single, 'I Love My Dog', went into the charts in October 1966. It was to foreshadow a career that, at one time, made Stevens one of Britain's most popular entertainers.

The origins of Cat's music were two-fold. The popular songs he was hearing in his teens, and the Greek folk tunes he grew up with. Indeed, later in his career, Greek instruments were evident on a number of his recordings.

Between 1966 and 1968 he had a string of hits including 'Matthew And Son', 'I'm Gonna Get Me A Gun', and 'A Bad Night', Yet towards the end of this period, his health failed him, due to overwork and physical neglect. In a

state of collapse, suffering from T.B., he spent three months in a sanitorium, where he had sufficient time to re-evaluate his work, the direction of which had been worrying him.

When he returned he was determined that he wanted an alternative to the commercial pressures of the big-business side of the music world, and during 1969 and 1970 he lived on profits made earlier – and devoted himself to writing songs of considerable personal significance.

There emerged a string of hugely successful albums, admired both in England and America. 'Tea For The Tillerman', 'Teaser And The Firecat' and 'Catch Bull At Four' and several hit singles – 'Lady D'Arbanville', 'Moon Shadow', Morning Has Broken', and 'Can't Keep It In' – ensured him a place

CAT STEVENS — a devout Muslem, he lives in seclusion

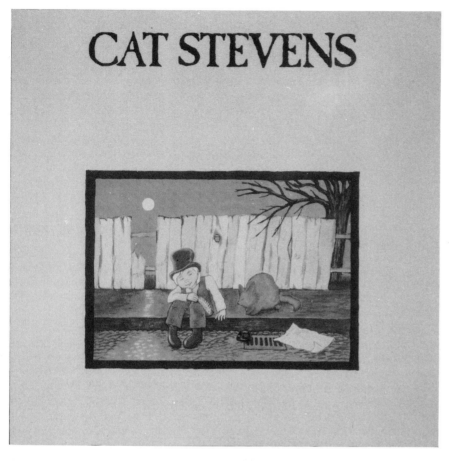

CAT STEVENS — 1972 album

of admiration on the highest echelons of popular music. His last chart single 'The Old School Yard', came in 1977.

However, by this time he was again subjecting his lifestyle to the closest scrutiny. Stevens became a Moslem convert and married a girl to whom he had *never* spoken, but whom he'd seen only at a London mosque.

The millionaire star with two careers behind him has now become a fanatical Moslem – renamed Yusef Islam – living the life of a recluse, shunning the world of showbusiness as much as possible. . . . and spending his days examining personal and religious issues. He has given up writing songs, too.

"I used to be a singer of songs, my songs. A lot of the time, I would be singing about finding the truth and about peace," he said.

"But I wasn't living it, so I was a hypocrite. I want to become truthful and I realised that first of all I have to get myself together before I can help anyone else."

SWEET
British. Male. Vocal/Instrumental Group.
Original line-up: Brian Connolly (vocals); Steve Priest (bass); Mick Tucker (drums); Frank Torpley (guitar).

The Sweet were formed in 1968 by Brian Connolly and Mick Tucker. They had both been members of a group called Wainwright's Gentlemen, which also featured the talents of Ian Gillan and Roger Glover, who later formed Deep Purple.

Initially, the group was signed to Fontana Records and their debut single 'Slow Motion', was released the same year. Later, however, they switched labels to EMI and released three not-too-successful singles – 'Lollipop', 'Get On The Line' and 'All You'll Ever Get From Me'.

In 1969, Mick Stewart was recruited on guitar to replace Frank Torpley, and a year later, he, too, was replaced by Andy Scott.

It was the same year, that the group signed a management deal with hit songwriters Nicky Chinn and Mike

Chapman – the 'brains' behind the recording success of Suzi Quatro and Mud. And within twelve months, after changing Sweet's rather sombre image to one much more colorful and exciting glam-cum-glitter-rock, Chinn and Chapman's special kind of hit-making magic started to work for the group.

They enjoyed their first British chart success in 1971 with 'Funny Funny' – and it was followed, over the next four years, with a stream of top-selling bubblegum-glitter-pop singles: 'Co Co', 'Alexander Graham Bell', 'Poppa Joe', 'Little Willy' – which established the group in America – 'Wig Wam Bam', 'Blockbuster' (their only British chart-topper in 1975), 'Hell Raiser', 'Ballroom Blitz', 'Teenage Rampage', 'Turn It Down' and 'The Six Teens'.

Yet, at the height of their success – and at one time they were certainly one of the top three groups in Britain – Sweet came in for tremendous criticism by the Press and public alike for the sexual nature of their act and stage antics. As a result they were banned from playing at many of the country's major venues.

In 1974, lead-singer Brian Connolly was seriously injured in a street brawl and suffered extensive damage to his throat and vocal chords, and for a while it was feared he would never sing again. Luckily, he recovered to lead the group on a massive assault on America – where Sweet had already established themselves as a major attraction and regularly headlined sell-out tours. The same year, however, they decided to branch out on their own, and left the hit-machine of Chinn and Chapman, in an effort to establish their own songwriting talents on record. Within months of the split, the group were back in the chart with their own composition 'Fox On The Run', followed by 'Action' and 'Lies In Your Eyes'. And by now, they had emerged as the *top* British teeny-rock group in the States, heading such rivals as T-Rex, The Bay City Rollers and Slade.

However, 1976 saw the departure of Brian Connolly, but the group continued to tour, though by now they had abandoned their glitter-rock image in favor of a much more heavy-metal approach.

Connolly returned to the fold shortly afterwards, and in 1978 Sweet made a dramatic return to the British chart with 'Love Is Like Oxygen'. But the success wasn't to last long – and by the middle of 1979, Brian Connolly was on his way again, leaving the group to concentrate on a solo career.

Today – now down to a trio – Sweet still tour, though their appeal is confined to European clubs and ballrooms . . . and the domestic University and college circuit.

THE SWINGING BLUE JEANS
British. Male. Vocal/Instrumental Group.

Original line-up: Ray Ennis (guitar); Ralph Ellis (guitar); Les Braid (bass); Norman Kuhlke (drums).

Formed in Liverpool in 1961 as The Bluegenes, the Swinging Blue Jeans followed virtually the same path to success as many of their Merseybeat contemporaries during the early '60s. Indeed, after playing the succession of local dance hall and club engagements – including the famous Cavern Club – they took the same route to Germany and appeared at the rapidly emerging Star Club in Hamburg.

In 1962, they were signed to a recording contract by HMV Records and their debut single 'It's Too Late Now' in 1963, just crept into the British charts at Number 30. But by the turn of 1964, The Swinging Blue Jeans had tasted success with their second single 'Hippy Hippy Shake' (a cover version of the Chan Romero song) which crashed into the Hit Parade and just fell short of the coveted Number 1 slot. Their follow-up release – another revival, this time of Little Richard's 'Good Golly Miss Molly' – followed suit, and their next single (yet *another* cover . . . of Betty Everett's classic) 'You're No Good', reached Number 3 in Britain. Both 'Hippy Hippy Shake' and 'Good Golly Miss Molly' registered strongly in America.

One of Britain's 'goodtime bands', The Jeans were essentially a visual group, and they could never hope to capture the excitement of their 'live' performances on record. And, after scoring in the charts once more with 'Don't Make Me Over' in 1966, their career went into a steep decline.

However, despite several line-up changes – Ray Ennis and Les Braid are the *only* original members still appearing with the band which now features Colin Manley and Ian McGee – The Swinging Blue Jeans are still

THE SWINGING BLUE JEANS — (l-r): Les Braid, Roy Ennis, Raplh Ellis, (top) Norman Kuhlke

going strong, touring Europe extensively where they are extremely popular in Germany, Holland and Scandinavia. They regularly return to the British cabaret circuit, while in America, they have headlined several 'Merseybeat' revival tours.

In 1979, they were plucked out of Britain's clubland to undertake a short concert tour of Britain – in yet another rock revival package – with fellow '60s stars Wayne Fontana (see **Wayne Fontana**) and Gerry And The Pacemakers (see **Gerry And The Pacemakers**). The tour also stopped off in London to play concerts at the Rainbow Theatre.

SYLVIA
Swedish. Female. Singer.

Swedish singing star Sylvia Vrethammer took the international pop charts by storm in the early 1970s with a massive world-wide hit, which became one of the most sung songs in the history of music – *and* an anthem to holiday makers on their way to and from Spain. 'Y Viva Espana'.

In the summer of 1974, the song rocketed into the British chart, where it stayed for a massive 28 weeks, reaching a highest position of 4. It also went on to sell over a million copies – *and*, not unnaturally, to top Hit Parades all over Europe.

Sylvia first sang the song in 1972 on the Canary Islands where she was appearing in cabaret. She later took it to Number 1 in her native Sweden, where she was already established as one of the country's leading entertainers.

However, she failed to consolidate her fantastic recording success – and in Britain only managed to creep into the Top Forty with her follow up single (another Spanish flavored song), 'Hasta La Vista'.

Although out of the recording eye for the latter part of the 1970s, Sylvia enjoyed outstanding success, appearing in concert and cabaret engagements, all over Europe where she is one of the Continent's biggest singing stars . . . *and* very much in demand.

In the summer of 1980, she toured Britain with Bert Kaempfert just prior to his tragic death.

TEN YEARS AFTER
British. Male. Vocal/Instrumental Group.

Original line-up: Alvin Lee (guitar); Leo Lyons (bass); Chick Churchill (keyboards); Ric Lee (drums).

Immortalized on celluloid in the movie 'Woodstock' in 1968 – their version of the classic 'Goin' Home' proved to be one of the most exciting (and most popular) sequences in the entire movie – Ten Years After emerged as one of the most successful British rock bands ever to tour America. Indeed, in a mere handful of years, they undertook no less than *twenty-eight* separate tours of the States, the majority of which enjoyed magnificent success.

The group was formed by Nottingham-born Alvin Lee. In 1964, he teamed up with Leo Lyons, himself a native of the Midlands city, and together with a drummer in tow, they went to Hamburg, Germany, to perform in various clubs. Back in England, the group scraped around for a meagre living which necessitated Lee and Lyons combining their group activities, with session work.

In 1967 they teamed up with Chick Churchill on keyboards and Ric Lee (no relation to Alvin Lee) on drums, and became known as The Jaybirds, later calling themselves Ten Years After. They landed a top-line residency at a London club and within weeks had signed a record deal with Decca Records.

For the next year, the group worked steadily in Britain and Europe, before they toured America for the first time – *and* later appeared at the Woodstock Festival, where they received huge acclaim. So much so, that they became a regular attraction on the U.S. tour circuit and spent most of their time *out* of Britain. Ten Years After built up a massive cult following on both sides of the Atlantic and their albums sold like wild-fire. The group's great attraction and appeal was built around the devastating guitar work of Alvin Lee, and he emerged as one of the most accomplished guitarists in modern-day rock.

TEN YEARS AFTER — (l-r): Leo Lyons, Chick Churchill, Ric Lee, Alvin Lee

In 1970, the group notched up their only British hit single with 'Love Like A Man'.

They returned home from America in 1973, and Alvin Lee took leave of absence from the group, built his own studio in his Berkshire house, and concentrated on a solo recording career. He released the first of several solo albums called 'On The Road To Freedom'. However, a year later, the group were back together again and back on the road, touring Britain. In May 1975 they undertook their last tour of America, and disbanded the same year. Ric Lee formed his own production company, while Leo Lyons also went into production and later worked with British rock group UFO. Meanwhile, Chick Churchill joined British recording company Chrysalis.

Alvin Lee, however, has continued to rock with the best of them ever since, and worked on several solo projects, including albums and singles. He also formed his own group, which toured as Alvin Lee And Co.

In 1979, he toured Britain with another new band – Alvin Lee Ten Years Later. And yet another group was formed in the fall of 1980, featuring Steve Gould (guitar), Mickey Feat (bass) and Tom Compton (guitar), to record a brand new album 'Freefall' on Avatar Records. A single 'I Don't Wanna Stop' was also released.

After forming his latest band Alvin told a London newspaper: "I'm definitely not re-forming Ten Years After. After Woodstock things got out of proportion, and we found it difficult to relate!"

JOE TEX
American. Male. Singer.

It was singing in the Church choir in his home of Baytown, Texas, that first made Joe Tex interested in music. It was the start of a career that would, in time, see him being hailed as Soul Brother Number 1, America's second most influential soul artist of all time . . . next to James Brown (see **James Brown**).

At 18, Tex won an amateur show in his home town – the first prize for which was a trip to New York. He went straight to Harlem's Apollo Theater, entered and *won* another talent show and was offered a 4 week engagement. As a result he turned professional.

He never looked back, writing and

recording through the '60s a string of hits, including 'Hold What You've Got' (his first million-seller), 'You've Got What It Takes', and the American chart-topper, 'I Want To (Do Everything For You)'. Hits followed hits, with Tex, who was born on August 8, 1933, established by then at the very top of the ranks of soul singers. His mixture of talents saw him as country singer, soul singer, soul leader and even preacher, all rolled into one, and *all* at the same time. His appeal was massive . . . and international.

However, at the end of the '60s, he had decided that he'd had enough of showbusiness and retired, to concentrate on his religion and the Church. His retirement was to be short-lived, and in 1972 he emerged once more

JOE TEX — used to rival James Brown

with another big success in the single stakes with 'I Gotcha'.

Although the '70s were *not* so productive a time for him as the previous decade had been, he did enjoy his first (and only) British single success in 1977 with the very much disco-orientated 'Ain't Gonna Bump No More (With No Big Fat Woman)'. It started a whole new career!

Today, he continues to work at what he knows best, writing and singing soul, although his music has always been tempered by a slight country bias.

THUNDERCLAP NEWMAN
British. Male. Vocal/Instrumental Group.

Original line-up: Andy Newman (keyboards); Jimmy McCulloch (guitar); John Keen (drums/vocals).

Formed in 1969 Thunderclap Newman enjoyed massive success with their debut single 'Something In The Air', which topped the British chart in the summer of that year. The record was produced by Pete Townsend, who met Andy Newman – a former Post Office engineer – at art school. They became firm friends, and Andy later composed 'Armenia City In The Sky' for The Who's 'Sell Out' LP.

The group was actually brought together by Townsend who had discovered lead-guitarist, Jimmy McCulloch playing in a Glasgow club. John Keen was a former roadie-turned-songwriter, and it was he who was responsible for writing the Number 1 song.

With their initial recording success, pressure was put on Thunderclap Newman to tour Britain, but even though they augmented the line-up with the inclusion of Jim Pitman-Avory and Jack McCulloch, Jimmy's brother,

for live engagements, they could never hope to reproduce their studio sound 'live' on stage. So concerts were a huge disappointment, which helped hasten the band's demise.

They split up in 1970, after releasing one album – 'Hollywood Dream' – and a further single 'Accident' which just crept into the British Top 40. Andy Newman and John Keen both later recorded well-received solo albums, while Jimmy McCulloch found recording and performing success with Blue, Stone The Crows and Paul McCartney's Wings. In 1979, he was found dead in tragic, yet unexplained circumstances, in a London apartment.

JOHNNY TILLOTSON
American. Male. Singer.

Vogues come and vogues go. Such was Johnny Tillotson's case. A teen idol by the early '60s, with his own distinctive pop/country sound, he had lost much of that appeal by the end of the decade, by which time his career had become more and more linked with the nightclub circuit.

THUNDERCLAP NEWMAN — (l-r): John Keen, Thunderclap Newman, Jimmy McCulloch

WHATEVER HAPPENED TO . . .?

Born in Jacksonville, Florida on April 20, 1939, he was enjoying local radio success by the time he was 10 in Palatka, to where he had moved in 1947. Within the next couple of years he had learned to play the ukelele and guitar, and by his mid teens was a regular on local TV, with his own band. He went on to Florida University to study journalism, but found that musical success impeded any academic career. And in 1959, sang for Cadence Records and soon saw his first U.S. chart hit with 'Dreamy Eyes'. After another hit, 'Without You', came his biggest success, 'Poetry in Motion', a Number 1 success on both sides of the Atlantic, selling 1,500,000 copies. He followed it with another success, 'Jimmy's Girl', before 'It Keeps Right On A Hurtin', which has since been recorded on numerous cover versions.

Then came U.S. Army service, but, despite his youth, the time was to betoken a waning in his popularity. When he left the Forces, Cadence Records had folded, and he was signed to MGM Records. His last British Top Ten hit was in 1963, with 'Out Of My Mind'.

Albums followed, and so, too, did more TV work. Then in 1968 he moved to California, where his career concentrated on a mixture of nightclub tours and TV acting.

During the 1970s, however, Johnny returned to his country roots and re-carved a successful singing career for himself, which has continued to this day.

His last scheduled appearance in England was due in the summer of 1980 when he was set to star alongside Johnny Cash and Glen Campbell at the Portsmouth Country Festival. Bankruptcy suits against the promoters resulted in the event being cancelled.

TINY TIM
American. Male. Singer.

In the late 1960s, when oddities and eccentrics abounded in the pop world, one figure stood above them all . . . for sheer weirdness!

Born Herbert Khaury in New York, in 1930, he became better known as Tiny Tim. And his career reached a bizarre zenith with, his marriage in 1969 to 'Miss Vicki' . . . on Johnny Car-

146

son's American TV show.

Tiny Tim started his career singing to small club audiences in lesser-known bars in the reasonably fashionable areas of New York City. Yet by the mid-sixties his wild eccentricity had picked him out for 'success'. The prestigious night clubs started to book him, and he became very much in-demand for television appearances. Audiences liked his falsetto renditions of old-time ballads, and his remarkable appearance – a 6ft-plus gangling frame, topped by a flowing mass of curly hair – added to his appeal. His face was something out of a waxworks. But then there was his ukelele . . .

British audiences switched on to him, if only because they couldn't believe their eyes or ears!

By now he had started to venture beyond New York. Legend has it that previously this was out of the question because he refused to use any WC but his own!

'Tiptoe Through The Tulips' was an undeniable success, and at one time Tim earned $100,000 a year. But as a novelty act, the Tiny Tim phenomenum was doomed. Although he had enjoyed a near-cult following, appearing on the same bill as top rock bands, audiences became used to this peculiar apparition and soon tired of him.

He faded from the limelight to the obscure New York bars from which he had come. And then the famous TV marriage ended in divorce.

Now, fighting a severe weight problem, he still plays the little clubs, along with his ukelele and 'Tiptoe Through The Tulips' hoping that one day his weirdness will once again be fashionable. His former wife, 'Miss Vicki', is a dancer in the same act!

In spring 1980, he told an American journalist: "I'm confident I *can* make a comeback, it's just getting a hit record. And that *is* going to happen. I've gone from rags to riches . . . and from riches to rags – you come up, you go down, and you come up again! It's just like an elevator.

"Right down in the basement – then back up to the top floor. Just watch me climb!"

TINY TIM — *waiting for the comeback*

THE TORNADOS
British. Male. Instrumental Group.
Original line-up: Clem Cattini (drums); Alan Caddy (guitar); Roger Jackson (keyboards); Heinz Burt (bass); George Bellamy (guitar).

The Tornados were brought together in the early '60s by hit songwriter Joe Meek as the backing group for singing star John Leyton. They had worked together in the past, however, as members of The Pirates, who backed Johnny Kidd . . . *and* actually landed the job with Meek, after answering an advertisement in a music trade p.per.

After touring with John Leyton for several months, the group went back on the road with Don Gibson – and later became the permanent backing group for Billy Fury.

In 1962, though, inspired by the recent launching of the TV satellite Telstar, Joe Meek wrote a tune to commemorate the event and named it after the orbitting space craft. When he needed a group to record it, he turned immediately to The Tornados. And they actually learned, arranged and recorded the number in precisely ninety minutes flat!

The record was released by Decca Records in Britain in the summer of 1962, and it entered the charts at the end of August. Before September was out, 'Telstar' was sitting at the very top

THE TORNADOS — *with Heinz Burt (second from left)*

of the Hit Parade, where it stayed for five weeks to become the biggest selling single of the year. A few weeks later, it went to the Number 1 slot in America, and in all, sold over a million copies.

The Tornados followed up their success in Britain at the beginning of 1963 with another instrumental smash – 'Globe-trotter', which reached Number 5 in the chart – and in all they enjoyed a further three moderately placed hits: 'Robot', 'The Ice Cream Man' and 'Dragonfly'. Yet, at the start of 1963, bassman Heinz Burt (of the peroxide hair) left the group, to go solo with his own backing group, The Wild Boys in tow. In August that year, he chalked up his first hit single with an ode to the late, lamented Eddie Cochran, called 'Just Like Eddy' which reached Number 5 in Britain. And for the next few years, he scored with four more hits – 'Country Boy', 'You Were There', 'Questions I Can't Answer' and 'Diggin' My Potatoes'. He also toured the country extensively, playing his own kind of rock 'n' roll on and endless stream of one-night-stands.

However, after a few years of minor success, he left the business and later worked on the production line at

Fords in Dagenham, Essex. Not long afterwards, though, he was tempted away from the motor trade – legend has it on the proviso that he *didn't* have to dye his hair blond this time round – and hit the road once more, playing clubs, cabaret engagements and dance halls, revelling in his former chart success. In 1974, he joined fellow 'old' rockers Marty Wilde and Billy Fury on a British rock revival tour, which proved quite successful.

Heinz has continued to rock ever since in Britain and on occasional excursions abroad, and in the fall of 1980 – like Marvin Rainwater (see **Marvin Rainwater**) – he appeared at the Hastings Town Football Club.

The Tornados, meanwhile, realizing that their halcyon days of chart success were over, turned their attentions to sessions where they have all carved outstandingly successful careers.

THE TOYS
American. Female. Vocal Group.
Original line-up: Barbara Harris; June Montiero; Barbara Parritt.

The Toys showed one facet of the '60s popular scene – the quick rise to fame, and the equally quick decline of fortune.

The girls all met at the Woodrow Wilson High School in New York, and on leaving decided to try and make a career in music for themselves.

They rehearsed frantically before

auditioning for Genius Records, who were greatly impressed with their ability and signed them to a recording contract.

Their first (and biggest) hit was Sandy Linzer and Denny Rendell's million-seller 'A Lover's Concerto', based on a Bach melody. It made the Top Ten in both Britain and America. Then followed numerous TV appearances for the threesome on both sides of the Atlantic, in 1965. And an American tour with Gene Pitney. The following year they had their second hit with 'Attack', and recorded a top-selling album, with the cumbersome title, 'The Toys Sing A Lover's Concerto And Attack'.

But that was it! The public had had enough of the gimmicky sound, and the threesome split in 1968 into obscurity.

THE TROGGS
British. Male. Vocal/Instrumental Group.
Original line-up: Reg Presley (vocals); Chris Britton (guitar); Pete Staples (bass); Ronnie Bond (drums).

Formed in Andover, Hampshire in 1966, The Troggs hit the chart-trail the same year, when they were signed to a management deal with Larry Page, and a recording contract with Fontana Records. And in the very first year of

THE TOYS — *rocketed to obscurity*

their formation, the band enjoyed *four* Top Ten singles in Britain with 'Wild Thing' – which later went on to top the American chart and sell a million copies – 'With A Girl Like You' – which topped the British chart and sold a million – 'I Can't Control Myself' and 'Any Way You Want It'.

The following year, they scored again with 'Give It To Me', and their third million-seller 'Love Is All Around', which was written by lead-singer Presley. At the same time, they developed an amazing fan following in America where their tours met with outstanding success.

Named after the mythical cave-dwellers Troglodytes (Troggs for short), the group's chart career ended abruptly in 1968 with their last hit single 'Little Girl', and they turned to European tours and British cabaret engagements to sustain them. In 1969, Pete Staples left, to be replaced by Tony Murray.

During the early '70s, however, they came in for immense criticism and even ridicule when a bootleg tape of a dire recording session (warts, four-letter words and all) was released on to the British market. Still, they resurfaced shortly afterwards with an intriguing version of The Beach Boys 'Good Vibrations' – a minor hit – and later rebuilt a substantial following for themselves on the British college circuit. In America, their appeal reached cult proportions.

Today, Reg Presley, Chris Britton, Ronnie Bond and Tony Murray are still making a sizeable living for them-

IKE AND TINA TURNER — *Ike now a producer; Tina singing solo*

selves with club and cabaret tours of Germany, Holland, France, Britain and, of course, America, where their popularity has never been in doubt.

IKE AND TINA TURNER
American.
Male Instrumentalist/Female Singer.

For Ike and Tina Turner there were two sides to their 1966 hit, 'River Deep, Mountain High', one positive, one negative. On the positive side, this masterpiece of production established them a major force in Great Britain; and on the negative, it heralded the temporary retirement of its producer, Phil Spector (see **Phil Spector**).

The song was not a success in the States, but in Britain it made headlines *and* the Top Five.

Ike Turner (born Clarksdale, Mississippi on November 5, 1931) met former Gospel singer Annie Mae 'Tina' Bullock (born Brownsville, Tennessee, on November 26, 1938) at a nightclub in St. Louis, where she had moved with her sister in the hope of carving out a living for herself as a singer. Ike Turner — who had been playing music since he was 6 – had by this time already been a DJ, and had had a successful career as an r & b artiste particularly with B. B. King and Howlin' Wolf. They married in 1958, and had their first million seller two years later with 'A Fool In Love' written by Ike. More hits followed, including 'I Idolize You' and 'It's Gonna Work

Out Fine', and they toured America with the 15-piece Ike And Tina Turner Revue: Tina on vocals backed by the four-girl group The Ikettes and Ike's Kings of Rhythm Orchestra.

The mid-'60s was to see their fateful meeting with Spector, who produced 'River Deep, Mountain High', which only made 88 in the U.S. The same year they had another big British hit with 'Tell Her I'm Not Home'.

In 1969 (when 'River Deep, Mountain High', was re-released and back in the British charts) the Turners toured the U.S. with The Rolling Stones. Their act became more and more suggestive, packing in fans wherever they appeared.

And so it continued into the next decade.

Early '70s hits included their own, distinctive versions of 'Proud Mary', 'Get Back' and 'Honky Tonk Women', before their classic 'Nutbush City Limits', written by Tina, in 1973, which sold a million.

But the highpoint of their partnership had already passed, and in 1976 they announced that not only was their musical partnership over, but so too was their marriage.

Since then Ike has continued to record and has emerged as one of the most respected producers in the business. Tina has continued to sing, packing in audiences all over the world, with her staggeringly sensuous stage performances. She toured Britain again in 1979 and played concerts and cabaret engagements to capacity business.

THE TURTLES
American. Male.
Vocal/Instrumental Group.

Original line-up: Mark Volman (vocals); Howard Kaylan (vocals); Al Nichol (guitar); Chuck Portz (bass); Jim Tucker (guitar); Don Murray (drums).

Yet another of the 'Goodtime' bands to emerge at the beginning of the Flower Power era, The Turtles were formed in Los Angeles in 1965. They had come together as a surfing band two years earlier (minus Murray and Tucker) and worked under the name of The Nightriders, before changing to The Crossfires. Then for nearly five years they presented their own kind

of folk-rock music with brilliant effect.

They enjoyed their first American hit in 1965 – the year Don Murray left to be replaced by John Barbata – with the Dylan song 'It Aint Me Babe', though Sonny and Cher's version (see **Sonny and Cher**) pipped them in the chart race and stunted their success. Yet greater success was to come their way in 1965 with the release of the masterful 'Happy Together' – their first British hit – one of the best pure pop songs ever written. It conveyed *everything* The Turtles stood for. Their follow up singles 'She'd Rather Be With Me' and 'Elenore' were equally effective.

The Turtles were heavily into satirical humor, which was strongly represented in their live shows. Yet they were doomed once they became tied up with the psychedelic scene . . . and lost their way completely.

The group broke up in 1970 in a flurry of lawsuits and counter claims, with Nichol and Barbata going into session work.

The hugely likeable Mark Volman and Howard Kaylan formed their own group The Phlorescent Leech (Flo) and Eddie, and later joined Frank Zappa And The Mothers Of Invention, with whom they had their own live set at concerts. They also recorded extensively with Zappa and appeared in his hit movie '200 Motels'.

In 1972, now back as a double act in their own right, they toured Europe and America and worked on sessions with Marc Bolan (see **Marc Bolan**) as part of T-Rex, but later split up to

THE TURTLES — *compilation album containing the 1967 hit 'Happy Together'*

diversify their talents in numerous other directions, including magazine and radio work – Mark Volman hosted his own radio show – and the inevitable sessions.

Today, however, back together *yet again* as Flo and Eddie, Mark Volman and Howard Kaylan are currently hosting their own Monday night radio show, 'Flo And Eddie By The Fireside', on New York's WLIR station. (The show is similar in format and zany humour to their successful radio series of 1978 for the KMET station in Los Angeles). They are also recording together again . . . and in the fall of 1980, laid down tracks in Jamaica for a projected 1981 reggae album called 'Prince Flo And Jah Edward I'. Flo and Eddie played several major concerts in Britain early in 1981.

CONWAY TWITTY
American. Male. Singer.

Conway Twitty's last scheduled big British appearance was at Wembley's Country Music Festival in London in April 1977. It never happened. Just prior to his arriving in England, a maniac issued a death warning against the singer, threatening to blow him up! Not unnaturally, Twitty stayed at home in Tennessee.

He was born Harold Lloyd Jenkins on September 1, 1933 in Friars Point, Mississippi; his stage name was chosen by his agent – with the 'Conway'-part being found on a road map in

Arkansas! and the 'Twitty'-part coming from the Texan town.

His father was in charge of a Mississippi ferryboat, on which he taught his son to play guitar. He proved an eager student and by the age of 10, he was regularly appearing on local radio. Two years later, he formed his own group – The Phillips Country Ramblers.

His great love as a boy was baseball and he was on the verge of being signed up by the Philadelphia baseball team, when he was summoned for national service with the Army. Two years in uniform, saw him playing with another group (made up of fellow servicemen) called The Cimmarons, and regularly performing on radio in Tokyo, to where he was posted.

Demobilized and back home in America, he formed yet another band and toured the States singing rock 'n' roll and soon became a big radio star. His manager Don Seat, whom he had met in the Army, helped to organize a recording contract with Mercury in 1957, and his first record success was 'I Need Your Loving'. A year later, he was signed to MGM with whom he recorded his multi-million-selling international chart-topper 'It's Only Make Believe', which legend has it, he wrote in five minutes flat!

Conway Twitty was now an emerging star and next followed radio and television appearances . . . *and* acting roles, in such movies as 'Sexpot Goes To College' and 'College Confidential'. He made more singles, too, including 'Story Of My Love', 'Mona Lisa', 'Is A Blue Bird Blue', 'C'est Si Bon' and 'Lonely Boy Blue' (his second million-seller). And started writing country songs, penning 'Walk Me To The Door' for Ray Price in 1960.

But as his rock 'n' roll audiences faded in the early 1960s, Conway turned to his first love – country music. He moved to Oklahoma City in 1965 and appeared with the group The Lonely Blue Boys (named after his big hit single) . . . and later starred in his own television series – 'The Conway Twitty Show'.

Not long afterwards he settled in Nashville and started recording country songs. In a ten year period from 1968 to 1978, he scored with no less than 33 Number 1 hits on the U.S. country charts. And his country metamor-

phosis was complete during the 1970s when, after teaming up with Loretta Lynn as a duo to make many singles and albums together – including a reworking of 'It's Only Make Believe' – the twosome received the coveted CMA Vocal Duo Of The Year Award on several occasions starting in 1972.

Today, he is still one of the most influential country singers in America and regularly tours the States, enjoying even more adulation and acclaim than in his rocking heyday.

In 1972, he was awarded the Indian title of Hatako-Chtokchito-A-Yakni-Tooa – which means 'Great Man Of Country Music.' It says it all.

RITCHIE VALENS
American. Male. Singer.

Ritchie Valens was born Richard Valenzuela on May 13, 1941, and raised in Pocoima, Los Angeles.

As a youngster, he sang and played guitar at school and in 1958, while still studying, he was signed to a recording contract by Del-Fi Records. His first release for the label was 'Come On Let's Go', which he followed with the million-selling 'Donna' (coupled with 'La Bamba') – a song he had written for his high school sweetheart Donna Ludwig. It reached the Number 2 slot in America, and registered his first chart success in Britain. His third single – 'That's My Little Suzie' – was only a minor hit.

His career as a rising rock 'n' roll star, however, was short-lived. On February 3, 1959, he was killed when the light aircraft carrying him, Buddy Holly and The Big Bopper (see **The Big Bopper**) to their next engagement on a gruelling U.S. tour, crashed in bad weather shortly after taking off from Mason City, Iowa. The Beechcraft Bonanza airplane smashed into a corn field at Ames, Iowa, killing its distinguished passengers instantly.

LEROY VAN DYKE
American. Male.
Singer/Songwriter.

Leroy Van Dyke, who is today a vital part of the Nashville Grand Ole

VANILLA FUDGE — only Carmine Appice remains in the pop limelight

Opry – performing regularly – was born on October 4, 1929 in Spring Fork, Missouri.

On leaving high school, he trained at the University of Missouri, where he earned a BS degree in agriculture. A stint in Korea with the U.S. Army saw him working for Army intelligence and entertaining his fellow servicemen in his off duty moments.

Back home in Missouri, he landed a job as a farm reporter for a local newspaper, before he decided to use his training to its best advantage, and became a livestock auctioneer. It was during this time, that he co-wrote (with Buddy Black) the classic song 'The Auctioneer' which he entered for a song-writing contest. Next, he was asked to sing the song on Arthur Godfry's 'Talent Scouts' show, which resulted in being offered a recording contract with Dot Records. When the record of 'The Auctioneer' was released, it sold nearly three million copies in 1956.

Leroy became a regular on Red Foley's TV show and later switched record labels to Mercury where he recorded the perennial favorite 'Walk On By' – his first British hit in 1962, which reached the U.S. Top Ten and remained in the Country charts for over 30 weeks! He followed it up with 'If A Woman Answers' and 'Black

Cloud'. And over the next eight years, he continued to make regular appearances in the Country chart. 'Louisville' in 1968 marked a major recording comeback to the national Hit Parade.

Since then, Leroy Van Dyke's musical presence has continued to be felt in Nashville, particularly at the Grand Ole Opry where he won the Connie B. Gray Award for his "outstanding contribution to the furthering of country music". Like so many of his country contemporaries, however, he works only when *he* feels like it, having amassed a great wealth of money – some people believe him to be a millionaire – from his song writing.

VANILLA FUDGE
American. Male.
Vocal/Instrumental Group.
Original line-up: Carmine Appice (drums); Tim Bogert (bass); Vince Martell (guitar); Mark Stein (organ).

So they come, so they go – some more distinguished than others. In the case of Vanilla Fudge it was just one musical achievement – a psychedelic version of Diana Ross and The Supremes' 'You Keep Me Hanging On', which made the British and American Top Twenty in the summer of 1967.

They were formed in 1965 as The Pigeons, changing their name to Vanilla Fudge in 1967. But as a group, they

lasted for just four years. And if Vanilla Fudge left any legacy – certainly their early work enjoyed some acclaim – it was as the first heavy rock band to emerge from America's East Coast. They envisioned their sound as a fusion of psychedelia and symphonic rock, taking many well known standards to give them their own 'heavy' treatment, including The Beatles' 'Eleanor Rigby'.

Latterly overreaching themselves, and perhaps taking themselves a bit too seriously, the group disbanded.

Bogert went on to play with Cactus, which had intended to be formed with Jeff Beck and Rod Stewart, and at the turn of the '70s formed Beck, Bogert and Appice with Carmine Appice. Later in the '70s he turned to sessions work. Martell took part in the Cactus venture, but then quit the music industry. And Stein formed a band called Boomerang.

Carmine Appice, however, has continued to work as a vital member of Rod Stewart's group, with whom he toured the world in 1980.

BOBBY VEE
American. Male. Singer.

Bobby Vee, born Robert Velline in Fargo, North Dakota, on April 30, 1943, idolized Buddy Holly. He was his favorite singer and he longed to emulate him. With this intention in mind, he'd formed a local pop group with his brother, who played guitar. It was ironic . . . because as a result of Holly's death in February 1959, Bobby Vee was launched on the road to stardom.

He says: "At the time, there was only one other group in my hometown of Fargo. And when Buddy Holly died in a plane crash on his way to play a concert engagement in our town, the local disc jockey sent out a message over the air asking for any groups in the area to help out, and fill in for Buddy. Our bass player made arrangements for us to appear even though we weren't very well organized. We only knew a handful of numbers, but we went out and bought matching sweaters and I picked up a new string for my guitar . . . and we were ready to perform.

BOBBY VEE — living off past glories

"We called ourselves The Shadows."

As luck would have it, an agent was in the audience and he took an interest in the up-and-coming new group, and started booking them out on engagements. Then in the summer of 1959, they scraped together five hundred dollars to make their first recording.

"It was with Soma Records in Minneapolis," adds Bobby. "They specialized in package deals for local bands. For the money, they would release two records for you in three States. So on June 1, we cut two vocal and two instrumentals, including my own song 'Suzie Baby', which soon after its release started to break locally. A representative of Liberty Records got to hear it and the label bought the rights to release it nationally."

Bobby himself was signed to the label and made his first single 'One Last Kiss' at the end of the year, followed by 'Devil Or Angel' – which reached the American Top Five. In 1961, he scored again with a Gene Pitney (see **Gene Pitney**) composition 'Rubber Ball' – his first British Hit Parade success – and followed it up with some of the all-time classic pop singles of the 1960s: 'How Many Tears', 'More Than I Can Say', 'Take Good Care Of My Baby' (his first American chart-topper, which sold a million copies), 'Run To Him', and 'The Night Has A Thousand Eyes'.

At the height of his career, he also recorded a tribute album to his great idol, Buddy Holly, performing on disc with Holly's former backing group The Crickets.

His run of American hits continued until 1970 – his last million-selling was in 1967 with 'Come Back When You Grow Up' which reached Number 2 in the charts – when he recorded less frequently, and for a while, he disappeared from the commercial eye. He did make a projected comeback during the 1970s under his real name of Robert T. Velline, though without too much success.

However, with the wave of nostalgia sweeping the world in the middle of the decade, Bobby reconsidered his future, reverted back to his original name of *Vee*, and set out to tour the American theaters and nightclub circuit singing his old hits *and* contemporary country-rock material.

Today, he continues to wallow in his former chart glory, which was consolidated in 1980 with the release and subsequent success of a 'Greatest Hits' album.

A projected European tour was scheduled for the summer of 1981.

GENE VINCENT
American. Male. Singer.

Gene Vincent was born Vincent Eugene Craddock at Maiden Point, Norfolk, Virginia on February 11, 1935.

In 1950 he lied about his age in order to join the U.S. Navy, and he later saw active service in Korea. However, in 1953 during a spell as a despatch rider on his hometown base in Norfolk, Gene was severely injured in a motorcycle accident, resulting in permanent injury to his left leg. And in 1955, he was invalided out of the service.

For the next year, Gene sang with groups on various local radio stations. And in 1956, he met disc jockey 'Sheriff' Tex Vincent, who was so impressed with the singer that he put together the best local musicians he could muster to back him on a demo tape, which was later sent to Capitol Records. Capitol, in turn, saw Vincent as their answer to Elvis Presley and signed him – and his backing group, The Blue Caps – to a contract. Their first single 'Be Bop A Lula', co-written by Vincent and Davis, was released . . . and it crashed into the American Top Ten to become one of the all-time rock 'n' roll classic songs.

GENE VINCENT

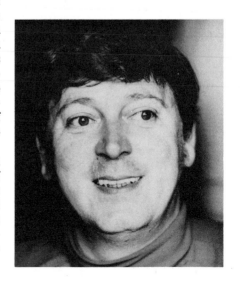

GENE VINCENT — his 1957 Capitol album

It was the start of a dynamic career for Gene Vincent which saw him chart with a string of exciting singles including 'Lotta Lovin' ', 'Race With The Devil', 'Blue Jean Bop', 'Jumps, Giggles And Shouts', 'Wild Cat', 'My Heart', 'Pistol Packin' Mama', 'She She Little Sheila' and 'I'm Going Home'. And he was also featured in several of the pop-rock movies of the day, like 'The Girl Can't Help It' and 'Hot Rod Gang'.

In 1959, after his career went off the rails through gross mis-management, Gene disbanded The Blue Caps and moved to England in the hope of re-establishing himself. It was just the right move to make.

He was signed to appear on Jack Good's hit television series 'Boy Meets Girl' (the sequel to 'Oh Boy!') . . . and it was Good who suggested that he change his image to accommodate the all-black all-leather look which became his trade mark. It was an instant success. A year later on April 17, 1960, he suffered another massive set-back in his career. While headlining a major British concert tour with Eddie Cochran, Gene was badly in-jured when Cochran's car, in which he was travelling, crashed after bursting a tyre, at Chippenham in Wiltshire. Cochran was killed outright.

Gene Vincent never really recovered from the accident. His left leg – already weakened from his earlier motorcycle crash in the early '50s – was shattered, and at one time it was feared it would have to be amputated. It was certainly never the same again.

For the next few years, Vincent's life and career went into steep decline. He was dogged by financial problems, again brought on by bad management – he never learned. And in despair, he found relief and solace in alcohol. By 1969 he was a wreck, grossly overweight and deep in debt. A year later, however, despite his problems, he made a brief comeback at the Toronto Rock Festival in Canada.

Gene Vincent died on October 12, 1971 from heart seizure, brought on by a bleeding ulcer . . . and a mass of worries. It was ironic, because he was on the verge of a spectacular career revival.

MARY WELLS
American. Female. Singer.

One song ensured Mary Wells' pop immortality – 'My Guy' – recorded in 1964. It was an enormous hit, clocking up sales of over a million.

Born in Detroit on May 13, 1943, Mary Wells started singing at the age of ten, and actually auditioned for a place on the Tamla Motown label in 1961, when, at 18, she came from no-where and presented the label with her own composition, 'Bye Bye Baby' – which became her first single release . . . and her first American hit.

A year later, she enjoyed a million-selling single success with the Smokey Robinson song 'Two Lovers' – and she emerged as the 'First Lady' of Tamla Motown.

By the time 'My Guy' was released in 1964, she was one of Tamla's most successful artists. The same year, she recorded 'Once Upon A Time' with Tamla's 'leading man' Marvin Gaye, *and* toured Britain with The Beatles.

Her career however had reached its summit, and she later left the Motown label for 20th Century Fox, followed by excursions to Atco and Jubilee.

The '70s saw no great commercial

MARY WELLS

153

success for Mary – with the exception of the 'My Guy' re-release in 1972 when once again it reached the British Top Twenty – although, by then, she was married to songwriter Cecil Womack, and had virtually retired from the business to concentrate on family life.

BARRY WHITE
American. Male.
Singer/Instrumentalist.

Enormous is perhaps the best way to describe Barry White – enormous in the terms of popularity. Enormous in the terms of physical bulk. And enormous in the terms of talent.

He was born in Galveston, Texas, on September 12, 1944, but at the age of six months, his family moved to Los Angeles. Coming from a religious family, too, Barry was influenced by the church and he started singing with the choir at eight. At ten, he was a virtuoso performer on organ, and at 12, he directed the choir.

In his teens, Barry joined a local r & b group called The Upfronts and spent the next two years singing and playing keyboards with them. A prolific songwriter as well, Barry enjoyed chart success in 1963 when Bob And Earl recorded his song 'The Harlem Shuffle', and he became their manager. Two years later, he scored again when Jackie Lee (Earl Cosby from Bob and Earl) recorded his song 'The Duck'.

Barry later moved into record pro-

BARRY WHITE — a millionaire and enjoying it

duction with Bronco Records and produced hits for Felice Taylor and Viola Wills. When Bronco folded, he continued to write songs, scoring once more with 'Under The Influence Of Love'.

In 1968, he met Linda and Glodean James, and Diana Taylor, and took over their management, to become their advisor and mentor. He groomed them for three years, signed them to the 20th century label and then as Love Unlimited they enjoyed outstanding success with 'Walkin' In The Rain With The One I Love'. He too, joined 20th Century Records, formed the Love Unlimited Orchestra, and started out on his own solo career once more. In 1973 he enjoyed two million-selling singles 'I'm Gonna Love You Just A Little Bit More, Baby' and 'Never, Never Gonna Give Ya Up', followed by a string of exciting hits – 'Can't Get Enough Of Your Love, Babe', 'You're The First, The Last, My Everything' (his only British Number 1 success) 'I'll Do Anything You Want Me To', 'Let The Music Play', 'You See The Trouble With Me', 'Just The Way You Are' and many more.

Now one of the most respected producers and performers in American music – and a shrewd business man as well, Barry White has never really been away from the commercial music scene. And he continues to involve himself with the industry, always searching for new innovations and new techniques.

In 1980 he was scheduled to make a concert tour of Britain, his first for some time, but ill-health forced him to cancel the trip – though a tour is rescheduled for 1981.

Today, he lives with his wife and their seven children in Los Angeles, totally engrossed in the business that has made him a millionaire.

DANNY WILLIAMS
British. Male. Singer.

Danny Williams was born in Port Elizabeth, South Africa on January 7, 1942, and started his singing career at the age of thirteen.

His first breakthrough to success came in 1959 when he appeared in 'The Golden City Dixies' in his native South Africa. The show travelled to London in 1960, where Danny was

DANNY WILLIAMS — a black belt karate instructor

signed to a recording contract by producer Norman Newell. His first record – 'We Will Never Be As Young As This Again' – was released in the spring of 1961 and just crept into the British Top 50. His second single, 'The Miracle Of You', reached 41. But, by the end of that year, Danny's third release 'Moon River' went on to top the chart.

He followed it up with four more chart singles in the early '60s – 'Jeannie', 'Wonderful World Of The Young', 'Tears' and 'My Own True Love' – and for a while he was one of the country's leading stars, regularly touring and appearing on all the top TV variety shows.

. . . And the tours continued well into the '70s, when he tasted chart success once more with 'Dancing Easy' – from the Martini TV commercial – in 1977.

Since then, although out of the commercial eye, Danny Williams has continued to work extensively with concert and cabaret appearances in Britain, and throughout the world. And he has become one of the busiest entertainers in showbusiness. Most recently, he has established himself as a major star in the Middle East, where he regularly appears.

Away from singing, Danny has developed another successful career, however, as a black-belt karate instructor.

He says: "Singing was not enough. People fall by the wayside in our business. I wanted an alternative – something I could escape to."

He has done just that – and today is one of the top instructors in England.

MARY WILSON
American. Female. Singer.

Mary Wilson was born in Greenville, Mississippi, on March 6, 1944, and it was at high school, in Detroit, that with friends Florence Ballard and Diana Ross she formed a singing group called The Primettes, as a 'sister' act to The Primes (later to become The Temptations).

At a school talent contest shortly after their formation, The Primettes were 'discovered' by record executive Berry Gordy, who signed them to a recording contract. In 1962, with a change of name, The Primettes, now The Supremes, had their first single – 'Your Heart Belongs To Me' – released on Berry's Tamla Motown label. Two years and six successful singles later, they clocked up a massive international success with 'Where Did Our Love Go', to herald the start of an amazing run of hit singles: 'Baby Love' (a Number 1 hit in Britain and America), 'Stop In The Name Of Love', 'Reflections', 'The Happening', 'My World Is Empty Without You Babe', 'You Can't Hurry Love', 'You Keep Me Hanging On', 'I'm Gonna Make You Love Me' (with The Temptations) and many, many more. Thirteen singles were released from 1964 to 1967 – and ten of them became chart toppers in America!

In 1967 Florence Ballard left to be replaced by Cindy Birdsong, and for the next two years, the group operated as Diana Ross and The Supremes. They reverted to the original name in 1969 when Diana Ross departed to pursue her own solo singing and acting career.

However, during the 1970s the

MARY WILSON — pictured with The Supremes

group thrived and enjoyed several other hit singles between 1970 and 1974, including 'Stoned Love', 'Up The Ladder To The Roof', 'Floy Joy', 'Nathan Jones' and 'Automatically Sunshine'. Then, when the hit records started to fade, Mary carried on by herself. With the help of two back-up singers – and billed as 'The Supremes' Mary Wilson – she continued to tour, playing concert and cabaret engagements in Britain, America and Europe. She gained particular success in Britain on the domestic cabaret circuit, where today she has become something of a permanent fixture.

STEVIE WINWOOD
British. Male. Singer/Songwriter.

A genuine prodigy, Stevie Winwood emerged at just 15, as part of the Spencer Davis Group (see **The Spencer Davis Group**). He was born May 12, 1948 in Birmingham, England, and as vocalist/pianist/guitarist with the group, wrote such top rock numbers as 'I'm A Man' and 'Gimme Some Lovin'.' Although The Spencer Davis Group achieved wide acceptance in Britain, and were much admired by the top U.K. artists of the time – including The Beatles – they never attracted an international following, and in 1967, Stevie left, to form Traffic.

They captured the mood of that summer with two hit singles: 'Paper Sun', and 'Hole In My Shoe', and later in the year charted with 'Here We Go Round The Mulberry Bush', the theme of the film of the same name.

In 1969, however, Traffic disbanded – temporarily – and Winwood went off to join the ill-fated Blind Faith, the first genuine supergroup, with Eric Clapton and Ginger Baker (see **Ginger Baker**) from Cream (see **Cream**), and Ric Grech.

The group stayed together for less than a year, and 1970 saw Traffic reform as a trio with Winwood, Chris Wood and Jim Capaldi. Their masterpiece was 'John Barleycorn Must Die', issued the same year. The line-up of the band was later augmented as the pressure of the work-load on Winwood mounted, but the quality was maintained, and the band's following grew.

In 1974, however, Stevie decided to retire, and retreated to a cottage in

STEVE WINWOOD — a big 1980 return with 'Arc Of A Diver'

Gloucestershire. He re-emerged two years later to take part in the 'Go project' with Stomu Yamash'ta and Klaus Schulze, and the following year released his long awaited solo album, entitled simply 'Winwood'.

1979 saw him making another comeback, playing for Georgie Fame and Julie Covington on tour – and, at the same time playing gigs as a keyboard artist in his own right, at various small and obscure British venues.

In December 1980, however, he was back on the recording scene with his long-awaited second solo album 'Arc Of A Diver'.

THE YARDBIRDS
British. Male. Vocal/Instrumental Group.
Original line-up: Keith Reif (vocals); Anthony Topham (guitar); Chris Dreja (guitar); Jim McCarty (drums); Paul Samwell-Smith (bass).

In a short, five year career, The Yardbirds built up a tremendous reputation for themselves as one of the most influental r & b groups in Britain in the early '60s. And at one time featured three of the world's most accomplished, and prolific lead-guitarists in rock music history – Eric Clapton, Jeff Beck and Jimmy Page . . . though not all at the same time.

The group was formed as the Met-ropolis Blues Quartet at Kingston Art School, in Surrey, in 1963, playing raw, uncomplicated rhythm and blues. They soon built up a large following in and around the London area, and not long after their formation – now working as The Yardbirds – they took over The Rolling Stones' residency at the Crawdaddy Club in Richmond, Surrey. It was here that Eric Clapton joined them, replacing Anthony 'Tops' Topham on lead guitar. Shortly afterwards, they signed a recording contract with Columbia Records and released their first album 'Five Live Yardbirds' and then followed The Stones once again, into their former residency at London's Marquee Club. A year later, they toured Britain and Europe with Sonny Boy Williamson, which spawned the album 'Sonny Boy Williamson And The Yardbirds'.

The group's first single for Columbia – 'Good Morning Little Schoolgirl' – had been released in the fall of 1964 and just scraped into the lower reaches on the British Top Fifty. At the beginning of 1965, however, they recorded 'For Your Love', which gave them their first Top Ten hit – and followed it up with more successful singles 'Heart Full Of Soul' (which reached Number 2 in 1966), and 'Evil Hearted You' (Number 3). In 1966, Clapton decided to leave and later joined John Mayall's Bluesbreakers, to be replaced by Jeff Beck. The same year, following successful tours of America where they were building a huge following and two more British hits – 'Shapes Of Things' (Number 3) and 'Over Under Sideways Down' – Paul Samwell-Smith left the group to become a record producer and later worked in the studio with Cat Stevens. Chris Dreja filled in on bass, while Jimmy Page was brought in on guitar. The band responded with what became their last his single together – 'Happenings Ten Years Time Ago'.

But before long, Jeff Beck parted company – and went off to form the first of several Jeff Beck Groups which initially featured Rod Stewart, Ronnie Wood, Vince Price and Jet Harris. Prior to the formation of the group, Beck enjoyed tremendous single success in his own right with 'Hi Ho Silver Lining! The Yardbirds, meanwhile, operated as a quartet and were even featured in the movie 'Blow Up'. They enjoyed several visits to America during this time where their 'live' album – 'Live Yardbirds' – was recorded in New York in March 1968.

The group officially disbanded in

July of that year, with Jimmy Page retaining control of the name 'Yardbirds'. He resurfaced shortly afterwards fronting the 'New' Yardbirds . . . which later re-emerged as Led Zeppelin, managed by the group's former roadie Peter Grant. Chris Dreja left the performing stage completely and became a successful photographer, while Reif and McCarty worked as a duo before teaming up with Keith's sister, Jane, to form Renaissance in 1969.

After recording the album 'Renaissance' the same year, Keith Reif left the group and worked briefly as a producer with Medicine Head, with whom he occasionally performed 'live'. In 1975 he formed the group Armageddon.

On May 14, 1976, he died at his home in Hounslow when the guitar he was playing suddenly became live and electrocuted him. McCarty meanwhile formed the group Illusion with Jane Reif.

THE YOUNG RASCALS
American. Male.
Vocal/Instrumental Group.

Original line-up: Eddie Brigati (vocals); Felix Cavaliere (organ); Gene Cornish (guitar); Dino Danelli (drums).

The Rascals – they called themselves The Young Rascals until they left their teens and decided to drop the 'Young' prefix – based their reputation on live performances, around their gutsy original songs. And their slightly eccentric appearance. But it gained them a following in New Jersey clubs, around 1965, particularly the Choo Choo Club in Garfield, where they made their debut in January 1965. Next followed a 3-month residency on The Barge, off Southampton, Long Island – where they were discovered and signed to Atlantic Records. 'I Ain't Gonna Eat Out My Heart Anymore' was their first single release and their first American hit, but it was 'Good Lovin' ', in 1966, which gave them their

THE YOUNG RASCALS — *finally broke up in 1972*

first Number 1 success.

The group's following mushroomed, and they became highly influential on the East Coast, inspiring such other contemporary groups as the Vagrants, and Vanilla Fudge.

Then in 1967, they recorded what was to be their major hit, 'Groovin' ', which marked a total change of style. Yet it was a record that captured the mood of that spring. The disc itself signalled the summit of their career, and although they had another U.S. Number 1 the following year with 'People Got To Be Free' and another hit with 'A Beautiful Morning', they were on the down path.

1971 saw big changes. Brigati and Cornish left, and Cavaliere and Danelli took on three new members – Ann Sutton, Buzzy Feiton and Robert Popwell.

The new line-up issued two albums, but, realizing they had lost much of their following, called it a day in 1972.

Danelli rejoined Cornish to form the moderately successful band Bulldogs. Cavaliere went solo, but later joined Treasure – with Rick Laird and Jack Scarangella – in 1977. And Brigati teamed up with his brother, David, for recordings and sessions.

Of the newcomers, Ann Sutton went into sessions notably with Gregg Allman, Ian Hunter and Paul Butterfield. Popwell later joined The Crusaders and Feiton also drifted into sessions and worked with Butterfield.

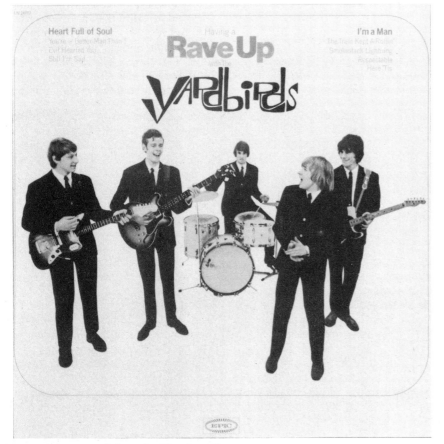

THE YARDBIRDS — *(above); The band's second American LP (1966)*

Z

ZAGER AND EVANS
American. Male. Vocal duo.

Zager And Evans' multi-million selling single 'In The Year 2525' in 1969, was one of the most futuristic songs ever written . . . telling a morbid tale of a changing world in distant years. It captured the public's imagination completely, yet if Zager And Evans could *really* have looked into the future – as the song suggested – they would have seen that 'In The Year 2525' was to become their only hit single.

The Zager And Evans success story itself is as fascinating as the song.

Born in Lincoln, Nebraska, Denny Zager and Rick Evans started their musical careers with the group The Eccentrics. In 1960 they decided to leave and go their own separate ways . . . and started working together as a Country and Western duo.

In 1968, after moderate success, they borrowed $500 and set out to make a record. Buying studio time in Odessa, Texas, they recorded 'In The Year 2525' – which Evans had written in 1964 – and then set about forming their own recording company, Truth Records, to distribute the 1,000 singles they had had pressed. Next step . . . they set about selling them to record stores all over America, from the back of their station wagon.

Soon the single caught on and many local radio stations started to play it, which in turn aroused tremendous interest with several major record companies – and they were eventually offered a deal with RCA.

'In The Year 2525' was released by RCA in the summer of 1969 and went straight to the top of the American Hit Parade, selling five million copies! And it established Denny and Rick as major recording artists, a position and status that looked secure when their debut album for RCA ('2525 Exordium And Terminus') was a sizeable hit the same year. However, they never managed to follow up their success and remained members of the 'one-hit-wonders' club.

After experiencing the international limelight for several years, Zager And Evans returned to their country roots, playing and singing in the small nightclubs from whence they had come.

THE ZOMBIES
British. Male. Vocal/Instrumental Group.
Original line-up: Colin Blunstone (vocals); Rod Argent (keyboard); Hugh Grundy (drums); Paul Atkinson (guitar); Paul Arnold (bass).

Formed as a school group in 1962, in the Hertfordshire city of St. Albans, The Zombies never realized their full potential. Indeed, long after their demise, a single 'Time Of The Season' taken from their album 'Odyssey And Oracle' went on to top the American Hit Parade – and to sell more than a million copies.

The group were initially signed to Decca Records in Britain after winning a talent competition in the London Evening News, and in the summer of 1964, they released their first single 'She's Not There', which became a Top Ten hit on both sides of the Atlantic. By this time, Chris White had replaced Paul Arnold on bass but the group couldn't follow up the outstanding success of their debut single, even though their second release 'Tell Her No' did eventually reach the lower reaches of the British Top Fifty in February 1965.

THE ZOMBIES — *with a youthful Colin Blunstone (far left) and Rod Argent (center)*

They split up in 1967 with Grundy and Atkinson going into the recording industry as producers. Colin Blunstone, however, set out on his own solo career under the name of Neil McArthur and in 1969 brought out an up-dated, revamped version of 'She's Not There', which made the Top Fifty. He later reverted back to his real name and clocked up several more hit singles in the early 1970s with 'Say You Don't Mind' (1972); 'I Don't Believe In Miracles' (1972) and 'Could We Dare To Be Wrong' (1973).

In the spring of 1981, Colin Blunstone singing with Dave Stewart, returned to the British Charts with a reworking of the old Jimmy Ruffin hit 'What Becomes Of The Broken Hearted' on Stiff Records.

Keyboard player Rod Argent, meanwhile, formed his own group – called simply Argent – which featured Russ Ballard (guitar), Jim Rodford (bass) and Robert Henrit (drums). He also worked very closely with Chris White on writing much of the group's material and production. For several years, the group enjoyed tremendous success both as a touring and recording band. They established themselves with three major hit records – 'Hold Your Head Up' (1972); 'Tragedy' (1972) and 'God Gave Rock 'N' Roll To You' (1973) and several albums. When the group finally split in the mid-'70s, Argent himself went into recording and session work, and later appeared on the Andrew Lloyd Webber/Don Black concept album 'Tell Me On A Sunday' featuring Marti Webb, in 1980.